DERAILING DEMOCRACY IN
AFGHANISTAN

NOAH COBURN

and

ANNA LARSON

DERAILING
DEMOCRACY IN
AFGHANISTAN

Elections in an Unstable
Political Landscape

Columbia University Press / New York

Columbia University Press
Publishers Since 1893
New York   Chichester, West Sussex
cup.columbia.edu

Library of Congress Cataloging-in-Publication Data
Coburn, Noah.
    Derailing democracy in Afghanistan : elections in an unstable political
landscape / Noah Coburn and Anna Larson.
        pages   cm
    Includes bibliographical references and index.
    ISBN 978-0-231-16620-1 (cloth : alk. paper) — ISBN 978-0-231-53574-8
(ebook)
    1. Elections—Afghanistan. 2. Democracy—Afghanistan. 3. Democratization—
Afghanistan. 4. Afghanistan—Politics and government—2001–   I. Larson,
Anna, M.Sc. II. Title.

    JQ1769.A5C63   2013
    324.9581—dc23
                                                            2013029061

Columbia University Press books are printed on permanent and durable
acid-free paper.
This book is printed on paper with recycled content.

Printed in the United States of America

c 10 9 8 7 6 5 4 3 2 1

JACKET DESIGN: Bryce Scimanski

References to websites (URLs) were accurate at the time of writing. Neither the
author nor Columbia University Press is responsible for URLs that may have
expired or changed since the manuscript was prepared.

CONTENTS

CONTENTS

4. A HOUSE OF SAND:
The Fallout of the 2005 Parliamentary Election

5. ENGINEERING ELECTIONS LOCALLY

6. THE UNINTENDED CONSEQUENCES OF
INTERNATIONAL SUPPORT

7. VIOLENCE AND VOTING

8. "THEY MAKE THEIR ABLUTIONS WITH
BOTTLED WATER":
Elites and the Decline of Accountability

9. INTERNATIONAL INTERVENTION AND
ASPIRATIONS OF REPRESENTATIVE GOVERNANCE

LIST OF ILLUSTRATIONS

ABBREVIATIONS

AIHRC	Afghanistan Independent Human Rights Commission
APAP	Afghanistan Parliamentary Assistance Project
AREU	Afghanistan Research and Evaluation Unit
DFID	Department for International Development (UK)
ECC	Electoral Complaints Commission
FEFA	Free and Fair Election Foundation of Afghanistan
IEC	Independent Election Commission
ISAF	International Security Assistance Force
JEMB	Joint Electoral Management Body
MoWA	Ministry of Women's Affairs
NATO	North Atlantic Treaty Organization
PDPA	People's Democratic Party of Afghanistan
SNTV	Single Non-Transferable Vote
UNAMA	United Nations Assistance Mission to Afghanistan
UNDP	United Nations Development Program
UNHCR	United Nations High Commissioner for Refugees
UNIFEM	United Nations Development Fund for Women
UNOPS	United Nations Office for Project Services
USAID	United States Agency for International Development

CHRONOLOGY

TIMELINE OF ELECTIONS AND OTHER MAJOR HISTORICAL EVENTS IN AFGHANISTAN, 1931–2011

1931   Nader Shah endorses a constitution allowing for a first elected National Council.

1933   Nader Shah killed, succeeded by his son Zahir Shah.

1949   National Council elections held under Prime Minister Shah Mahmud. "Liberal parliament" formed.

1952   Second set of elections under Prime Minister Shah Mahmud.

1953   Internal coup—Mohammed Daoud Khan, a cousin of the King, overthrows Shah Mahmud as prime minister.

1963   Prime Minister Daoud resigns.

1964   New constitution introduced by Zahir Shah formally establishes open democratic elections and a bicameral parliament. Introduces universal suffrage—women given the vote.

1965   First relatively free parliamentary elections.

1969   Parliamentary elections.

1973   Former Prime Minister Daoud overthrows the monarchy and establishes the Republic of Afghanistan. No parliament exists until 1977.

1977   Daoud announces a new constitution that takes away many powers of parliament and the judiciary. Afghanistan becomes a one-party state.

1978   "Saur Revolution" occurs: Daoud and family assassinated, People's Democratic Party of Afghanistan (PDPA) takes power with Nur Mohammad Taraki as president.

1979   Soviet invasion. President Taraki assassinated; Hafizullah Amin becomes president for three months. Amin then also assassinated and succeeded by Babrak Karmal.

1985–86   New constitution. Local elections held in a few government-controlled areas of Kabul.

1987   Dr. Mohammad Najibullah becomes president. Ratifies a new constitution, specifying a parliament elected by popular vote and a president elected by parliament; makes provisions for local and provincial councils.

1988   Elections held, but only in government-controlled areas.

1989   Russian troops leave Afghanistan.

1992   Najibullah steps down after the collapse of the regime; civil war follows.

1996   Taliban take Kabul, killing President Najibullah.

2001   Fall of the Taliban with U.S. military intervention; internationally sponsored Bonn process of rebuilding the Afghan state begins.

2002   Emergency Loya Jirga officially selects Hamid Karzai head of the Transitional Administration.

2003–2004   Constitutional Loya Jirga drafts and ratifies new Afghan constitution.

2004   First presidential elections; Karzai elected to office.

2005   Parliamentary and provincial council elections.

2009   Presidential and provincial council elections; Hamid Karzai reelected as president after Dr. Abdullah Abdullah agrees to forgo a runoff.

2010   Parliamentary elections.

2011   Karzai establishes Special Court to rule on fraud in the 2010 elections, initially refusing to inaugurate parliament.

DEMOCRACY DERAILED?

By 2010 it was clear that the international intervention in Afghanistan had not unfolded according to anyone's expectations. The early estimates of a three-year engagement made by diplomats and policymakers after the initial invasion in 2001 seemed, in hindsight, incredibly short-sighted. With a government perceived by many of its citizens as predatory, an insurgency gripping large areas of a country that had initially welcomed the presence of NATO forces, and countless failed development projects, Afghans and internationals alike were left wondering, what had gone wrong? Opinions varied. Was it due to the failure to include the Taliban in preliminary negotiations at Bonn? Were the corrupt fumblings of President Hamid Karzai and his advisors to blame? Was it the shift in American focus towards Iraq? Or was Afghanistan truly the graveyard of empires? Surprisingly missing from many of these debates have been the series of elections held in 2004, 2005, 2009, and 2010.

In the post–Cold War world order, it has often been assumed that the best way to create stability and build public support for a new government in the wake of international interventions in post-conflict contexts is to combine economic aid with the sponsorship of a series of elections and other state-building projects. In part the result of an emphasis by policymakers in the 1990s on the liberal peace thesis, building on the claim that democracies do not go to war with one another, this approach has seen the international promotion of democratic elections in countries as diverse as the former Yugoslavia, East Timor, and Iraq.[1] In Afghanistan, after four fraudulent and violence-plagued trips to the polls, however, it is clear that this formula is flawed: elections have not contributed to stabilization at all.

As the international community transitions out of Afghanistan, many Afghans and international actors have dismissed elections as failed experiments in democracy. However, a combined decade in the country looking at issues of local politics and governance, and discussing these with Afghans across the country, has left us with a more disturbing question: Have elections actually contributed to the failure to establish a legitimate, representative government in Afghanistan? What if some of our most basic assumptions about what elections do are in fact unfounded? Is there a better way to understand elections and their impact on local politics? This book is our attempt to explore some of these questions.

We believe a careful look at the local political landscape in Afghanistan demonstrates that the way in which elections have been implemented over the course of the international intervention has cumulatively contributed to the destabilization of Afghanistan, and the widening of the gap between the government and the Afghan people. Representative governance, that is, a form of political resource management in which elected representatives make decisions for the good of a given community, has suffered as a result. This is not to say that elections should not have occurred in Afghanistan at all, nor that the country was in some way "unready" for them. Rather, we argue that the way elections were manipulated by the Afghan political elite, with the support of international actors who viewed elections as technical procedures, as opposed to part of a broader political process, constitutes the root of the problem.

If the elections were so damaging to representative governance in Afghanistan, why were more people not commenting on them at the time?[2] At the 2001 Bonn Conference the international community was intent on holding elections, and when presidential polls took place in 2004, Afghan voters were quick to embrace them. But the tendency of international actors and the world media to look at elections as individual, technical occurrences meant that all focus was placed on issues like voter turnout, the number of female participants, and, latterly, fraud. Little attention was paid to the realpolitik of it all—for example, the way that local commanders and other political figures were using elections to solidify and formalize their authority. This lack of understanding was only furthered by the ambiguity and murkiness that pervade Afghan politics, which have left both outside observers and Afghans themselves struggling to understand or predict the political dealings going on among the elite.

This book does not look at the technical aspects of elections in Afghanistan as much as it focuses on the wider political processes that were taking place at the time. Drawing on and combining comparative theoretical perspectives of elections, post-conflict intervention, sovereignty, and sociologist Pierre Bourdieu's notion of habitus, it explores the way elections played out in terms of the failure of opposition groups to counterbalance President Karzai's tightening grip on power, the role of violence and instability in daily political life at the local level, and the increasing distance perceived between Afghans and their national government.

The title of the book, Derailing Democracy, is not meant to imply that elections are solely, or even primarily, to blame for the failure to establish a truly representative government in Kabul. However, it is meant to suggest that electoral processes did contribute to this failure. Specifically, it implies that the international community's focus on technical aspects of the elections and the tendency of both the American government and the international media to see the simple holding of elections as a sign of success diverted the gaze of both Afghan and international observers from the more significant political processes that were taking place at a deeper level. Those looking for quick answers on how internationally sponsored elections should be held in post-conflict situations will be disappointed. However, we do hope that the Afghan case will offer some suggestions on both an academic and a more practical level as to how we can sharpen our approaches and better understand how elections reshape the lived political experiences of all involved. This appears to be a timely moment to reflect on these issues, as Afghan and international actors plan elections in 2014 and, more broadly, consider their responses to political uprisings in the Arab world and beyond.

This work both benefits and suffers from the fact it is coauthored by an anthropologist and a political scientist. While certain sections were written by one of us more than the other, the book has ultimately evolved from a four-year dialogue about governance and elections with Afghan colleagues and numerous other Afghanistan analysts, over cups of tea, late suppers, and pages of elections returns. The result is a work that treads the line between political science, political economy, and anthropology, and this may be problematic for some. We are sure that some political scientists may complain about our limited use of quantitative data, while some anthropologists may argue that we are focusing too much on structures and processes. Ultimately, however, we believe that this blending of approaches is critical in understanding politics as a "lived experience." While this is more than a set of processes, it often takes place with a keen awareness and interpretation of certain processes and rules. These, of course, can be followed or broken in different ways, and partly why the Afghan elections are fascinating is the way in which rules have been both followed and broken, but an awareness of the rules still shapes the way that politics is lived and decisions are made.

The issues of how individuals and communities respond to these structures and processes, and how these responses shape politics, are what occupy us for most of this work. Elections are one such process that we feel is a useful venue for observing politics in action. Particularly in Afghanistan, where competition is often hidden and motives are veiled, elections have been a rare case of at least quasi-public and active political debates. Furthermore, while the international community's focus on elections seems to grow about six months before an election and peters out a month or two after, part of our argument is that a careful look at the past election cycles in Afghanistan reveals some important insights about how elections and other processes have long-lasting effects on politics in Afghanistan, far beyond the experience of a presidential or parliamentary poll every four or five years. Making policy recommendations is not the primary goal of this book, but if we were to make one central point to diplomats, policymakers, and others in the rapidly expanding international intervention industry, it would be that elections should never be viewed as isolated events, due to the simple fact that this is not how their participants view them.

Part of our focus on the lived experience of politics plays out in the biographic sketches and descriptive sections that begin each chapter. Beyond being what we hope are colorful interludes, these illustrate the ways in which individuals are making decisions in Afghanistan today, reminding us that when it comes to political struggles, very little is inevitable and decisions must be understood within their complete social, economic, and cultural contexts.

Another way in which lived experience is explored throughout the book is through the alternation of chapters on local- and national-level perspectives. As we explain in chapter 1, we feel that this approach is helpful to the portrayal of elections (and particularly parliamentary polls) as a local-national nexus, influenced by and influencing political structures within both local communities and the higher echelons of national government. Much of the book is also primarily written in the past tense; while we do make some statements concerning how Afghan politics and elections operate that we hope can be generalized, the current political situation in Afghanistan is so unstable that a change to the electoral process as currently implemented is likely.

In order to protect the identities of those we interviewed, all the names have been changed except for high-level, recognizable government officials.

The foundation for much of this book is research that we conducted on representative governance at the Afghanistan Research and Evaluation Unit (AREU) in 2008–2011. This research presented us with the opportunity to think about specific aspects of elections and democracy in Afghanistan, providing the seed for many of our more general reflections on elections found here. The greatest debt we owe is to the team of researchers and friends at AREU who worked with us throughout the process. In particular, without Mohammad Hasan Wafaey, Farid Ahmad Bayat, Anisa Nuhzat, Maryam Safi, Muneer Salamzai, Zahir Sediqqi, Sediq Seddiqi, and Yahyah Rahmini, this project would never have been completed.

In addition, our thinking about elections in Afghanistan was aided more generally by Paula Kantor, Shahmahmood Miakhel, Scott Worden, Martine van Bijlert, Zubair Ahmad, Thomas Ruttig, Thomas Barfield, Whitney Azoy, Deborah Smith, Paul Wordsworth, J. Brian O'Day, Tim Luccaro, John Dempsey, Andrew Wilder, and Zuhal Nesari, as well as time spent working with or for a variety of organizations including the National Democratic Institute, the United States Institute of Peace, the Center for Russian, Eastern European, and Eurasian Studies at the University of Michigan (with special thanks to Douglas Northrup and Juan Cole), the Anthropology Department at Skidmore College, the Organization for Social Development and Research and the Post War Reconstruction and Development Unit at the University of York. We are grateful to Oliver Lough in particular for his help with the writing process, and to Carl Larson and our other friends in Kabul who have kept us in good humor along the way.

DERAILING DEMOCRACY IN AFGHANISTAN

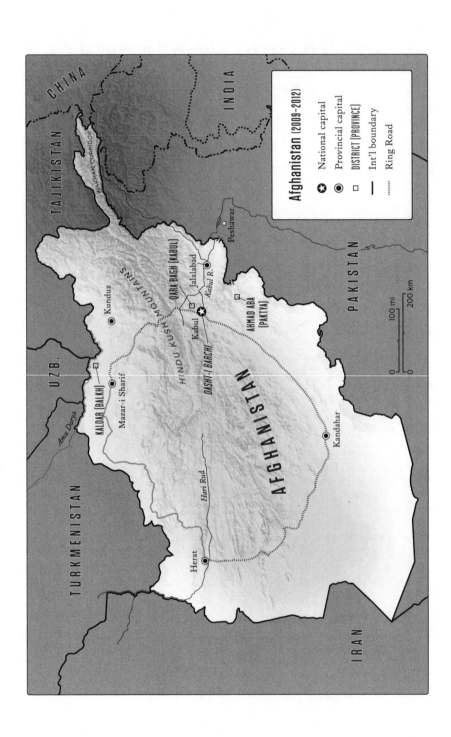

1

UNDERSTANDING ELECTIONS IN AFGHANISTAN

RUZ GOLDI

I N NORTHERNMOST AFGHANISTAN, *before the bend in the Amu Darya that sends the river north to be swallowed up by the Uzbek desert, live many of the country's Turkmen. Settlements here are not as remote as those in the high mountains of the Wakhan Corridor or in the rugged valleys of Nuristan, but the population is still isolated, despite the proximity of the busy border crossing into Uzbekistan and the relatively wealthy city of Mazar-i Sharif. Unlike other parts of the Turkistan Plain, which stretches across the northern limits of the Hindu Kush, the land is not particularly fertile, and the farmers who live here remain poor.*

Limited economic opportunities have reenforced quasi-feudal land tenancy agreements between rich landowners and the rest of the population, particularly in the district of Kaldar. This continues to bind communities together in tight networks based on economic cooperation between close relatives. Coupled with the importance of maintaining relationships between families, these bonds have meant that strictly arranged marriages, often accompanied by high bride prices, remain typical. In the course of a casual conversation, one elderly man spoke of remarrying after his first wife had passed away, leaving him with a young daughter. The second marriage had left him 600,000 Afghanis ($30,000) in debt once the ceremony expenses and bride price had been paid. With the three working members of his family bringing *in only around 55 Afs (a little more than a dollar) each per day, the man was forced to rely on his relatives and connections to a few rich landowners for credit to keep his head above water.*

The town of Hairatan at the border crossing with Uzbekistan provides something of a contrast to the poverty and slow pace of life in the rest of the district. This busy transit point has grown substantially in recent years and is primarily inhabited by Tajik Afghans who have moved there from other parts of northern Afghanistan. In the rural areas, away from Hairatan, most residents speak only Turkmen, often struggling to communicate with the Dari-speaking Tajiks who inhabit the bazaar and control most of the trade passing through the area. In fact, many Turkmen in rural areas rely primarily on radio stations broadcasting from Uzbekistan as their source of information and entertainment, and have only limited knowledge of Afghan affairs. For many of these people, a group of Dari-speaking Turkmen merchants living in Hairatan have become important community interlocutors who help facilitate business and political relationships across the divide. In recent times, no such figure has been as important as Ruz Goldi.

For someone newly arrived in the area, pinpointing the role of Ruz Guldi is not as straightforward as it might seem. A major landowner, businessman, and former commander, who is widely considered to be the primary leader of the Turkmen in the area, Ruz Goldi won a seat in the Wolesi Jirga, or lower house of the Afghan parliament, in 2005. Despite this, his role as a local elder (though in fact he is closer to middle age) remains primary. When we first arrived in the area and asked residents who their representative was, many explained that they had no parliamentarian, apparently unaware that Ruz Goldi had in fact taken on this role after winning the election in 2005. Similarly, the demands the community placed on Ruz Goldi—holding feasts, providing hospitality, providing credit, negotiating with commanders in the area—are not demands that most in the West would associate with an elected representative. Ruz Goldi's position was in some ways one that could not be earned simply by winning an election; it could only be earned over time, through family connections—and was protected by performing certain social rituals and maintaining particular political relationships. When one young man was asked how one could become like Ruz Goldi, he answered, somewhat bemused, "No one can become like Ruz Goldi, because only Ruz Goldi is Ruz Goldi!"

Like many leaders in Afghanistan today, Ruz Goldi first made a name for himself fighting against the Soviets. He studied until eleventh grade, when he joined a jihadi group fighting out of Pakistan. He returned to Afghanistan in the late 1980s once the Soviets had withdrawn, but while the Soviet-installed President Najibullah was still in power. Under the Taliban, his family moved to Turkmenistan and he later spent time in Kazakhstan, Tajikistan, Iran, and Germany. Following the fall of the Taliban, he joined the interim government and worked in the Ministry of Economy and the Ministry of Labor and Social Affairs before running for the Wolesi Jirga in 2005.

During his term in office as a parliamentarian, he worked on a series of projects for members of his community; he expressed concern about how poor economic conditions were leading to the use of very young girls in the weaving industry, and that young children were often given small amounts of opium to keep them quiet while their mothers worked. Central to his political agenda, Ruz Goldi also attempted to address the erosion of valuable farmland along the Amu Darya as the river shifted its course to the south.

As with many Afghan politicians, Ruz Goldi relied on a carefully cultivated network of allies in order to secure resources for his followers. He was able to convince Ustad Atta Mohammad Noor, governor of Balkh Province, to come and inspect the erosion along the riverbanks, in the hope that he would then raise the issue with President Karzai. But while such connections to important patronage networks are often the keys to getting things done in the area, they are far from reliable; thus far, no work has been started to shore up the slowly eroding riverbank.

In Kaldar, government and service provision are not always linked in the ways that many would assume. In addition to the government, a series of overlapping NGOs provide services that are often confusing to local residents. Pointing to a school, one man said, "I don't know who made this school for us. There is just a board with some words written in a foreign language." Similarly, although Ruz Goldi was a representative from the area, not all residents felt represented by him. This is particularly true of the Tajiks living in Hairatan, and one explained to us that Ruz Goldi was "the parliamentarian from this area, but we cannot raise our issues to him for he is representing his own [Turkmen] people . . . [and] he has bodyguards."

Despite his strong support among the Turkmen population, Ruz Goldi failed to win reelection to the Wolesi Jirga in 2010, securing only 7,656 votes compared to 10,787 for the bottom-placed winning male candidate in the province.[1] *When preparing for the elections, he lacked some of the enthusiasm of other candidates we had interviewed. When asked about his campaign techniques, he said, "I don't want to make promises to the people. I will tell them that we have to do our jobs in accordance with the law. We want to serve the people, mostly by finding jobs for the unemployed and doing something about education and narcotics."*

One reason he lost his seat appeared to be the competition from candidates associated with the well-oiled political machine of former Northern Alliance figures, headed in the region by Governor Atta, that successfully mobilized the area's Tajik voters.[2] *Many of these voters, as well as the governor, had connections with the Jamiat-i Islami political party—the largest component of the Northern Alliance and still capable of mobilizing strong political support in the north of the country. Young men from Mazar came into the area the days leading up to the election and were particularly active on Election Day, promising that other candidates were more likely to supply them with resources and, in some instances, demonstrating this by paying certain more apathetic Turkmen to vote for Tajik candidates supported by Governor Atta.*

However, speaking with Ruz Goldi after the election, he was remarkably unperturbed about the entire process and said that now that he had lost, he was looking forward to paying more attention to his multiple businesses, which he felt he had neglected during his time in parliament.

Ruz Goldi did not identify himself primarily as a parliamentarian, and neither did his constituents, which seemed to take some of the sting out of the loss. Instead, his position as a parliamentarian was just one of several ways he maintained his authority and political legitimacy among the Turkmen. At the same time, the parliamentary elections were one of multiple political struggles taking place across Afghanistan over the distribution of political and economic resources. Significantly, they were also not always the ones that local communities felt were the most important. While the international community in Kabul painstakingly debated technical aspects of the voting process, for Ruz Goldi and voters in Kaldar, elections were not really about representative governance. Rather, they were places for different patronage networks to compete with each other, where resources were transferred, where different ethnicities and other local groups renegotiated local balances of power, and where the ruling elite attempted to solidify their control of the national-

level political system. In fact, Afghan elections were so tied into other political pro-
cesses, it suddenly seems necessary to ask whether the international community actu-
ally missed the true story of how elections have reshaped politics in Afghanistan.

WHAT ARE ELECTIONS?

Before we begin, we should start by asking a seemingly simple question: what
is an election? Most definitions of elections consider them a critical component of democratic politics—a means through which to institutionalize
political equality by giving individuals an opportunity to cast equal votes for a
potential representative of their choice on a regular basis, or, for others, a site of
contestation for governmental office.[3] Even more simply, elections are formal
decision-making processes that allow a population or constituency to choose
an individual to hold public office. These relatively uncritical definitions mark
a distinction between the population and the individual who is to gain authority from public office. This corresponds to the way in which, moving away
from the direct participation of citizens in decision-making that characterized
Athenian models of the democratic process, most elections in contemporary
contexts facilitate representation of the population by the elected individual,
assigning representative responsibilities to the public office.

In theory, elections are held in order to quantify popular support for certain individuals with the aim of creating a representative, or at least as representative as possible, government, that is held to account by further elections.
For some scholars, such as Robert Dahl, this is the only feasible method of
scaling-up democratic politics to the national level.[4] The extent, however,
to which the population can be adequately represented by an elected individual has been widely debated. For example, the proponents of deliberative democracy call for a far greater degree of popular participation at the
local level in the periods between national elections.[5] Nevertheless, practical limitations mean that many states rely on elections as the sole means
through which representative decision-makers are chosen, at the same time
allocating a significant degree of decision-making authority to the position
of public office.

To counterbalance the potential monopolization of power that could result from this kind of system, elections are usually held at regular intervals to make sure that individuals are subject to the competitive gaining or regaining of public confidence through the popular vote. As political scientist Adam Przeworski notes, this has the effect of "institutionalizing uncertainty" in that those holding public office have to contend with the potential limits on how long they can hold their position.[6] It is precisely the ability of ordinary voters to limit the authority of those in office that is at the heart of most conceptions of democracy. Such an analysis describes elections as systems that create winners and losers, where the winners are granted political office, often becoming the very embodiment of the state itself. This implies a vision of the state that conforms to Max Weber's rationalist, bureaucratic model of legal authority and a monopoly on legitimate violence assigned to the state and those who represent it.[7]

But in the Afghan case, we found some of these assumptions about what elections do troubling. For a start, Weber's model cannot be applied to a state like Afghanistan in which the monopoly of violence is not held by state actors exclusively or automatically,[8] but is constantly being renegotiated by a range of different actors in different geographical areas.[9] Also, for many Afghans we spoke to, like Ruz Goldi, the elections were not simply about winning and losing, and political *authority* was not tied explicitly to political *office*. Yet despite this, the entire electoral process still had real repercussions on local politics. How, then, should we go about unpicking these nuances?

ELECTIONS AS STRUCTURES THAT STRUCTURE

With some of these issues in mind, we believe that an approach that blends anthropology and political science is particularly effective for reevaluating our understandings of elections, especially in the Afghan context. In the social sciences, elections have (with a few notable exceptions) been part of the domain of political science.[10] Anthropology, historically rooted in the study of non-Western societies, has little history of studying elections, even while they are deeply shaped by issues that have traditionally interested anthropologists, such as kinship, nationalism, and class.[11]

Political science approaches are useful for understanding the structures and procedures of elections, but by focusing on them as specific events—and events that are primarily conceived of in terms of their contribution to a democratic politics or democratization—they tend to miss the way they are embedded in multiple layers of political and cultural struggles that may or may not be directly associated by voters with "democracy" within both communities and nations.[12] Elections take place within certain political cultures, but just as importantly, elections can reshape those political cultures. For this reason we have attempted to analyze elections as a part of wider political processes and debates, beyond those of democratization per se, that are encapsulated by Bourdieu's notion of "structuring structures." In Bourdieu's approach political and social processes like elections shape the actions and decisions of the individual, but these decisions in turn reshape how processes play out again in the future. In this way, elections are structuring structures: they create a certain political world for individuals, what Bourdieu calls "*habitus*," or what we prefer to call "political landscape."[13]

We use this phrase because it emphasizes how the political setting in which individuals live alters their choices. As Bourdieu, we perceive political practices as becoming embodied in individual actors, but not in a deterministic manner. For most of those we spoke with, one of the strongest beliefs was the way that they could work to reshape political systems through many different approaches: by bringing their problems to tribal elders or NGOs, by organizing as a community around a certain issue, or in some cases, even by resorting to violence. We believe this notion of political landscape and the processes that take place within it, such as elections, do not dictate how an individual makes choices, but do shape the way that individuals think and feel as they make their choices. Landscapes have contours, which make it easier to move in some ways than in others. Within such a landscape, processes, like elections, (1) shape the way that individuals make decisions, but (2) are then reshaped by the political practices and norms of the community.

Take rural Paktya as an example. In this mountainous Pashtun area in southeast Afghanistan, elections have altered people's perceptions of the local political landscape. On the one hand, elements of democratic elections as they have been promoted in Afghanistan since 2004 shape and change the way politics is understood for anyone socialized in rural Paktya: the way that ballots are cast suggests that everyone (including women) gets an equal vote in the determination of leadership. The simple act of entering a polling station alone and marking a ballot emphasizes individual political agency in a way that is not necessarily typical in an area where the rights of the individual are often secondary to group politics. At the same time, the system of candidates competing for votes emphasizes an adversarial (as opposed to negotiated) approach to selecting leaders. These new elements of political decision-making, introduced via elections, contrast with older consensus-based decisions made by community elders within a village council, for example, and influence the way individuals now perceive certain issues such as the role of local elders, individualism, and women's rights.

On the other hand, however, elections are themselves structured by a series of existing political ideals and notions that in turn shape the way voters perceive and act in the election experience. In Paktya, strong tribal ties and an emphasis on kinship lead individuals to vote together as a family more frequently than would be expected in Western elections, for example. This in turn shapes campaigns, in which candidates try to secure entire blocs of votes. In this case, while individuals' political experience is being reshaped by elections, the political landscape that these individuals inhabit (and the communities of which they are a part) is also reshaping the elections themselves.

In some instances clashes can occur between accepted social norms and the new political processes of elections, leaving voters to debate and reformulate aspects of their political worlds. As a result, while the one-person/one-vote balloting system suggests that all individuals have an equal voice in the election process, in conservative Paktya it is rare for women to leave their large family compounds to express that voice. The mere extension of voting rights to women has created a good deal of debate at multiple levels of Afghan political society across the country over the wider role of women in the public sphere. While in many instances these debates reflect political conflict, there is also a certain amount of opportunity for individuals to negotiate and create new forms of power. For example, a common recent form of fraud has involved men coming to polling centers with a stack of voter registration cards and asking to cast votes on behalf of their "female relatives" (many of whom do not actually exist). This strategy exploits a combination of the modern technical nuances of the balloting process and local conservative values to secure more votes for a family. At the same time, in some areas women have been able to cast votes independently and without intimidation at polling centers, negotiating a new, albeit limited, political space in the public sphere.

In order to fit some of these elements into our analysis, we study the part elections play in the process of political ordering and structuring of society, but at the same time look at how elections themselves are being shaped and structured by other social and political conditions. Elections may therefore provide a structure within which an individual must make a series of choices (to vote or not to vote, to vote collectively or according to differing individual convictions, etc.); but at the same time, the way elections are understood culturally, the history of previous elections in the country, and many other factors will all shape how they are held and how choices are made. For example, we will see that fraud in the elections of 2004, 2005, and 2009 directly contributed to fraud in 2010, since political actors incorporated increasingly sophisticated means of manipulating the system and saw electoral fraud as a viable political option.

Viewing elections with this broader lens leads us to expand the kind of questions we ask about them far beyond simply establishing who won or lost. How was the election won? What resources were used? How do people talk about the election in relation to other political struggles? What groups gained or lost political capital? What types of rhetoric, old or new, were used to mobilize voters? What does this mean on both a macro and micro level for politics within a community?

POLITICAL PERFORMANCE

When viewing elections as part of the political landscape, it is important to observe that they are constantly being interpreted by participants according to cultural understandings of politics and how political processes should function. But how does this happen? Elections, beyond selecting winning candidates, are also a part of long histories of symbolic political performance and ritual, filled with deep (though not always simple) meaning in which the entire community participates. Those that participate in elections use and manipulate political symbols to both convince voters how to vote, but also attempt to define and reshape the meaning attached to elections themselves. In his study of political rituals and politics, David Kertzer points out that in rituals such as elections, these "symbols do not arise spontaneously, nor is the continual process of redefinition of the symbolic universe a matter of chance."[14] Aspects of the election process have become ritualized. The act of lining up at polling stations, giving political speeches, are not isolated events, but are parts of meaningful political patterns.

Elections themselves are symbols, as are their various components such as the ballot box or the dye-stained finger that proves participation in many countries. The abundant images that surround elections, like election posters, are used by candidates to elicit certain responses and shape the way that voters feel about both elections and politics more generally. Moreover, these symbols may be manipulated by political leaders, the media, or even international organizations in an attempt to convey certain messages to those participating in these rituals. Images of Karzai voting publically on Election Day convey a very different political message than attacks in which insurgents have set ballot boxes on fire. While elections do not have as long a history in Afghanistan, symbols still abound and were often discussed by voters. Candidates and other political leaders use these symbols and political language to convince voters that their vision of a political future for Afghanistan is the correct one.

These symbols, like all other symbols, are also embedded within a cultural and historical context that needs to be taken into account when analyzing how individuals and communities understand elections. In this sense, it is unhelpful to think of elections in Afghanistan since the U.S.-led invasion as "new." Even while certain electoral procedures are novel, the selection of representatives to govern a political community is deeply embedded in the Afghan political experience. This experience includes previous legislative elections in 1965 and 1969, but also a range of other political processes that Afghans use to select leadership, ranging from "traditional" *loya jirgas* ("grand councils" held at the national level) to voting for

FIGURE 1.1 Street with campaign posters. (Reprinted by permission of Farid Ahmad Bayat)

contestants on Afghan music programs.[15] Candidates regularly adorn both their campaign posters and stump speeches with symbolic imagery that has deep cultural resonance in Afghan political history, drawing on religious imagery or idioms of kinship or tribal ties. Ashraf Ghani, for example, a figure often accused of being too Western as a result of having spent many years abroad, used an image of the Koran holder as his chosen symbol on the ballot paper during the presidential election of 2009, implying a commitment to Islamic values. In contrast with this, a younger candidate campaigning for parliament in 2010 flaunted his modern outlook by using the symbol of a laptop computer.[16]

Considering elections as political ritual is important because it highlights the fact that these are processes that Afghan voters perform in, by going to polling stations and attending community meetings about the elections. Elections have had long-lasting repercussions in determining both who has access to certain types of political and economic resources, and how politics is performed and lived within communities. Instead of

FIGURE 1.2 Campaign posters.

seeing elections as fixed occasions for public participation or events to be judged as legitimate or illegitimate, free and fair or fraudulent—we think it is more useful to see elections as part of a near-continual process of local political negotiations and struggles over the meaning and distribution of power in which individuals are deeply embedded. Since the beginning of the current international intervention in 2001, this struggle over both power and meaning has taken place in parallel with debates over the value and concept of democracy.

DEMOCRACY?

Primarily because elections are often assumed to be one of the most representative ways in which to distribute power according to the will of the people, a close association is often made between elections and democracy. Two claims are often made in the literature about the connection between the two: first, that "representative" democracy cannot occur without elections; but second, that elections alone do not constitute democracy. [17] Thus, it follows that elections form a fundamental base from which a democratic politics can develop but that this development is far from guaranteed.

Neither of these claims addresses the *kind* of democratic politics that elections might produce in a given context, however, and in fact, the seemingly simple association between elections and democracy turns out to be rather complex. In recent decades, both anthropologists and political scientists have debated the various definitions and manifestations of democracy. Political scientists, for example, have differentiated between formal, participatory, social, and liberal democracy in terms of the rights and expectations of citizens;[18] between multi- and two-party democracy in terms of the different structures or institutional frameworks around which democratic participation occurs;[19] or between direct, deliberative, and representative democracy in terms of the methods of connection between citizen and state.[20] In an attempt to move past debates over how to classify governments and political systems more broadly, scholars have attempted to separate the formal composition of democratic institutions from the social and political characteristics of democratic states—or to "disentangle democratic systems from the actual distribution of democratic values."[21] Across both disciplines, distinctions have been made between constitutional, procedural, process-oriented, and substantive democracy and there have also been numerous attempts to subclassify democracy even further with the addition of a wide variety of adjectives—from monitory, cosmopolitan, and discursive to delegative, hollow, and illiberal, to name but a few.[22]

Given our focus on elections in Afghanistan, we attempt to avoid debates over whether Afghanistan is or is not a democracy, or whether it is currently undergoing a process of democratization (or even de-democratization), since doing so does little to help us understand how political processes are being experienced on the local level by Afghans.[23] Indeed, for many Afghans we spoke to during interviews, elections and democracy were separate subjects that had relatively little connection to one another. At the same time, however, Afghans are very much aware of and involved in debates over elections and to what extent elections offer them access to political power. For this reason, we see elections as political processes in which citizens are theoretically allocated equal access to political opportunity, and democracy as a system that *guarantees* equal access to and accountability over political power.

In focusing on this primary value of "political opportunity" and its attributes (such as access to economic opportunities), we downplay other "democratic values," often conflated with liberal constitutionalism and emphasized in Western political discourse.[24] Our respondents simply did not prioritize values such as freedom of the press or freedom of religion, which are enshrined in Western conceptions of democracy. Afghan voters we spoke to during research conducted for this book saw elections as parts of political processes that were more closely related to questions of whether someone had the political capital to open a business or arrange a marriage alliance than to these other values perhaps more closely associated with democracy in the West. Prioritizing access to political power in particular allows us to temporarily put to one side historically Western concepts, like civil society, to which democracy is often attached. When we consider democracy as a system that guarantees equal access to and accountability over political power (and elections as processes that ideally facilitate this), it suddenly becomes much easier to conceptualize an Islamic democracy, or any other of the numerous types of democratic systems that exist outside the confines of Western, liberal contexts.

We realize that this approach is controversial in nature, and that readers may object to our disregarding of liberal values that have come to define what democracy means from a Western perspective. We do not intend to suggest that these liberal values are necessarily inappropriate or inapplicable in the Afghan context. These are debates for Afghans to hold among themselves, alongside decisions about the terms on which they see Afghan democracy developing. Rather, in focusing on democracy as a system first and foremost guaranteeing political opportunity, we seek conceptual clarity to analyze if and how elections since 2001 have promoted this most central of democratic values. If, as this book contends, they have not done so, and in fact have contributed to the decline of political opportunity among voters, then fundamental questions about the purposes of post-conflict elections need to be addressed.

We feel that a combined approach drawing on both anthropology and political science is useful to the study of this juncture between the processes of elections and the values they potentially promote. A holistic analysis of elections in Afghanistan requires both a "top-down" and a "bottom-up" approach. By viewing elections as structuring structures, as opposed purely to events that are necessary to the onset of democratization, it becomes apparent that elections can reshape individual values and concerns, but that values and concerns can also reshape how elections are performed. In Afghanistan, for example, cultural norms in certain parts of the country mean that women who rarely leave family compounds are unlikely to vote in elections. At the same time, however, the act of holding elections and participating in campaigns has led youth in many cities to increasingly demand more equal access to political authority. Form alters values, while values alter form.

The current international intervention in Afghanistan has created a situation in which the meanings of terms like "democracy" and "human rights" are particularly disputed.[25] Much of this is due to the fact that the definitions and implications of these terms often have (and are certainly perceived by Afghans to have) clear political agendas. When embassies in Kabul talk about promoting democracy in Afghanistan, they often seem to imply a highly Westernized version of the term which would make it easier for the West to understand and to deal with the Afghan state on the international stage. Afghan definitions, on the other hand, often emphasize the importance of Islam, and in many cases are tied to the need to guard against a perceived imposition of imported Western values. Some of these definitions have little or no connection to the holding of elections, which are seen by many as wholly unconnected to the language of democracy. As such, while elections continue to shape and be shaped by political values within Afghan communities, there is not necessarily a sense among these communities that these processes are linked to democratization, whatever this might entail.

ELECTIONS AND DEMOCRATIZATION

In the post–Cold War order, elections have been promoted as part of international interventions in peacebuilding in post-conflict contexts.[26] Implicitly invoking the logic of the liberal peace thesis, which contends that democracies do not go to war with one another, they have been promoted largely as a means to usher in a political settlement between parties in warfare and to "legitimize" transitional governments that have been set up in the interim.[27] As Simon Chesterman observes, however, elections have become so entrenched within blueprints for international intervention in these circumstances that "they are staged because they are part of an accepted template of what typically happens toward the end of a peace operation."[28] In spite of this, some scholars contend that democratization—meaning the move away from an authoritarian form of political regime—can occur through elections, given the way in which in and of themselves they generate incentives and interests among key actors that lead (over time) to the emergence of democratic politics.[29]

In Afghanistan, as elsewhere, the international community has prioritized elections in the hope of quickly establishing a legitimate, democratic regime.[30] But elections have largely failed to achieve this goal—indeed, in many ways, the rapid promotion of elections has actually contributed to increasing the insecurity of the country's political landscape. In many instances, elections in Afghanistan have actually encouraged violence, stagnation, and the inequitable distribution of resources, conditions that most commentators would consider very undemocratic. As Edward Mansfield and Jack Snyder have demonstrated convincingly in regard to other contexts, the Afghan case reveals that so-called "democratic transitions" can in fact exacerbate rather than alleviate conflict.[31] This is a recurring theme throughout this book. For the time being, however, a key issue in untangling the relationship between values and processes is the complex nature of sovereignty in Afghanistan. When explored and unpacked, this can shed light on the multiple structures of authority that render election processes so complex in the Afghan context.

ELECTIONS AND SOVEREIGNTY

One of the most glaring problems with a strict procedural definition of elections that describes them as granting authority in the Weberian bureaucratic-rational legal sense is that such a definition assumes that the state functions according to a distinctly modern, Western ideal. In the Afghan case, a major issue with this assumption is that sovereignty—typically understood as a position of ultimate political authority—does not reside with the state (or elsewhere) as a single, consolidated entity. Instead, sovereignty is constantly contested and negotiated by government officials, community leaders, religious figures, businessmen, and others. Simultaneously, however, the international community has treated the Afghan state since the U.S.-led invasion in 2001 as if it were such a bureaucratic-rational legal entity.[32]

Recently, both political scientists and anthropologists have begun to question how useful the classic definition linking the state and sovereignty actually is. Distinctions have been made between different types of state sovereignty, such as Stephen Krasner's conceptions of international legal sovereignty, Westphalian sovereignty, domestic sovereignty, and interborder trade sovereignty.[33] Such a complication helps us analyze the complexity of sovereignty and the need to move beyond an all-encompassing term, but it does not address a more fundamental issue: case studies, both from today and historically, demonstrate the fact that sovereignty is almost constantly contested and shifting. To counter this, states use the fiction of absolute sovereignty in an effort to organize and control populations.[34] They attempt to reinforce this notion of hegemony through the performance of sovereignty, as explored in both Foucault's classic study of the spectacular performative violence of punishment during the medieval period and his vision of the near constant monitory state of the panopticon.[35] But as numerous studies have shown, there are few grounded cases in the world today where such hegemonic forces actually completely dominate the political landscape. Instead, sovereignty is constantly disputed, and individuals in each society remain locked in debate over what the state is and where the bounds of its sovereignty are. These tests of sovereignty can range from an American drone strike in Pakistan to the nonviolent protester during the Arab Spring whose passive resistance publicly exposes the state's inability or unwillingness to assert authority.

This understanding has some useful implications for our study of elections, along with the representative government that they claim to create by giving people the right to endow a state with absolute power. In reality, the abilities of both sides are severely curtailed: citizens rarely have the full range of rights promised by most definitions of democracy (particularly through the racialization and gendering of citizenship),[36] but states also do not have the hegemonic control that Foucault's vision of the panopticon suggests. Instead of understanding elections as strictly defining winners and losers, which then grant the state sovereignty over the people, it is thus more useful to see them in the context of this constant debate over sovereignty, where the definitions of power and authority are never clear or as static as they seem.

SOVEREIGNTY AND POWER IN AFGHANISTAN

While sovereignty is debated in all political societies, from small acts of resistance to large public demonstrations, the case of Afghanistan is extreme.[37] Beyond decades of fighting, this tension over definitions has deeper roots in Afghanistan's long history of tension between tribes on the periphery and a weak state at the center, compounded by social values that emphasize both individualism and the group.[38] This has created a political landscape in which the government is not just treated warily, but where its position in local political life is questioned daily on almost every level.

Dispute resolution in Afghanistan, for example, rarely takes place within the state court system. Instead, there is a vibrant informal justice sector that relies on local elders and religious figures, and mechanisms such as *shuras*, or councils, and jirgas, which are generally ad hoc bodies of close male kin brought together to resolve a specific dispute or discuss some other political issue. However, these mechanisms are rarely completely independent of the state and often look to get their decisions certified by government officials. More often than not, though, they turn to district governors or chiefs of police instead of officials in the weaker judicial branch such as judges and prosecutors.[39] This means that the ability to ultimately resolve disputes is not just contested between government officials and these supposedly non-state actors; it is actively disputed even within formal government structures.

Closely related is the way in which governance at a local level often involves a series of compromises between the district governor, local elders, former mujahideen commanders, and, in some areas, members of the Taliban or other insurgent groups. These groups all vie for control of territory, allocation of resources, and influence over social ordering. Such a system suggests that sovereignty as understood by local communities has much less to do with formal governance structures outlined in the constitution than it does with a constant struggle over authority and legitimacy within the communities themselves.

The situation has been further complicated in recent years by the role of the international community in development, but also in programs that focus on governance and rule of law. The international military's strategy of "clear, hold, build" in insurgent areas demands a presence of local Afghan government personnel that the central government is often unable to provide.[40] As a result, the military and private contractors funded by the United States Agency for International Development (USAID) and other donors have set up independent local councils to make governance decisions in some areas, creating a system with often tenuous links to the national government. Across the country, the provision of development aid, often circumventing but sometimes in cooperation with local government officials, weakens the image of the state as a provider of resources. Furthermore, state monopoly of violence is challenged by the role of international military troops who were called on by many communities to provide security during the 2009 and 2010 elections.

We feel it is a mistake to view these elements of international intervention as separate from the Afghan political system. Instead of creating pure parallel structures, these groups and programs are instead intertwined with local politics, sometimes strengthening the position of local government officials, sometimes weakening them. Within election campaigns themselves, some candidates have gained political capital from their relationships with NGOs or other international actors, while others have used anti-Western rhetoric to mobilize voters. In such cases, it is thus vital to analyze the international presence as integral to local political systems as we seek to understand the impact of elections on a local level.

In addition, the insurgency has further eroded the ability of the Afghan government to claim sovereignty. Beyond demonstrating the government's inability to assert its own authority across much of its territory, the insurgency also sets up another, competing system of governance and rule of law in many areas. Almost all of the provinces in the country had Taliban "shadow governors" by 2009, accompanied in many places by an active system of Taliban courts.[41] As the international military began its troop "surge" in 2009, its embrace of counterinsurgency theory worked off the assumption that most of the communities supporting insurgents were not doing so for ideological reasons, but because almost eight years of international intervention had failed to meet communities' most basic demands of security, effective governance, and justice. It appeared that the Taliban, in some instances, were actually delivering "government services," such as justice, more efficiently than the internationally backed national government.

Furthermore, the insurgency fits into a more than thirty-year trend of increasingly questioning state legitimacy. Since the communist coup in 1978 brought to power a highly unpopular government, almost all subsequent governments have failed to establish legitimacy among a significant percentage of the population, reinforcing the idea that state legitimacy and sovereignty is constantly debatable and open to being quickly, and brutally, reshaped. The commonly perceived failure to establish sovereignty has deeply shaped politics, even in those areas furthest from the insurgency, because it has served as a constant reminder that state power is far from absolute.

Recent literature exploring weak state systems and the "shadow state" has focused in particular on how non-state figures use state apparatuses in order to enrich themselves, while simultaneously (and ironically) deepening the penetration of the state into society.[42] But in the Afghan context, the dividing line between state and non-state actors is often far from clear.[43] Ahmed Wali Karzai, the half-brother of the president assassinated in 2011, was head of the provincial council in Kandahar Province, generally acknowledged leader of the Popalzai tribe, commander of a sizable militia, on the CIA payroll, and, depending on whom you believe, a facilitator of the opium trade or, perhaps, the drug kingpin of the South. With kin connections to the president and a formal post himself, he was not only a government official, but deeply tied to the state. At the same time, however, many would argue that most of his authority came instead from his tribal links and his ability to threaten violence. Certainly no other head of a provincial council (in most provinces a weak and sidelined institution) was as influential anywhere else in the country. In fact, it is arguable that it was Ahmed Wali Karzai himself who gave the Kandahar provincial council its influence, and not the other way round; now that he is dead, the council has declined in status. Ultimately, Ahmed Wali Karzai challenges almost every conventional model for understanding political power.

While Ahmed Wali Karzai may be a rather extreme example, there are few government officials in Afghanistan today who do not have some alternative source of political capital due to links with tribes, militia groups, political parties, or merchants. Similarly, there are very few supposedly non-state figures— such as those same tribal elders, militia members, party members, and merchants—who have not tried to reinforce their political capital by developing relations with government officials or institutions. As a result, in Afghanistan, terms like *state actor* or *non-state actor* are not only oversimplifications, but they often disguise the numerous other sources of power which are in play.

On a more local level, elected representatives including parliamentarians and provincial council members are often grouped together with other local leaders in most Afghan political discussions. They are expected to provide their followers with hospitality and serve feasts on holidays, combining these elements of more "traditional" influence with the influence they have gained through their government posts.[44] Elected officials are not thought of as a separate class of political leader, but live on a spectrum that includes an incredible array of different actors. While religious leaders, commanders, and parliamentarians may look very different to the outside observer—from the clothes that they wear to the way they describe their own authority— these figures are all competing in the same local arena, often using similar personal networks.

These examples serve to demonstrate just how unbounded sovereignty can be in the Afghan case. As a consequence, the link between the Afghan state, government officials, and sovereign political authority cannot be assumed to function in the same way as it does in Western Europe, for example. Olivier Roy describes this relationship between community and state in Afghanistan as one of "externality and compromise."[45] This means that while communities are rarely without connections to the state, their relationship with it is the subject of continuous renegotiation and bargaining, with processes of realignment often involving violence in some form.

In fact, even the link between state and territory is at some points tenuous in political narratives about Afghanistan. The Durand line designating the border between Pakistan and Afghanistan has yet to be recognized by either side; many Afghans still consider Peshawar to be part of greater "Pashtunistan," an issue that remains a source of tension to this day.[46] In addition, the alleged presence in Pakistan of figures such as Gulbuddin Hekmatyar[47] and Mullah Omar (widely believed to be supported by Pakistan's Inter-Services Intelligence) leads many Afghans to argue that there is no such thing as purely domestic politics.[48]

Much of this is due to the tumult of not just the past decade in Afghanistan, but the past century, as the old pattern of struggle for political legitimacy, previously confined to the Mohammadzai subtribe of the Durrani Pashtuns, was upset.[49] The factional fighting during the civil war period in particular highlighted with devastating clarity just how open this struggle for national political legitimacy has become. On a local level this has been even more severe, with certain areas changing hands repeatedly between pro-Soviet forces, jihadi parties, other local militias, and the Taliban.

In addition, contested authority at both a local and a national level has raised important questions not just over which individuals should rule, but over what *type* of individual should have political authority. In some areas, particularly during the Taliban period, religious figures became more important; during the civil war, local commanders took on increasingly central roles, and government bureaucrats saw their positions rise during the Soviet period, fall during the civil war, and rise again with the American invasion. This has made the very nature of what the government should look like and how sovereignty should be understood a source of constant debate. These questions have put a particular premium on the framing of political narratives to portray certain groups as more or less legitimate. As a result, narratives about the nature of sovereignty and which groups or figures should command power at both the local and national level have more recently become a crucial aspect of the election process.

With multiple sources of political legitimacy and no clear divide between state and non-state actors, elections in Afghanistan cannot really be simply about "winners" and "losers." This is because the legitimacy "won" in an election by a given candidate is in itself not enough to establish a political position and must be supplemented by other means of authority. Conversely, local leaders also use positions in the provincial council or Wolesi Jirga to augment other forms of authority, which are based on their positions as tribal leaders, religious figures, or simply as influential individuals. By the same token, the legitimacy "lost" by a candidate failing to gain political office in a state institution through elections can also be regained through other means, such as threats of violence, decisions about capital investment, or the use of government connections to secure resources for a community.

The most useful way to understand elections in our analysis is thus as one of many interconnected venues of political contestation. Elections themselves have come to be one of the more important sites for struggle because they are a particularly public venue in a political landscape that has put an increasing premium on secrecy and a lack of transparency. In this sense they can be analyzed as a type of political theater in which actors not only attempt to win positions but also publicly posture, demonstrating their influence or attempting to increase their status within communities. At the same time, the fact that elections are now being held in Afghanistan on a regular basis means that they are beginning to become ritualized. All of this serves to demonstrate the fact that elections in Afghanistan are a dynamic process, with recent changes such as an increase in corruption to lower numbers of participants continuing to alter the ways that elections reshape Afghan political life.

We feel that this approach to elections is important not only because it highlights how elections have shaped politics in Afghanistan (and, of course, how politics in Afghanistan have shaped elections) but also because looking at them as lived experiences that take place within certain political landscapes suggests ways to further the study of elections in other settings.

STUDYING ELECTIONS

This book is based on a compilation of evidence gathered by the authors and a team of Afghan researchers based at the Afghanistan Research and Evaluation Unit (AREU) between 2008 and 2011. It draws out and examines a number of key themes that emerged from a number of different, but related, research projects on various aspects of governance in Afghanistan, including political parties, elections, democratization, internal parliamentary dynamics, and relationships between representatives and their communities. Over seven hundred interviews were conducted in total.

The research was primarily ethnographic in the sense that researchers focused on a specific series of communities and attempted to understand the local political landscape in its entirety and how it was shaped by social and cultural issues. Most of the interviews took the form of semi-structured conversations with respondents on and around these different subjects, with an emphasis on stories and local examples of how national politics were playing out on a local level. We also spent time in bazaars, schools, polling stations, the waiting rooms of district government offices, and other public spaces, conducting less formal interviews. Interviews were not confined to electoral issues, but often became wide-ranging political discussions that offered insights into local politics as they were being experienced by those in the community. In particular, we attempted to focus on the disputes or conflicts that were most discussed within the community, and then to study how those issues played out during the election process. Moving beyond simply focusing on electoral processes themselves, we were able to observe how elections and campaigns were actually affecting the major political issues in the area.

While we also conducted interviews with diplomats, election officials from the international community, and other international actors involved in the process, the overarching focus of data collection was on gaining Afghan perspectives from a variety of different geographical areas and across a spectrum of social groups. Over the course of the research, interviews were conducted in Kabul, Balkh, Parwan, Nangarhar, Nimroz, Ghazni, and Paktya Provinces. These provinces represent diverse social, ethnic, economic, and political landscapes, each with their own particular political dynamics. This diversity allowed for an exploration of how far elections are framed by localized political and social contexts. We also attempted to interview from as broad a range of groups as possible, including men, women, youth, religious leaders, elders, literate and illiterate people, those with full-time salaried positions in government, shopkeepers, laborers, and farmers. Even more significant was the intentional mix of urban and rural perspectives involved.[50]

As a result of our approach, our analysis is both local and national. While this may at times produce a confusing number of actors, the combination is important because it ultimately reflects how voters themselves perceived the elections. Local political issues often had ties to much larger, national-level struggles, especially given the tendency of groups to try and link their communities to national-level patronage networks through avenues such as ethnically based political parties. For example, understanding candidates' use of local land disputes in Ghazni Province to mobilize voters requires an awareness of the political history of the relationship between Pashtuns and Hazaras—the dominant groups in the province—at a national level. In general, our focus shifts with chapters 4, 6, and 8 often focusing on national issues (while looking at their local implications) and chapters 5 and 7 focusing on local issues (while linking them to national-level debates). While it can be challenging to follow these issues at different levels simultaneously, any attempt to learn from the recent Afghan elections that does not endeavor to do so is bound to miss either the ways that political issues actually played out in people's lives, or the way that they shaped national-level political issues.

In order to gain more ethnographic depth, we have chosen to focus on four districts where we spent much of our time in particular when analyzing politics at a local level. These areas were the focus of a substantial proportion of our research work and provide particularly useful contrasts between each other. We also feel that these examples help to tell the story of Afghanistan's elections most effectively. The areas are Dasht-i Barchi and Qara Bagh in Kabul Province, Kaldar in Balkh Province, and Ahmad Aba in Paktya Province. While elections are national- and provincial-level processes, many of the central issues are extremely localized, and this local, ethnographic focus allowed us to deal with issues in more depth in these four areas.

TABLE 1.1 DISTRICTS OF FOCUS

DISTRICT	PROVINCE	SETTING	ETHNICITY
Kaldar	Balkh	Primarily rural	Primarily Turkmen
Ahmad Aba	Paktya	Primarily rural	Pashtun
Dasht-i Barchi	Kabul	Urban	Primarily Hazara
Qara Bagh	Kabul	Densely settled rural area	Tajik/Pashtun mix

As a result of this approach there are certain key political issues that will return repeatedly in various chapters. In Qara Bagh, a semi-urban ethnically diverse district in northern Kabul Province, disputes over government land and internationally or government-sponsored building projects were particularly important. In Kaldar, the position of the Turkmen vis-à-vis other ethnic groups and the area's poor economic conditions shaped much of local politics. In Ahmad Aba, a primarily Pashtun district dominated by the Ahmadzai tribe, the relationship between the insurgency and local instability was the prevailing issue. And in Dasht-i Barchi, an urban area in western Kabul, it was the tension between young, increasingly urbanized Hazara residents and their communities of origin in Ghazni and Bamiyan Provinces that dominated conversations. These issues are all primarily local, but were deeply linked to issues across the country; issues with the insurgency in Ahmad Aba, ethnicity in Dasht-i Barchi, and development in Kaldar all had parallels in numerous other parts of the country.

Qualitative, semi-structured interviews provided our primary method for gathering data, given our focus on lived political experience as described through the stories of Afghans themselves. This allowed a focus on people's perceptions of elections, as opposed to the precise processes and regulations that were often not followed.[51] For example, while we often tried to verify rumors of fraud or manipulation, we ultimately believe that the perception of fraud is more important than fraud itself, since this dictates popular responses to the new government and to the elections themselves as well as other political processes. Similarly, in the Afghan case, rumors of power and a reputation for resorting to violence can have just as much effect as actual access to things like weapons and government positions.

In addition to this, we conducted some limited quantitative polling, most systematically before the presidential and provincial council elections of 2009. However, beyond presenting serious methodological challenges and consuming large amounts of time, such polls often miss the diversity of issues from district to district, leaving a rather incomplete picture of local political issues.[52] In this respect, the research leans further in the direction of anthropology than political science, but can be seen through an interpretative lens of social explanation. As such, we see political processes such as elections not as structures that remain constant in any environment, but rather filled with meaning assigned by their participants in a manner that reflects the specific circumstances of a given location or community.

THE ROAD AHEAD

With the groundwork established here, the following chapters of this book deal with all elections that have taken place since the U.S.-led invasion in 2001. However, their focus is primarily on the 2009 and 2010 elections, not only because we gathered the most data during this period but also because they demonstrated most strongly how elections can serve as venues where political power is contested and redefined. In particular, communities and individuals learned much from the election process of 2004 and 2005 and adapted their political strategies accordingly. In doing so, they reshaped how elections were contested, ultimately contributing to increasing instability, corruption, and political stagnation.

As a result of this focus, the book proceeds both chronologically and thematically. Chapters may refer to events taking place in other periods as well, but we have made an effort to keep each chapter as contained as possible. Chapter 2 gives a brief history of elections and governance processes in Afghanistan, while chapter 3 looks specifically at the process of setting up elections following the U.S.-led invasion. Chapter 4 focuses on the failure of the Wolesi Jirga to create an effective opposition force to President Karzai, particularly following the elections of 2004 and 2005. Chapter 5 focuses on the presidential and provincial council elections of 2009 as a context for understanding the ways that local communities and individuals have attempted to manipulate elections, and some of the repercussions of these practices. Chapter 6 focuses on the period between the 2009 and 2010 elections and the failure of the international community to create lasting reforms. Chapter 7 looks at the role of violence and instability in elections, particularly the Wolesi Jirga election of 2010. Chapter 8 looks at the aftermath of the 2010 elections, in particular, and how the process has been manipulated at a national level by Karzai and other members of the ruling elite. Chapter 9 is a conclusion that attempts both to look forward into Afghanistan's political future and to generalize some of the lessons of how the social sciences understand elections in other contexts as well.

2

OF BALLOTS AND BOUNDARIES

A Brief History of Political Participation in Afghanistan

THE POLLING STATION

*A*UGUST 20, 2009. *Election Day in Kabul fell on a particularly hazy summer morning. Security concerns kept many people indoors initially, the streets feeling eerily empty. As the morning progressed, however, the city's intricate network of alleyways, side roads, and paved thoroughfares became gradually busier: dozens of schools, clinics, and other public buildings across the province were briefly transformed into hives of activity as people turned out to cast their votes. One polling center, located in a small village school between the districts of Istalif and Qara Bagh, was crowded for much of the morning, the main road outside choked with parked cars, pickup trucks, and a few conspicuous SUVs.*

Inside, balloting was taking place across four different empty classrooms. Women voted in another building around the back of the school, the blue line of burqa-clad voters barely visible from the men's polling center. Across other locations in the district the separation between men's and women's voting varied. In several more conservative areas, the two were entirely separate from each other and a good distance away. In other centers across Qara Bagh, however, men and women simply lined up on opposite sides of the same school courtyard, visible to each other across the playground.

A low wall surrounded the school grounds and a policeman stood by the empty volleyball court, frisking men one at a time as they entered through the narrow gate. The police watched sternly as onlookers and those who had already voted milled around curiously watching the process, but there were no serious attempts to return inside to cast a second vote. On a low table next to the policeman was a small pile of knives that he was holding while their owners voted. Inside the gate there was a line of about forty men snaking up to the actual school building itself. Most of the men were not standing, but crouched in the shade of several mulberry trees. Although it was still early, the heat of the day was approaching fast and shade was in short supply. Another couple of policemen, including the commander of the police unit assigned to the polling center, leaned back on chairs at the entrance to the building, letting in a few men at a time.

Inside, classrooms had been cleared of their desks, which had been tossed haphazardly into the courtyard to make way for a series of five-foot-tall cardboard cutout booths, each with a pen attached with a length of twine. Although they had been arranged in a semicircle to provide a degree of privacy, with the confusion of men moving around the room it was still fairly easy to watch how others were voting.

There were several officials in the room, marked by the plastic vests they wore over their shirts with the Independent Election Commission (IEC) logo printed on them. These men attempted to keep order as voters jostled their way through the school's dark, narrow hallways. Inside one of the classrooms, voters submitted their laminated registration cards to the scrutiny of an elderly election official seated at a small table. If he was satisfied that the voter and the card matched (and in several instances he was not), he would write down the voter's name and identification number on a sheet in front of him and punch a hole in the card to show it had been used. He then took the index finger of the man's right hand and dipped it in a small container of ink—the permanence of which (or lack thereof) was to be the source of many debates in the media in the ensuing days.

At the next table, another official was handing out ballots, giving two to each voter. The first was the presidential ballot, a long page with the details of 42 candidates divided into two columns. Each candidate was represented by a number, a photo, their name, and a symbol. Symbols ranged from pieces of fruit through gas canisters and aircraft to books and pens. Some of the symbols that were most suggestive included that chosen by Hamid Karzai: the scales of justice.

FIGURE 2.1 Election Monitors at a Polling Station

The second ballot was for the provincial council; at twelve pages long, it looked more like a glossy magazine. These candidates were also represented by their name, number, photo, and symbol, but in this instance there were so many pages that confused voters often struggled to find their candidates among over 500 pictures. After voting carefully in the presidential election, many voters seemed to simply mark their provincial council ballots randomly. One old man, in a show of exasperation, tried to ask an IEC staff member for help. The official walked over and pointed to a figure on the ballot. He then turned, shrugged, and asked, "What can I do?"

In addition to IEC officials and voters, there were also a series of monitors or agents from each of the local candidates, marked out by the laminated cards they wore around their necks. As the room became more crowded, the occasional squabble broke out between the tightly packed voters and monitors as IEC staff attempted unsuccessfully to stop new voters from entering. Although each candidate was supposed to be able to assign only certain accredited monitors, in several instances monitors leaving the polling station simply took off their cards and handed them to others taking their place.

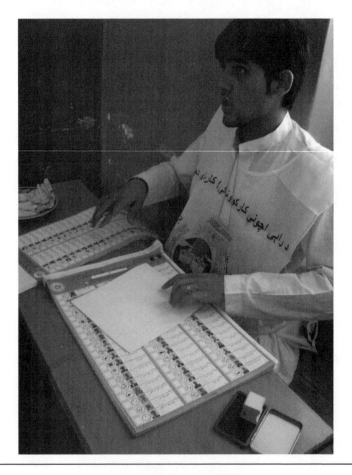

FIGURE 2.2 Provincial Ballot

While most voters waited patiently in line, there was clearly some tension at several points during the process. In an effort to keep those who had already voted away, the chief official at the station at one point attempted to clear the entire area, telling the men sitting around in the street outside that they had to move back to the village center, a little ways up the road. When the police came out, they grudgingly began to shuffle back, but only staying a couple of steps ahead of the police officers.

After some murmuring a short local elder in a gray turban came forward to speak with the official. Their discussion gradually grew more heated: Whose right was it to observe the elections? The official, perspiring lightly in a button-down shirt, explained that it was his duty alone to enforce state regulations, while the elder with a vigorous sweep of his arms to toward the men behind him, suggested the process should be watched by the entire community. Eventually, the local police commander intervened. Having listened from a few steps back, he made it clear that he would not let the election official use his officers to clear the area, but also did not say that he agreed with the elder. Sensing that he had lost the argument, the official compromised and let men back into the surrounding field, but not into the school grounds themselves. Somewhat exasperated, he turned back inside.

Across Afghanistan, elections brought out similar tensions and negotiations about how the polls should be conducted and more generally how political processes should work, ranging from the rather gentle disagreement described above to armed attacks. In virtually all cases, however, it became clear that this was a community process, and one which, in its ability to draw lingering crowds and provoke heated debate, resembled other forms of local decision-making and leadership selection that have evolved within Afghan communities over years. An understanding of these practices in the context of Afghan history sheds some important light on the contours of the political landscape onto which elections after the American-led invasion were imposed.

EARLY ELECTIONS: PARTICIPATION AND PROCEDURE AT THE LOCAL LEVEL

To begin to look at how elections fit into wider patterns of governance and local politics in Afghanistan, it is important to place them within political and historical contexts that extend far beyond the events of the past decade.

While some hailed the 2004 and 2005 elections—the first to be held following the international intervention in 2001—as the first steps toward an Afghan democracy, there were nonetheless precedents in place: earlier elections, but also a history of community consultation in the selection of leaders, that affected the way in which the polls played out.

The year 2004 may have marked the first fully participatory election for a national leader that had ever taken place in Afghanistan, but it was not the first election for many older Afghans. Prior to 2004, relatively free parliamentary polls had taken place in 1949, with the establishment of the so-called Liberal Parliament (1949–1952).[1] Later, during what is sometimes referred to as the "decade of democracy" (1963–1973), parliamentary elections took place under the reforms and new constitution of Zahir Shah in 1964, and again in 1969. This fledgling electoral cycle was cut short in 1973 by a coup in which Mohammed Daoud Khan (a cousin of the king and former prime minister) put an end to the constitutional monarchy and declared the beginning of the Republic.[2]

These early parliamentary elections were in many ways the forerunners of those to be held in 2005. There were obvious parallels, including the way in which candidates were directly elected as individuals, not (officially) party members, at the local level to serve in the lower house of the bicameral parliament in Kabul. In the 1960s, a set number of seats were allocated to each of the then twenty-eight provinces, dependent on population estimates, comprising a total of 216 representatives (as compared with 249 today). These elected officials represented a much smaller population, however.[3] Official constituencies were also smaller, and the number of seats and candidates per constituency significantly lower.

The Municipal Law of 1947 also began the process of electing some of the officials in towns and cities of over 10,000 residents.[4] Towns were split into wards or neighborhoods, called *nahiyah*, which would each formally elect two representatives to form the municipal council. Relatively few candidates competed in these polls: in Kabul, for example, in 1962, only three candidates competed officially for the two seats in each of the ten nahiyah.[5]

At the time, the government was openly rejecting candidates at all levels when they did not meet with the approval of the ruling elite, making election processes for parliamentary and municipal councils hardly free or transparent.[6] There was also a widespread sense among voters in Kabul that the central government controlled the outcome of elections regardless of the popular vote, although, as Louis Dupree notes, few Kabulis appeared to have taken part in municipal polls.[7] Despite this, in interviews we conducted a number of older people talked about the "old system" as more appropriate to the context, and more representative. With smaller official constituencies for parliamentarians, voters in these elections were more likely to be familiar with the candidates and, as a consequence, these people claimed in retrospect to have felt some connection to their representatives. In conversations we had with respondents about the parliament, people talked about the concept of *ashnai*, familiarity, as of real significance to their feeling represented. Whereas for Afghan parliamentary elections now, a candidate's potential constituency constitutes an entire province; in 1965 and 1969, candidates competed for seats in much smaller electoral districts. In Kabul city, there were five districts (each comprising two nahiyah) and thus five seats available for parliament, each confined to a specific district constituency. Candidates for the seats in these five urban constituencies numbered no more than seven in each.[8]

More generally, the memory of these earlier elections made older respondents particularly likely to speak of a period when they felt that they had a certain say in selecting their representatives. Even among younger voters, the 1960s and 1970s were considered a golden age of stability, despite much of the active political repression of dissidents undertaken by the government during this period. As we will see in later chapters, this contrast only made communities more critical of the internationally sponsored elections after 2004.

One problem with the "old" system, however, was that its apparently greater propensity for representation was also a weakness in terms of its inability to encourage cross-ethnic or intergroup interaction. According to the 1960s method, for example, a candidate needed only to convince his kinfolk and wider community of his ability to stand for the parliament or municipal council without having to court the communities on the other side of the road. As electoral districts were smaller, they were often ethnically homogeneous.[9] In a sense, this was convenient, reflecting the complete lack of structures or institutions—such as political parties—that could facilitate greater interaction between otherwise separate groups at a local level. This meant that even while elections allowed a degree of public political participation, elected bodies presented little real challenge to the king or other members of the small ruling elite, who retained a tight grasp on the entire process. (See Chronology: Timeline of Elections and Other Major Historical Events in Afghanistan, page ooo.)[10]

POLITICAL PARTIES:
PARTICIPANTS AT THE FRINGE

Although they did not provide coherent platforms for electoral competition at the time, parties did exist in Afghanistan in the 1960s. In some respects—for example, through their active newspapers and membership lists—they functioned more as parties, in the Western sense of institutions organizing political activity, then, than most of Afghanistan's current political parties, which gained much of their status as militias fighting against the Soviet Union. Nevertheless, they were unable to secure formal recognition as political organizations from the ruling monarchy. A bill authorizing parties' existence was drafted and passed by parliament in 1968, but was never signed by the king.[11]

Zahir Shah's hesitance to grant formal approved status to parties could be seen as part of an existing trend: since the early twentieth century, political organizations had been marginalized by successive leaders who viewed these groups (sometimes accurately) as a potential source of violent, regime-threatening opposition.[12] Principally for this reason, leaders endeavored to limit political activity among their opponents—whether it was Amanullah Khan's imprisonment of his uncle Nasrullah in the early years of the century, after claiming the throne for himself; the government's dissolution of the newly formed Student Union at Kabul University in 1951; Zahir Shah disallowing party newspapers and refusing to sign the party law; or Daoud and his intolerance of opposition during his presidency; or even the rival factions of the People's Democratic Party of Afghanistan (PDPA) and their brutal, paranoid persecution of each other.[13] This history of an intolerance of competition pushed opposition groups to the fringes, preventing them from partaking in or critiquing the affairs of government in a manner that resonated with the public.[14]

During the Soviet occupation, political parties increasingly began to resemble violent, military factions whose support bases were often ethnically determined. The Soviet period had forced many of the Islamic parties established in the decades before the Soviet invasion to flee across the borders to neighboring countries, where they were able to conduct their activities more freely. These groups' rise to prominence in Pakistan and Iran also facilitated a stockpiling of weapons and resources that would be put to use in the large-scale destruction of Kabul in the civil war that followed. On the one hand, the Soviet era consolidated the mujahideen parties' support bases among different sectors of Afghan society—not least because these parties used their influence to control distribution of foreign aid in refugee camps and the areas they controlled across the borders.[15] But on the other hand, continuous shifts in party leadership and alliances, particularly in the early 1990s, demonstrated to many Afghans the superficiality of their leaders' promises and their brazen desire for power. Given their vivid memories of this violent and manipulative reputation, it is little wonder that most Afghans we talked to considered the prospect of empowering parties after the 2001 invasion to be hazardous at best.

The importance of these parties and their activities during the jihad and civil war periods leads many outsiders, particularly those who attempt to compare Afghanistan to the Balkans, to put ethnicity at the center of processes of political identification. Yet in the Afghan context, political negotiations and alliances happen just as much in spite of ethnicity as they do because of it. Historically, Afghanistan has been ethnically diverse and even in the more homogeneous areas, such as the Pashtun south, it is common to find pockets of Tajiks or other ethnic groups, particularly in the cities. In areas where Pashtuns do dominate, groups divide themselves further along tribal lines, and even further, by lineage—it is not rare to encounter men feuding with their cousins, but allied with their neighbors of different tribes. At a higher level, this means struggles *within* a given group over its control are in many instances more intense and violent than struggles *between* various groups. Partially in response to these tensions, Afghanistan has a long history of political alliances, but also business partnerships and marriage arrangements, which cross ethnic and tribal lines.

This can make organizing politics according to ethnic identity a challenging prospect for a would-be party; and as a consequence, it is something that occurs for the most part only during periods of stress and conflict. During these times, people's willingness to trust those outside their immediate kin is understandably lessened. For this reason, ethnicity became critically important as a mobilizing tool during the civil war period, but later diminished as local groups—often from the same ethnicity—competed with each other for resources immediately following the U.S. invasion. Evidently, ethnicity remains a potent rallying cry in leaders' attempts to mobilize supporters and has resurfaced in recent years as the threat of insurgency has increased. As a general rule, however, if ethnic divides are not reinforced by other political or economic alliances, they tend to have minimal political impact on the daily lives of most Afghans.

BEYOND ELECTIONS: PARTICIPATION WITH A WIDE-ANGLE LENS

When looking at political participation throughout Afghan history, it becomes apparent that elections are only a part of a much more interesting story of public interaction with governance structures in the country. Thomas Barfield argues that at the national level much of the political history of Afghanistan since the founding of the modern Afghan state in 1747 is the story of an expanding notion of political legitimacy, both in terms of who could legitimately rule the country and whose job it was to choose the ruler.[16] This can be traced in part through the common Afghan political narrative about the selection of political leaders through tribal councils or loya jirgas.

Often cited as a "traditional" Afghan institution for selecting a leader, the institution of the loya jirga has changed significantly in the past 250 years, although its "traditional" nature has often been emphasized to mask what has actually constituted real political change. The jirga that selected the country's first ruler, Ahmed Shah in 1747, was a rather limited, rubber-stamp affair made up of only Abdali Pashtuns (later known as the Durrani Pashtuns). The next loya jirga was not held until 1915 (by King Habibullah), followed by a handful of others in the early twentieth century—in 1930, 1941, and 1955. These were held to ratify Nadir Shah's accession to the throne, to affirm a position of neutrality in the Second World War, and to proclaim support for the king's stance on Pashtunistan, respectively.[17] Although the participants would be selected from a slightly wider section of social elites as time passed, these meetings continued to be mostly formalities, with the group acknowledging preordained leaders or issues that had already been settled through complex, behind-the-scenes political negotiations. Despite this near-constant elite manipulation, the loya jirga remains an important process which many Afghans speak about as a quasi-democratic institution with deep roots in Afghan history.[18]

Far beneath the national-level negotiations that loya jirgas would supposedly symbolize, ad hoc *jirgas* (or councils) largely based on principles of consensus have existed as local-level decision-making mechanisms for years.[19] In Dupree's terms, these "rough and ready democratic institutions"[20] have in turn been augmented and shaped by a fierce cultural focus on individual equality and the belief that all men, particularly Pashtun men, are entitled to a certain level of self-determination.[21] Community leaders—maliks or khans—selected to lead these groups of elders often inherit their positions, but are still ratified and in other cases selected by the consensus of the group.[22] This in turn generally leads individuals in these positions to be responsive to those that they represent.

These bodies address a range of local issues, from dispute resolution to more general questions of local governance. The legitimacy of decisions made within jirgas is usually (but not always) generated through group consensus, often reached over periods of several days for complex issues. Acceptable "just" outcomes often involve both parties in a dispute taking some responsibility for its resolution—whether financially or through an agreement to accept the verdict. Oftentimes, agreements can be enforced through a proposed penalty, such as a small fee or the threat of having to provide food for the community. As Dupree describes, "the final decision [of a jirga] is binding on all involved parties and once announced is always considered unanimous. If a man does not abide by the jirga decision, his neighbors descend on him and force him to hold a feast for the entire village or camp."[23] This can often prove more of an incentive to keep to the bargain than any monetary sum.

However, while jirgas can be idealized as operating in this way, in reality such bodies are today often open to corruption and manipulation by those with certain political, economic, or military resources. In some instances, these bodies are the preserve of rich and powerful families and others often lacking the means to remove members should they abuse power.[24] In particular, the past three decades of instability have given powerful individuals a range of avenues for bypassing community consensus in establishing their authority. These include both the increased number of weapons available and funds from outside sources, such as international funds during the jihad, revenue from the narcotics industry, and even NGO support. In this way, those vying for local leadership positions are increasingly able to insulate themselves from some of the deeply democratic values historically associated with them. One of the results of this is the growing tendency of urban Afghans to complain about the corruption and conservatism of how politics based on the jirga system continues to work in the provinces. In the course of one conversation in the late spring of 2010, a teacher from Nangarhar both praised the jirga in his district of Jalalabad city as a locally accepted form of decision-making and criticized it bitterly as a corrupt manifestation of the power held by one family in the area.

It is often also common to find standing councils of local leaders, or shuras, in many parts of the country. These can be as small as gatherings of respected men in a local mosque, or as large as district- or tribal-level shuras. Historically, these bodies have played an important role in local governance, though as Chris Johnson and Jolyon Leslie point out, it is likely that in many parts of the country their role expanded rapidly during the jihad period.[25] During this time, communities realized that NGOs, aid groups, and others often preferred working with groups that appeared to be representative, giving them an incentive to set up these "traditional" bodies even if they did not have them already. However, while such local gatherings of elders may not have the deep histories that they occasionally claim to possess, their presence suggests that the *idea* of a decision-making body chosen by community members to represent them is not a foreign concept. Furthermore, by discussing them in idealized terms, there is often the sense that such groups *should* be representative and responsive to community needs, even when they are not.

Despite this emphasis on community participation, neither jirgas nor shuras are inclusive of the entire community, and their meetings rarely involve women, young men, or members of minority groups.[26] Newcomers or returnees to a given village or urban area can also be excluded, as one migrant recently returned from Iran told us in an interview in Nimroz Province in May 2010, relating how he had been systematically sidelined from local decision-making processes. Nevertheless, the existence of indigenous governance bodies that emphasize some degree of equality and representation should dispel the notion that Afghanistan is somehow culturally ill-equipped to handle democratic processes. Indeed, far from being a mechanism functioning with little or no connection to the state, these bodies also have a history of interaction with the central government, albeit negotiated. Existing jirgas and shuras have over the years formed the basis of different kinds of local councils—at the village, district, and provincial levels—which were semi-formalized in the twentieth century during Zahir Shah's reign. Writing in the early 1960s, Dupree describes the procedures used to select members for these councils.[27] To a greater or lesser degree, the state was involved in vetting candidates for council membership, and yet while these were not elections in the formal sense of the word, community involvement was formally considered a necessary part of the process.

These experiences—often personally remembered by the older generation—meant that Afghan individuals and communities came to the elections in 2004 with clear ideas about both what a representative and an unrepresentative government could look like. Unfortunately, this long history and evolution of decision-making practices was rarely acknowledged by international agencies in the years that would follow—many of whom would instead insist on the importance of "building the capacity" of Afghans in a variety of local governance issues, often paying lip service to "traditional" institutions and practices while emphasizing new programs as if they were building a democratic politics on an entirely blank slate.

3

ELECTING THE PEACE?

Afghanistan's Fast-Track Democracy

BA YAK GUL, BAHAR NAMEESHA (A SINGLE FLOWER DOES NOT MAKE SPRING)

*T*HE TREACHEROUS CLIMB *up the Kabul mountainside had to be made on foot: despite the best efforts of Hamid, our accomplished driver, the wheels of the white Corolla simply spat and spun for several minutes on the icy slopes. On leaving the vehicle at the bottom of the path, still a good 500 feet above the smog-soaked city, the best we could do on that freezing January morning was to remain upright on the slippery 45-degree incline, edging our way gingerly toward the parliamentarian's simple home. By the time we reached her two-roomed stone cottage on the mountain, we were an hour late for our interview.*

Unperturbed by the tardiness of our arrival, the parliamentarian greeted us warmly and immediately apologized for the humble surrounds in which she was hosting us. As we had arranged to meet during the 2006–2007 winter recess of parliament, at the end of its first year in office, she had been unable to procure a room in the legislative building on the other side of town. The heater was acting up, and so again with many an apology, she disappeared into the opposite room and returned with an enormous campal *(thick blanket) to cover the three of us (two female researchers and herself), and, cradling our steaming glass teacups for extra warmth, we began our conversation.*

Representing the remote province of Nuristan, the parliamentarian was keen to talk about the problems experienced by the women of the area. "There are so many difficulties for women, it would be impossible to count them. You shouldn't consider me as a typical example, as I am a wakil *(representative), and I am educated—but this is unusual for women. . . . There are no rights for women, they do not have the right to select a husband, or to go to school, and there is a lot of violence against them. If you have time I will take you to Nuristan and there you will see that many women do not even consider themselves human. The government does not work in these areas because there are no roads. They have no contact with the government and it does nothing for them." Instead, she explained, the province was controlled primarily by the provincial governor, who had connections with several influential members of Gulbuddin Hekmatyar's organization, Hizb-i Islami, and who controlled a network of commanders who had avoided Disarmament, Demobilization and Reintegration (DDR) processes by trading in their old weapons for cash and retaining their newer, more expensive models. Maintaining a close relationship with Hamid Karzai, the governor was able to access the patronage of the central state apparatus while functioning as a largely autonomous ruler in the region.*

After some time, the conversation turned to the subject of the Ministry of Women's Affairs (MoWA), established as part of the rebuilding of the Afghan state administration following the fall of the Taliban. And on this issue, the parliamentarian was unabashedly critical: "I think MoWA sounds beneficial in name but is in fact useless. . . . We support MoWA in parliament just to show the world that it exists and to show them that we are working for women in Afghanistan. But rural women do not know about MoWA—they do not know what it is for. We support it because of what the world would think if we did not. In the past few years MoWA has been also only for show, organizing workshops and getting funds, but it has not had a proper strategy. For example, last year it acquired funds to make women's gardens in three provinces. I am from Nuristan, and here women work very hard on the land, carrying baskets of wood, tying their children on their backs and taking them with them to work—they work like men. There are forced marriages there, where very young girls are married to old men, and family violence is common. MoWA does not think about these things, it thinks about gardens for women. I think having ministries like MoWA demonstrates the weakness of Karzai's government as he thinks about relationships and not about responsibilities."

As the discussion continued, this theme of the superficiality of change, primarily as a means to demonstrate "progress" to the outside world, recurred several times with reference to different examples—this was not limited to DDR efforts or MoWA but applied to the reintegration of warlords in parliament, to internationally sponsored women's caucuses in parliament, and to elections. It applied again and again to the way in which change in Kabul was mistakenly taken to indicate change in the country as a whole—a perspective to which the parliamentarian, as a Nuristani, repeatedly returned. While for many in the international community the establishment of these institutions signified steps on the road to democracy, Afghans we spoke to appeared far more skeptical of the depth of change that could be forged through what were often rushed, superficial, and symbolic "solutions."

As we left the cottage, bending to put back on our winter boots and outer layers while exchanging pleasantries and offers of future khedmat, *or assistance, with our research, it was difficult not to reflect on the critical words of the parliamentarian. Her blunt statements had clearly highlighted the void between the international ideas of what reserved seats for women might encourage, and the reality of provincial allegiances holding much stronger than connections to other female parliamentarians for the sake of promoting administrative change at the national level. Making our way carefully back down the still slippery mountainside, women were hanging washing to dry on makeshift lines outside of much smaller, dirtier homes as the sun began to melt the ice on the ground. Scolding grubby children as they did so, and glancing up with some skepticism at the clumsy foreigner slipping and sliding down the path, they seemed a world away from the life of politics and legislation that their neighbor had begun.*

STATE-BUILDING: A STORY OF CHANGE AND COMPROMISE

Soon after the initial military invasion of 2001 had ended, the United Nations hosted a conference in Bonn, Germany, to hammer out the process of rebuilding the Afghan state. This was considered a way for the United States and the international community more generally to compensate for lives and infrastructure lost in the invasion, and—less discussed, but more central—as a means to secure the region and prevent it from serving as a base for terrorism in the future.[1] The conference gave rise to what would later become known as the "Bonn process"—a series of state-building initiatives which laid out the groundwork for a new division of powers, with the establishment of an interim government, the drafting of a constitution, and preparations for elections in 2004 and 2005. In many ways, this indicated a potentially radical shift in the way Afghanistan was governed.

Yet throughout the debates and deliberations that would pervade this new process, it was possible to divide roughly the otherwise diverse views of policymakers into two different approaches. The first of these was that Afghans' generally positive view of international assistance in the immediate postwar period provided a major opportunity to promote change and development in the country, primarily through large-scale state-building processes. Agencies promoting women's interests, such as UNIFEM (United Nations Development Fund for Women), were among the major proponents of this view, seeing an opportunity or "policy window" through which to cement improvements to women's status as citizens, for example through the establishment of MoWA. The second approach, favored by Karzai and United Nations (UN) Special Representative Lakhdar Brahimi, among other key policymakers, was more conservative and prioritized stability and consensus over radical change.

Both of these stances were flawed, however. On the one hand, the assumption that new, state-of-the-art governmental structures could be built from scratch was belied by the remnants of many an institutional culture that survived in the rubble of the Kabul administration. Imagining that a return to the "status quo" would be possible, on the other hand, was also a grave error. Those romanticizing the days of the monarchy or the ascendancy of the civil service under the PDPA's Soviet-style socialism were neglecting to remember the changes that had taken place since these eras. In particular, they overlooked the way in which the very systems that had brought a limited degree of peace and prosperity to many during these earlier periods had been used and usurped by new, power-hungry elites, establishing themselves in place of those they had murdered or forced to flee.

What ultimately resulted from these conflicting approaches was a mixture of both—but with the second prevailing far above and beyond the first. The new Constitution of 2004, for example, was based largely on the king's Constitution of 1964 with very few amendments, save radical exceptions such as the provision for reserved seats for women in provincial councils, the lower house of parliament, and the senate. The electoral system also was molded around the second approach in an attempt to ensure it suited "the Afghan way," sidelining parties as a potential source of division and conflict. MoWA was established, but held little influence over administrative affairs. The changes that had been made paid lip service to global norms of "best practice": they did affect the way in which the new post-Taliban state developed, but lacked the substance to challenge the increasing influence of existing powerholders. As the parliamentarian from Nuristan concluded, many of these changes were adopted purely to suggest to the world that change was being made.

* * *

Contributing to the superficial nature of institutional change in Afghanistan at this time was how low a priority establishing a stable government seemed to be for many international actors. In a speech in February 2003, then-U.S. Defense Secretary Donald Rumsfeld declared that his country was not in the business of nation-building, making clear that this would be a task for the Afghan themselves.[2] Indeed, as Francis Fukuyama later described, in Afghanistan this was to be "a strategy of nation-building 'lite,' involving a rapid transition to local control and a tough-love policy that leaves locals to find their own way toward good government and democracy."[3] Fundamentally, this was a mission in the aftermath of 9/11 to ensure that Afghanistan, previously dubbed a "failed state," would never again provide a safe haven for terrorist activity. However, when applied to the realities of the Afghan context at the time, the agenda of the United States and other nations with troops in the country became increasingly expansive and less clear-cut. As Astri Suhrke has noted, this led to the "cascading of policy objectives" as more and more activities were added to the international mandate of intervention.[4] The blurred boundaries between short-term military stabilization and longer-lasting state-building aims were in some sense intentional, in that the "clear, hold, build" strategy and later counterinsurgency (COIN) efforts incorporated some aspects of state empowerment and reconstruction[5]—but there were also inherent contradictions between the two. These contradictions could be seen in international attempts to secure a basic political framework on which stable democratic institutions might be built. This framework—a new constitution, an established executive, and a functioning, elected legislature—was considered important as a means to facilitate the stabilization of the country. As such, this was the efficiency argument for state-building: that its potential contribution to the overall goal of stabilization alone would justify its presence in the overall strategy. But the quality and sustainability of the democratic institutions to be installed were never prioritized—these measures arguably were not so much an end in themselves but a means to achieve a broader security goal.

On a local level Afghans also became increasingly skeptical of the intentions of the international community. In conversations we had over the years it was common for people to point out the inconsistencies in international activities in the country, something that contributed to both a rise in conspiracy theories and a general resentment of the international presence in many areas. In the early days this often took the form of complaints against the presence of warlords in parliament: elections had been implemented, but the lack of international commitment to disarmament and candidate vetting had allowed the same old powerholders to prosper.[6]

Resulting from the mix of stabilization and state-building was a contradiction in terms of decision-making. Although as part of the state-building agenda efforts had been made to establish a sovereign administration and legitimate legislature, the urgency of military stabilization programs required most decisions concerning the presence of troops and the allocation of aid resources to be made by international policymakers and donor governments. These decisions often completely bypassed Afghan sources of authority, such as the parliament or provincial councils, in a manner clearly visible to the public—dramatically undermining people's confidence in their government's own decision-making abilities. Returning to the discussion of sovereignty in chapter 1, this was a critical demonstration of the way in which the Afghan state's *performance* of sovereign rule did not correspond with its actual ability to make executive decisions. This problem was compounded by a growing aid reliance over the decade of intervention which further undermined the government's accountability for national resources. Ministry officials were not forced to justify spending to their own citizens, but rather to international financial institutions and donors instead.[7] And perhaps most significantly, in a high-profile, costly, and dangerous war, the urgency of stabilization required that expediency trump process: the need for international actors to obtain information, to keep certain individuals "on side," or to achieve results quickly was often considered a higher priority than the need to ensure that political processes were institutionalized.[8] As we discuss in chapter 6, this would be the case with the figure of Pacha Khan Zadran, a commander from Paktya whose connections with the Haqqani network meant that his wavering allegiance to the Afghan government was encouraged by international actors at the cost of holding him to account for the deaths he caused in several successive uprisings in the region. In cases like these, personal connections were emphasized and exploited by international actors in ways that contradicted the democratic principles they preached.

The exercise of building the Afghan state in the aftermath of the fall of the Taliban was thus characterized by simultaneous processes of change and compromise—of the establishment of a basic democratic machinery that was consistently undermined by the demands of ongoing conflict and the instability this created. New institutions were not established in a vacuum, but affected and were affected by the context in which they were created. This became particularly evident in the results of international actors' emphasis on three key factors during the Bonn process: "tradition," legitimacy, and timing.

INTERNATIONAL PREOCCUPATIONS: "TRADITION," LEGITIMACY, AND TIMING

At the helm of the Bonn process, Lakhtar Brahimi and his colleagues designed a five-year exercise that would set up a series of sequential governing bodies (the emergency authority, interim authority, and transitional authority), concluding with presidential and parliamentary elections. Along the way, this process would be guided and ratified by the "traditional" means of holding loya jirgas, starting with the Emergency Loya Jirga in 2002 and moving on to the Constitutional Loya Jirga in 2003. In comparison to other international interventions in the aftermath of conflict, such as in the Balkans or East Timor, the approach in Afghanistan was more cautious, not insisting on the installation of "democracy" per se but carefully phrasing planned reforms in terms of promoting "responsible and representative government," for example.[9] As described by a diplomat closely linked to the negotiations that led to the Bonn Agreement, James Dobbins, the components of Bonn "drew heavily on traditional Afghan modalities for national decision-making," a factor which "clearly enhanced the legitimacy of the process in the eyes of the population as it went forward."[10]

But was this really the case? As described above, the "tradition" of the loya jirga in Afghanistan has been called into question in recent academic scholarship on the issue.[11] Furthermore, the so-called legitimacy of these events was undermined by a widespread concern among Afghans that decisions had been taken behind closed doors before they happened, particularly in the case of the Constitutional Loya Jirga in 2003.[12] Assumptions of legitimacy through tradition can be dangerous, obscuring the fact that tradition in itself is a social construct, often created and molded to suit the purposes of the powerful. Rather than providing a solid base of legitimacy for the process of rebuilding government, Brahimi's plan to incorporate several loya jirga–based events—supported strongly by American ambassador Zalmay Khalilzad—appeared to some to be a means of fast-tracking the until-recently-obscure Karzai into office, carefully staged to ensure that no opponent would carry as much political clout. Under ideal circumstances, this would then have led to the establishment of a pro-U.S. government that could assume control of Afghanistan's affairs as quickly as possible. Whatever the actual intention of incorporating these "traditional" institutions—whether a sincere attempt to establish what was thought to be a popularly legitimate council, an underhand means to secure Karzai's presidential seat, or a mixture of both—the loya jirga model did not succeed in merging supposedly traditional structures with a new democratic politics, largely because the personalities involved and the means through which they were selected did not correspond with local understandings of legitimacy.

ATTEMPTING TO CREATE
LEGITIMACY FROM THE TOP

The inclusion of loya jirgas in the Bonn process seemed to promote the impression among international actors, as implied by Dobbins and colleagues above, that the legitimacy box had been checked, and permanently so—by doing things "the Afghan way." Ultimately, however, any kind of decision-making chosen at this stage would not mask the underlying political reality: this was about post-Taliban power-grabbing and the question of which groups would control the resources attached to the most prominent government ministries.

In the run-up to the 2004 elections, there seemed to be little doubt on the part of international actors that Hamid Karzai would present a "legitimate" candidate and replacement for the king as head of state. Any question of a return to a constitutional monarchy had been dismissed, largely by the United States, in preference for a presidential system that resembled its own. But Karzai's legitimacy, in the eyes of Afghans, would not be derived solely from his performance at the polls—instead, it would come from similar sources that had brought about widespread public support for Zahir Shah during his realm. Karzai came from a family of Popalzai leaders, historically linked to the monarchy and politically powerful. He did not have blood on his hands and had played a role in the fight against the Taliban in Kandahar. These characteristics would serve him well: long before the election took place, his legitimacy as a personality was already established to a certain extent.

Beyond the perceived legitimacy of particular individuals, however, and beyond the way in which the outcomes of the initial loya jirgas may have been more important than the processes through which participants were selected to take part,[13] there was a need to ensure that the processes of elections were considered legitimate by the voting public. But the internationally conceived agreement at Bonn made no provisions to ensure that electoral processes would be perceived as legitimate means to select representatives in the long term. How would the representatives elected to these bodies actually interact with the public? What would be the source of ashnai that so clearly defined what representation meant to the members of the public we spoke to? In a context where many parts of the country—like Nuristan, as described by the parliamentarian above—had limited contact with central state institutions and had historically governed themselves in a relatively autonomous manner, there was little to imply that people would automatically consider themselves "represented" by elected officials. The implicit assumption was that once the presidency, the parliament, and the provincial councils were established, there was no turning back—the merits of these new entities would speak for themselves and periodic elections would be enough to ensure their continued status as representative bodies. But there was no international strategy beyond elections—no series of benchmarks or expectations of what the president, the parliament, or provincial councils should achieve during their terms of office, no game plan for governance.[14] Again, this approach fit with the idea of nation-building "lite"—this was a task for the Afghans themselves. Without a mechanism for assessing public perceptions of parliamentary performance between elections, for example, all emphasis was placed on representative bodies achieving legitimacy from the composition and characteristics of their members. This was a politics of presence: who was elected was more important than what they did once in office.

TIMING OF ELECTIONS

A third factor emphasized by international actors during the Bonn conference was the necessity of a compact time frame for intervention. Initial predictions about the time and resources required in Afghanistan were shockingly optimistic, and for all actors involved, even the most experienced of diplomats, this was expected to be a short engagement.

At first, these short-term horizons did not seem to present too much of a problem to stabilizing the country. Given that the Taliban had been defeated with surprising ease and were no longer posing a threat, international military engagement remained minimal. In 2003 much of the resources and attention that had been so critical in sustaining the fragile progress that had been made in Afghanistan were diverted to support the invasion of Iraq.[15] However, within two years it became clear that military objectives would need to take precedence once again as insurgent activity increased and the size of the territory outside Afghan government or international military control grew. Accordingly, time frames were lengthened on a yearly basis, and expectations—documented in a series of communiqués from successive international conferences on the subject of the intervention—adjusted.

One of the imperatives set down in Bonn was the need to hold elections as soon as realistically possible. The assumption was that this would ensure that the legitimacy of the new leader of Afghanistan would be established through the will of the Afghan people, and be recognized internationally as well. Tempered by the experience of running elections quickly in the aftermath of the war in the former Yugoslavia (which were scheduled a mere nine months after the end of the conflict there), international actors proposed a slightly longer time frame, of two years, for Afghanistan.

Even two years, following three decades of war, however, was a quick turnaround: why hold elections so soon after the end of the war? Far from being considered *too* soon, the presidential poll in 2004 was seen by many Afghans and internationals at the time as a welcome historical landmark—according to two experts: "the first opportunity in [Afghans'] long history to elect their leader through a direct process."[16] Turnout on Election Day certainly reflected this optimistic view, at nearly 80 percent of registered voters, and it was not surprising that widespread enthusiasm to participate was interpreted by international observers as Afghanistan's embrace of democracy. Furthermore, it led some to suggest that the roadmap used and implemented by the United Nations Assistance Mission to Afghanistan (UNAMA) to carry out these initial polls was a model to be emulated, providing "one template for setting conditions for what turned out to be rather successful elections."[17]

Glossed over in most retrospective reports, however, was the way procedural details were rushed and shoddily managed—no lasting database of voters was compiled, while indelible ink marking voters' fingers easily rubbed off, resulting in multiple voting in many places.[18] As in other cases of internationally sponsored elections in post-conflict countries in the decade before, this was an example of international actors emphasizing "form at the expense of substance."[19] Also, unlike the generally *outcome*-focused Emergency and Constitutional Loya Jirgas, the process of the elections being reliable and trustworthy was particularly important because, for the 7.4 million Afghans who cast their ballots, it was a lived experience that brought national-level politics into their local communities.

ELECTION DAY, 2004

To the casual observer, the presidential election of 2004 represented an astounding turn of events: three years after the ousting of the Taliban, four-fifths of registered voters arrived at the polls to cast their votes directly for the president for the first time in their country's history, all in a relatively secure environment. A clear majority was gained by a single candidate, Karzai, and most procedures seemed to have worked well.

Preparations for the polls had been somewhat fraught, however. One of the fallouts from the international focus on achieving state-building outcomes in the shortest possible time frame was the highly flawed voter registration process. Without exact population figures to begin with—the most recent statistics dated back to the Soviet occupation and even then covered only half the country—the process of conducting an election in Afghanistan was always going to be difficult. This problem was compounded by the UN's apparent refusal to entertain the idea of an electronic registration system, choosing instead a manual procedure that involved the distribution of physical paper registration cards that would be hole-punched when votes were cast.[20] Accordingly, there was no way to ensure that people had not registered more than once under slightly different names; a number of people we spoke to after the registration process talked about collecting ten or more cards, which could then be sold at a profit. Others would jokingly ask who we were voting for as foreigners, sometimes referring to a stunt pulled by a journalist who had registered Britney Spears to vote in Kandahar.

The lack of foresight demonstrated here was astonishing, especially in light of the ambitious electoral cycle set out in the constitution. Even worse, the physical nature of the data collected from the voter registration process in 2004 meant that records were not kept and a new process had to be carried out in 2009, again using a manual system that was neither reliable nor sustainable. The presence of ghost voters was widespread, along with the many invented women represented by their "husbands" at the polling stations in more conservative areas, and whose votes were generally (although illegally) accepted.[21] All post-2001 elections in Afghanistan therefore need to be considered with this in mind: there is no way to know whether any of the results collected reflected the actual number of votes cast, or whether they represented a proportionate slice of the actual Afghan population's views. These were not simply questions of statistics, and all of these issues were discussed in local communities. The entire process was already marred by technical irregularities before campaigning even began: young men talked about how the system could be cheated, people compared flimsy registration cards, and rumors started about politicians who were manipulating the system. On Election Day itself, fraud was a fairly common occurrence according to the accounts of Afghan observers and participants we collected. After a flawed registration process, the counting of ballots also turned up a number of irregularities that were not lost on the Afghans watching the process. Even while international commentators were applauding voter turnout, most Afghans were aware of how meaningless many of these numbers truly were. Technical flaws almost immediately had people discussing their potential political repercussions, which were even more resounding in future elections.

Scrolling down the list of eighteen candidates for the presidency, most were familiar faces whose participation shaped future public opinion about the Afghan government more generally. Alongside Karzai were the Panshiri Tajik Yunus Qanooni, a prominent Northern Alliance personality; Mohammad Mohaqqeq, a Hazara leader; and Abdul Rashid Dostum, the notorious Uzbek commander with a reputation for leaving hundreds of Taliban in metal containers in the northern deserts. All of these key ethnic minority leaders were campaigning in spite of the fact that most assumed that they could not win. Following the brutal reinforcement of ethnic divides during the civil war and later under the Taliban (perceived by many in the north not only as Islamic fundamentalists but primarily as Pashtun nationalists), there was an assumption that the population would vote largely along ethnic lines, which they did.

In this respect, leaders of the country's non-Pashtun ethnic groups ultimately seemed less concerned with winning the presidency—since Pashtuns formed the largest minority in the country and were likely to vote for Karzai now that the king was no longer a potential contender and since no other viable Pashtun candidate emerged—than they were with demonstrating their strength relative to other ethnic groups. As a consequence, they worked hard to convince their followers that using their votes to demonstrate group strength was vital to securing their fair share of resources from the newly formed government. For ethnic leaders like Dostom, the more votes they secured, the more they demonstrated on a national level the strength and political solidarity of their ethnic group going forward.

One notable absence in this race was Burhannadin Rabbani, the founder of the Jamiat-i Islami Mujahideen Party (often referred to simply as Jamiat), who had occupied the presidency as the country descended into civil war in the early 1990s. Ageing and frail, he was still formally recognized by the UN as president when the international intervention began, and yet he did not campaign himself to regain the title. Instead he traded his support for Karzai in the days before the election, in exchange for Karzai's selection of his son-in-law and the brother of the celebrated mujahideen leader, Ahmed Zia Massoud, as vice president. While never acknowledged in any public statements, rumors about this deal—mixing marriage, kinship, and politics in a way that the Afghan ruling elite had done for centuries—circulated widely. This was one of the first of a series of backroom bargains that Karzai would make during the election process. The result ensured that Karzai received some of the Tajik vote with the rest going to the only major Tajik candidate, Qanooni.

Bargaining of this kind that took place among the political elite over the course of the elections closely reflected the discussion among many ordinary Afghans, who viewed these first elections as part of the process of dividing power between the country's ethnic leaders. This would set the stage for similar political games in the forthcoming parliamentary polls. A technical detail that would affect the process of the parliamentary elections significantly, however, was the choice of electoral system—the Single Non-Transferable Vote.

SINGLE NON-TRANSFERABLE VOTES

Despite attempts to simplify the process, the new constitution called for the presidential election to be followed by the rapid implementation of a rather confusing series of additional polls. The president and the lower house of parliament, or the *Wolesi Jirga*, were to be elected every five years. Provincial councils would be elected every four years and would send one representative to the *Meshrano Jirga*, or upper house. This would be composed of one-third provincial council members, one-third presidential appointees, and one-third winners of district council elections (which are yet to be held, in spite of being planned to take place every three years).[22] Both Wolesi Jirga and provincial council elections were designed to be held on the provincial level, with the number of seats per province based on rough population estimates given the lack of accurate census data. This system created a good amount of confusion among voters, with many, particularly but not exclusively in rural areas, not distinguishing between these different types of representatives in their discussions.

All of these elections are conducted using the Single Non-Transferable Vote (SNTV) system, chosen by policymakers at the time on account of its innate simplicity. It works as follows: each voter, having registered, has one vote for one candidate. There is no option to express ranked preference or choose based upon party. Within each constituency (an entire province for presidential, parliamentary, and provincial council elections), an unlimited number of candidates can stand without a required platform or party affiliation, with those receiving the highest number of votes securing the seats (except for those reserved for women).[23] While ostensibly the easiest way to conduct an election in a country of over 80 percent illiteracy with no history of universal suffrage, there have been a number of problems with the system.

One issue concerns the large numbers of candidates registering for parliamentary and provincial council elections. As long as potential candidates meet basic criteria set out in the electoral law (mainly holding Afghan citizenship, being over a certain age, or not holding a government position while campaigning), they are able to run for office. In both 2005 and 2010, this resulted in parliamentary candidate numbers ranging widely from province to province, particularly in 2010, from 11 (Nimroz) to 625 (Kabul), corresponding roughly with population figures.[24] This in itself led to lengthy ballot papers in a number of provinces, which made locating candidates a difficult task despite the inclusion of candidate photos and symbols to help illiterate voters. Because the system does not require candidates to stand as political party members, they could not be grouped or distinguished from one another based on formal affiliations, either. Most candidates ran as *be-taraf* (independent), a Dari term literally meaning "without direction."

In terms of votes gained, the large numbers of competing candidates meant that unless certain groups (such as ethnic minority leaders, local elders, or the educated elite) were able to enforce their own limitations on the numbers of candidates they thought could represent them—selecting one per community, for example—there was little chance of preventing the division of votes between candidates, or of any one candidate gaining enough votes to secure a seat. By the time preparations were being made for elections in 2009 and 2010, the need to choose one or two individuals in a community rather than split the local vote between many was a well-known strategy across the country—but was easier described than implemented in practice.

Tribes, geographical villages or districts, and ethnic groups all stood to gain much in terms of links with Kabul and the ability to promote local projects nationally from the election of a representative—these goals varied widely as will be discussed in more depth in following chapters. However, all types of communities that tried but struggled to reduce the number of candidates standing for election within the community generally saw local candidates fail. Evidently, however, some communities were better able to organize themselves than others, and thus it became clear in 2009 that there was a differential favoring communities that were able to prioritize the need for a representative in parliament over and above the need to prevent unrest between competing candidates at the local level.

The question of which electoral system would be appropriate in the post-invasion context provoked considerable debate among policymakers and analysts preparing for the first round of elections. Queries included whether or not SNTV could facilitate the building of a functioning democratic system. Its propensity to encourage a large number of independent and formally unaligned candidates was clearly problematic, but no clear voice emerged to suggest an alternative. As one report details, UNAMA did eventually decide to oppose SNTV, but too late to make a difference.[25]

In 2008 one international commentator, describing the atmosphere among the international community at the time, told us: "In 2004–05 there was a huge amount of discussion about the electoral system. Everyone was saying that SNTV was terrible, that we needed some kind of regional proportional system instead. The story goes that one of Karzai's advisors was explaining to the cabinet about one type of regional proportional system, and made such a hash of it, that the reaction from the cabinet was like, if you can't explain it to us, then how in the world is the Afghan public going to understand it?" However, the decision was made, and it soon became clear that SNTV served a number of high-level Afghan political interests while creating chaos for local communities of which many local leaders would take advantage. SNTV made the process of choosing a candidate to vote for simple perhaps, but made the outcomes incredibly complex and easy to manipulate from above. Without any requirements of party affiliation, it discouraged organized opposition and increased the likelihood of a disorganized legislature that would not be able to counter executive decrees or decisions effectively.

THE 2005 PARLIAMENTARY AND PROVINCIAL COUNCIL ELECTIONS

In spite of these significant and obvious problems, plans and preparations for the parliamentary and provincial council elections of 2005 were quickly rolled out. Again, these elections appeared to run smoothly, on the surface, but the results were far from straightforward. Due to a combination of SNTV, a first-past-the-post method of distinguishing winners from losers, and an allocated number of seats per province, some candidates won with tens of thousands of votes while others scraped through with as low as 1,500. The resulting mixture of parliamentarians thus included prominent military or factional leaders, alongside teachers, elders, mullahs, and university students. The mix was strikingly diverse—and perhaps an indication of the variety of sources of legitimacy inherent within Afghan society at the time.

Another consequence of the system was the way in which tiny margins separated winners and losers (in one case separated by as few as three votes).[26] This meant that among the hundreds of candidates competing for a given number of seats in a province, a huge number *nearly* won due to how thinly the votes were spread. This left a bitter taste in the mouths both of many losing candidates, who felt their numbers had been counted incorrectly, and of voters, who decried the number of votes "wasted" on unsuccessful candidates. As one parliamentarian from Kabul told us: "I used to tell people that a vote is about trust and that they should cast their vote for those that deserve it. A single vote affects a person's success or failure, so they should be very careful."

As with the presidential elections, a number of Afghans we spoke to both at the time and in retrospect talked about incidences of fraud that they had seen taking place—incidences that were not documented in later reports for Electoral Observer missions. These included stories of boxes of votes being thrown into rivers, boxes being unlocked and tampered with overnight or on the journey to the central counting center, and intimidation at the polling booths. Turnout was also considerably lower this time than in the previous year. Final figures indicated that approximately 6.4 million (almost 50 percent) registered voters turned out at the polls in 2005.[27]

Like the election in 2004, the 2005 elections were orchestrated by the Joint Electoral Management Body (JEMB). Theoretically a joint Afghan-international implementing agency, it also encompassed a complaints commission and a media commission. However, due to the short time frame in which preparations could be made, the elections were largely an international affair, and the international actors involved allocated little time for the transfer of skills to Afghan electoral officials. In one respect, this was intentional—as one UN staff member working on elections in 2005 put it, "this wasn't supposed to be a capacity-building exercise." However, the lack of capacity-building—intended to occur between elections but largely deprioritized by inadequate donor funds—resulted in a handover to Afghan control for the second round of elections in 2009 and 2010, which was rushed, inadequate, and underfunded. By that time, to replace the JEMB, an Independent Electoral Commission (IEC) and Electoral Complaints Commission (ECC) had been established to be the primary agents of electoral organization, whose respective roles were to oversee the planning and implementation of the polls, and the processing of complaints.

Beyond this, a new grievance that arose in the 2005 elections came from a number of male candidates, both successful and unsuccessful, who were particularly scornful of the reserved seats system introduced for women, in which

27 percent of seats were set aside for female candidates in the Wolesi Jirga, and a further 25 percent in provincial councils. This meant that women could win seats with much lower vote counts than their male counterparts, and thus technically "unseat" men who had gained what would otherwise be enough votes to win a place in parliament.

THE RESERVED SEATS SYSTEM

While president in the early 1990s, Rabbani and his conservative religious allies had put together a strict code of conduct for women dictating the terms of their behavior and dress. In the context of a brutal civil war for control of the capital, daily life for women under this regime constituted not only the forced submission to these stipulations but the constant threat of rape, abduction, maiming, and murder.[28] These were dark, dreadful times. Emerging from these experiences, however, were women and their daughters whose formidable coping strategies enabled widespread underground activity when the Taliban—far better known in the international media than their predecessors for their oppression of women—imposed their own repressive codes. Hearing women tell their stories of the atrocities of the civil war, one could be forgiven for concluding, initially, that the advent of the Taliban provided welcome relief in its enforcement of confinement to the home. But the brutally enforced homebound seclusion and exclusion of women from the public sphere that followed put paid to any such expectations, earning the Taliban a richly deserved global reputation as the creators of a monstrous, archaic regime. With the fall of the Taliban, it was therefore little wonder that Afghans and internationals alike began looking for systematic means to redress past inequity and suffering.

One of the distinct features of the Bonn process was the strong emphasis on women's participation throughout. The various stages of the process were punctuated by many lengthy and heated meetings filled with the speeches of determined Afghan matriarchs, bold young activists, and impassioned Western feminists. This ultimately facilitated an unprecedented prioritization of women's interests—in the reservation of 10 percent female seats out of the 1,600 at the Emergency Loya Jirga; in the subsequent establishment of

MoWA; in Afghanistan's signature of the international Convention for the Elimination of all forms of Discrimination Against Women (CEDAW) in 2003; and in the provision of a reserved seats system for women candidates in elected bodies from the provincial level up that was constitutionally guaranteed. As a result of this, 27 percent of seats in the Wolesi Jirga (68 in total), 22 percent in the Meshrano Jirga, and 25 percent in the provincial councils were allocated only for women. These were significant gains, forging a new space for women in the political and public sphere that was established in writing and strongly backed by the international community.[29]

Women had also been part of the constitutional drafting commission (two out of the nine members) as well as the constitutional review committee (nine out of thirty-five members). The particular women involved had, for the most part, been active in civil society initiatives illicitly promoting women's activity under the Taliban; many went on to become senior figures within the Afghan government, while others continued to promote their own organizations' work, attracting substantial international funding and acclaim. They were certainly not afraid to state their views publically—indeed, the Emergency Loya Jirga was deputy-chaired by the later Minister of Women's Affairs, Sima Samar, and throughout the conference the voices of female delegates rang loud and clear across the tent in which the meeting was held, rebuking Rabbani and others in person for their past crimes.[30]

A conference organized jointly by UN agencies and MoWA in March 2003 and a further meeting in Kandahar in the same year saw the participation of a number of Afghan women's groups, who made their demands for greater women's participation in public office clear.[31] In this way, then, the inclusion and participation of women during the Bonn conference, while strongly encouraged by international actors such as UNIFEM and northern European donors in particular, was clearly also the result of pressure from prominent Afghan women themselves.

The reserved seats system itself, however, emerged as the result of policy transfer processes recommended by international experts on drafting constitutions in newly democratizing states. The introduction of legislative quotas had already become global best practice, following the recommendations compiled from the UN Conference on Women in Beijing in 1995, at which the idea of a

30 percent "critical mass" of women in legislative office had been affirmed as the minimum number needed to have an impact on legislation.[32] Since this time, the direct link between presence and influence has been called into question, and there remain numerous problems in the assumption that numerical quotas can in fact generate "impact," and that women, purely by merit of *being* women, will represent "women-in-general" in parliament.[33] As the representative from Nuristan had described from underneath a blanket on that bitterly cold morning in January 2007, the connection between women parliamentarians and their female constituents was far from clear. This was to be an example of yet another supposedly technical change that would affect the political landscape in Afghanistan, but in ways unanticipated by its international proponents. It would also be compromised by existing political norms, such as women's allegiance to kin and ethnic ties over and above their connection to other women, and like other measures of institutional adjustment introduced during the state-building process, in some instances did more harm than good.

A SENSE OF WHAT WAS TO COME

The electoral process established in Bonn presented Afghans with a wide range of new rules about how they would go about selecting their leaders. However, these rules were not established in a vacuum. As structuring structures, they affected the political context but were at the same time manipulated by candidates and voters, both of whom integrated them into local political processes with which they were more familiar. In addition, the changes that had been brought about by Bonn were compromised by the series of shortcuts taken by international actors, whose priorities lay not in nation-building but in quick-fix solutions to the problem of establishing a state in a short time frame. Unfortunately, both the new electoral rules and the political context in which they were applied ultimately contributed to an increasing sense of alienation of voters from their government, culminating in the disastrous Wolesi Jirga elections of 2010. The following chapters tell the story of how this came about.

4

A HOUSE OF SAND

The Fallout of the 2005 Parliamentary Election

CONVERSING IN THE DARK

*T*WO MILES TO *the southwest of Kabul's central mosque and markets, just beyond a mountain lined by the old city walls, sits the Afghan parliament. Abutting the once-beautiful, then-war-ravaged, and now once again fashionable district of* Kart-e Se *or Third Quarter, it is housed in an unassuming and unattractive modern construction. Hard to spot from the main boulevard, the building is encased in concrete slabs and barbed wire—cursory measures to deter the numerous suicide attacks that have struck the area since 2001. A further two miles to the south are the bombed-out ruins of Darulaman Palace, the building once intended to serve as Afghanistan's first parliament. Built in the 1920s, it formed part of the progressive vision of King Amanullah, whose plans to develop a functioning, elected legislature were halted abruptly by his deposition and an ensuing civil war in 1929. This haunting shell is one of the few remaining structures from that tumultuous period of enforced and rapid political change.*

Always intended as a temporary location for the lower and upper houses, the current parliamentary building resembles a gloomy secondary school. Inside is a warren of dark corridors, closets, and side-offices, adorned with elaborate carpets and portraits of eminent politicians of times past. In winter, however, no measure of fine upholstery can mitigate the freezing cold in these peripheral spaces; as temperatures drop, a parliamentarian's political influence can be gauged in part by their ability to procure a bokhari—*an electric, wood-, or gas-burning stove found in most Afghan houses— and by the length of time they choose to keep it alight. During these months, inviting visitors into well-heated rooms is a mark of status as aides and other parliamentary workers huddle next to their stoves in draftier offices.*

By contrast, the central room hosting the lower house plenary is bright and open, refurbished in 2004 by international donor agencies, boasting a semicircular arrangement of tiered seating where representatives gather for daily debates. Places for the 249 members are arranged alphabetically, leaving men and women interspersed in a rather radical, if politically unhelpful, manner. This arrangement is also a physical reflection of the current nature of parliamentary membership—representatives are considered, and often consider themselves to be, individuals, without fixed physical or political proximity to ideological groups or parties.

Debates in this room are often unstructured, frequently ending without resolution. The order of contributors (and length of contributions) is controlled, usually, by the Speaker of the House—a position which between 2005 and 2010 was occupied by Yunus Qanooni, a charismatic Panjshiri Tajik who exercised significant influence over parliamentary proceedings over the course of his reign. The content and quality of speeches varies enormously. They are, with some regularity, used by representatives to voice political concerns apparently unrelated to the topic of discussion, creating a rather disjointed debate style that jumps abruptly from one topic to another. The mere mention of an international agency can prompt a lengthy diatribe in Dari or Pashtu against NATO's presence in the country, or a statement concerning the need for paved roads in one province might lead to a succession of parliamentarians listing similar needs in their own regions. As many parliamentary debates are televised—filmed from the glass-fronted media balcony above the proceedings—a chance to speak on a subject can provide a key opportunity for representatives to demonstrate their active role in debates to constituents wealthy enough to afford televisions. This is not necessarily a concern for all parliamentarians at all times; it is not unusual for midterm discussions to be poorly attended and for the occasional representative to be caught indulging in a gentle snooze.

In light of often chaotic or soporific debates in the central chamber, events in the corridors and passageways surrounding it are often more politically potent than the posturing within. The greeting embraces of eminent ethnic leaders, the hushed conversations of aspiring liberals, or the immediate parting of crowded hallways to make way for prominent former mujahideen—such as religious conservative and Paghman strongman Abd al-Rabb al-Rasul Sayyaf or his now-deceased Badakhshani counterpart Burhannudin Rabbani—can reveal as much if not more of the stuff of political bargains as the observation of official debates. The dimly lit spaces around the legislature provide a backdrop for the shadowy, informal deals and allegiances that are made, broken and remade in the course of a parliamentary term.

* * *

Elected to the Wolesi Jirga in 2005, both Sayyaf and Rabbani are interesting examples of the small group of the elite parliamentarians holding considerable influence in the House. Both religious conservatives and academics educated in Cairo, they made lasting connections with the Muslim Brotherhood in the 1960s. Both also have a history of political activism in Kabul, where, on their return from Egypt, their campaigns among university students involved the organization of opposition to the increasingly secular policies of the Soviet-backed government. Forced to flee to Pakistan, Rabbani continued his political activism through the strengthening of his Jamiat-i Islami Party, and later, in the early 1990s, became president of Afghanistan following the collapse of Najibullah's government in 1992. During his reign, he was never able to bring the various mujahideen factions together and ended up presiding over some of the bloodiest fighting of the recent decades. Although ousted by the Taliban in 1996, retreating to his home province of Badakhshan, Rabbani continued to wield significant influence in the north. While never as widely beloved as his ally Ahmed Shah Massoud, he became de facto leader of the Northern Alliance, which would eventually defeat the Taliban in 2001 with the financial and later military support of international forces.

As the last president before the Taliban regime, Rabbani's actions and behavior throughout the Bonn process were thus critical to the success of the proceedings—and his support for the adoption of an internationally ratified agreement for the roadmap ahead was by no means given. Initially backing the initiative but then calling it insignificant, Rabbani's contradictory stances and demands for delays appeared to reflect the need to demonstrate an authoritative voice in the face of potential disenfranchisement. While his Northern Alliance was well represented at Bonn, and by far the strongest of the Afghan factions present, there were divisions within the ranks and a great deal of political bargaining taking place. Ultimately, however, Rabbani threw his support behind Karzai at the last minute, withdrawing his own candidacy for interim leader at the Emergency Loya Jirga in 2002.

These dynamics of authority thus comprised the background to Rabbani's candidacy in the parliamentary elections. Winning 26,422 votes, the former president easily commanded the highest vote count in Badakhshan in 2005 (with a margin of victory of over 12,000 votes) and continued to wield significant authority in the parliament in spite of his habitual absence therein. Few dared to contradict him, and when he did attend his presence in the legislature engendered a tangible awe and apprehensiveness.

Maintaining the leadership of the Jamiat Party, Rabbani was rumored to be resistant to change—to the extent that party decisions were rarely made and meetings inconsequential without him. Although in 2011 Ahmed Zia Massoud was informally appointed to the party leadership, this decision was not formalized, and the lingering authority of his father-in-law remained intact until later that year. On September 20, as he attempted to hold discussions with a Talib representative in his role as head of the High Peace Council, Rabbani was killed by a bomb hidden in the turban of the emissary, who was visiting him at his home. Having apparently been told by other officials attending the meeting that the visitor was a friend, no searches were carried out and there was nothing to prevent the attacker detonating his explosives once inside the private residence.

In the last years before his death, while over 70, Rabbani's age if anything seemed to increase his charisma and influence, and younger parliamentarians would scurry out of his way as he walked the halls in parliament. Summoning another politician for a brief conversation, he would ask him to visit his extravagant home on the outskirts of town to discuss a certain issue, while asking another whether international funds had been used to pave a road in Badakhshan. He would the enter the bright central hall to make a brief appearance, but it was there in the corridors, away from the television cameras, that most of the real political negotiations were playing out.

A HOUSE ON THE MARGINS

At the end of 2001, Afghanistan had reached a critical juncture. Northern Alliance leaders, the majority non-Pashtun, had ousted the Taliban in collaboration with U.S. forces. But if the anarchy of the early 1990s was to be avoided, a leader acceptable to all Afghans had to be found and established within a secure institutional framework to ensure that competition for control did not degenerate once again into violent civil war. It soon became clear that various international actors, most notably the United States (along with a strong contingent of Pashtun delegates in the Constitutional Loya Jirga), believed a robust presidential system to be the framework of choice, reasoning that a powerful figurehead would generate a sense of stability and control.[1]

Voices opposing this model came largely from Northern Alliance leaders, who considered a power-sharing arrangement to be more beneficial to the non-Pashtun ethnic minorities. This group felt their interests would be better represented by a strong parliament, functioning alongside a figurehead president. While following this path risked a re-ethnicization of politics, in potentially emphasizing divisions that lay along ethnic fault lines, this seemed for some to be the only way to ensure an effective opposition to a potentially predatory government, and to counter the perceived prospect of Pashtun dominance.[2] From the perspective of many Pashtuns, however, the Northern Alliance was already in a strong position, having defeated the Taliban militarily, having had the support of the Americans in order to do so, and as a result having effectively reclaimed territory in the north and west as their own. The stirrings of ethnically based tension and opposition to government that would reemerge at various points during the first parliamentary term were thus already visible.

With concerns over these tensions winning the day, the new Afghan constitution created a strong presidency, giving the president power to appoint ministers and governors, and to veto parliamentary decisions. As a consequence, the new parliament's potential to take on a role of executive oversight was questionable from the beginning.

* * *

While decision-making in the new state was to be highly centralized, the choice of a presidential system actually led to the proliferation of competing sources of power and patronage. Although Karzai obviously had the backing of the international community, it quickly became clear that he was highly dependent on this temporary source of economic and political capital. It was unsurprising then that regional powerholders maintained and expanded their own informal and often cross-border networks for revenue generation, in spite of their publically demonstrated allegiance to the central government. Governor Atta in Balkh, Governor Sherzai in Nangarhar, and Ismail Khan in Herat are just three of a number of provincial strongmen whose capacity to govern in a semiautonomous manner in their respective regions became evident quickly following Karzai's election.

Attempting to establish the president as the only formal source of real power and patronage also meant that the power networks of other actors such as these regional powerholders remained informal and were not subject to public limitation through elections, for example. The administrative structure ensured that personal relationships were a much more effective means to access state resources than parliamentary politics, which, as we discuss below, was often a disorganized and unwieldy affair. Future deadlocks in parliament over ministerial appointments, ethnic disputes, legislative amendments, and timings of elections would all need to be dealt with through personal payoffs and bargains, rather than institutional procedures. At the same time, these deals and negotiations created a precedent, resulting in a parliament whose increasing dependence on executive patronage would render its activities extremely weak by the beginning of its second term.

Opposition politics, whether in the form of the Westminster Model, a two-party system, or multiparty coalition framework, has widely become an assumed prerequisite to the building of democratic institutions, both in academic and policymaking circles.[3] Indeed, the presence of parties able to compete in active opposition to the government is a key criterion in some frameworks for measuring levels of democracy.[4] This is largely because it encourages open critique of government policy and the provision of popularly accepted alternatives, as well as ensuring an immediate replacement for a government that has been voted out of power. It also provides an incentive for checks and balances to be applied to government policy and activities.

Different forms of opposition politics vary greatly, however, and while prevalent are not the only means of political organization in existence.

Northern Ireland, for example, has an assembly divided along party lines but without an official opposition—majorities are gained by forming consensus within or across groups in the Unionist or Nationalist blocs, similar to the so-called "Grand Council" model put forward by consociationalist theorists.[5] Some might label this method impractical and even "tribal" given its lack of emphasis on policy and its tendency to suffocate any independent groups or smaller parties outside the two major factions. Nevertheless, in a post-conflict setting this arrangement has brought together warring sides that had previously opted for violence instead of vote counts.

As in Northern Ireland, the need to end violence and generate some form of stability within the political system was a major imperative for delegates at Bonn, those drafting the constitution, and international donors, all of whom hoped to prevent (in the short term at least) further outbreaks of conflict. Nevertheless, in the Afghan case this concern appears to have trumped a longer-term view of how people might legitimately raise their voice against the government in future. Ultimately, stifling the development of a legitimate parliamentary opposition encouraged the proliferation of informal bargains and politicking between leaders and the government that would soon eclipse the formal systems in place. Over the course of the first parliamentary term, this was to debilitate the legislature, rendering its attempts at government oversight essentially impotent.

THE HISTORY OF OPPOSITION AS A THREAT AND THE PARTY PROBLEM

There has never been much of a functioning political opposition to a government or monarch in Afghan history, if by "functioning" we mean a combination of publically legitimate, institutionalized (in the sense of existing beyond the lifespan of an individual leader), and peacefully active groups politically opposing the policies of government. As discussed in chapter 2, this has been the case for a number of reasons, not least the tendency for successive regimes to see opposition as a threat, generally responding violently to any perceived challenges to the ruler of the day.

FIGURE 4.1 Darulaman Palace.

In the nineteenth-century reign of King Abdurrahman, which followed a series of depositions and assassinations, such a hard line on dissenting groups was an apparent, if brutal, act of political necessity.[6] Twenty years after Abdurrahman's death, the assassination of his son and successor Habibullah resulted in a similar power struggle that would also leave its victor Amanullah wary of political opponents. However, determined to modernize Afghan politics, the new monarch nonetheless undertook the building of a new parliament at Darulaman Palace. As it turned out, this most progressive of leaders had not been wary enough, either of his more ambitious compatriots or of the machinations of the British Raj, and in 1929 a succession of tribal revolts brought about his downfall. Bloody struggles for the leadership once again ensued; Habibullah Ghazi, an ethnic Tajik empowered by the Ghilzai tribes, ruled for nine months before being deposed and executed by Amanullah's cousin Nadir Shah, who himself was assassinated in 1933. The throne then fell to his son, the 19-year-old Zahir Shah, ruling initially under the stewardship of his uncles, who had clearly learned the lessons of the generations of rulers before them: opposition, if not stifled, could quickly overthrow those in power.

Zahir's reign lasted for forty years—Afghanistan's most stable period in the past two and a half centuries. During this time, the country was internationally recognized by the League of Nations. The country maintained a position of neutrality during the Second World War and, as a buffer state, became a key component in the foreign policies of the Soviet Union and the United States during the Cold War. Indeed, its reliance on politically motivated aid from these countries was to increase exponentially during Zahir Shah's reign.[7] This was to further solidify Afghanistan's long-standing position as a rentier state highly dependent on external sources of income—although in this case the rent-seeking behavior of its government was based on its geostrategic position rather than, as in other states, on natural resources.[8] The stability of this macroeconomic bargaining position depended very much on there being only one interlocutor with whom foreign governments could negotiate— and on his ability to make decisions without the kind of delay a transparent, accountable government would involve. This was a political system that was effective as long as there was a steady stream of foreign income; while these resources continued to flow to tribes on the periphery, these groups had greater incentive to maintain their local autonomy than go through the trouble of overthrowing what was in reality a fairly weak state.[9]

While Zahir Shah would attempt toward the end of his reign to modernize the political landscape in Kabul through the formation of an elected national assembly, opposition groups were generally quashed, as they had been in earlier decades, with leaders either imprisoned or forced to operate underground. Efforts to suppress opposition would only increase after Daoud Khan's coup d'état, when voices opposing the government were also subject to violent repression, imprisonment, and forced exile in Pakistan, where the roots of the later resistance to the Soviet invasion began to take hold. Successive regimes led by communist leaders, Mujahideen groups, and the Taliban continued the trend of responding violently to challenges to their authority.

Given this history, it is unsurprising that attitudes among Afghanistan's political elite toward the development of a political opposition did not change with the signing of the Bonn Agreement. In keeping with his predecessors, Karzai also developed a distaste for opposing voices, attempting to either sideline or win over almost all potential competitors. An indication of this was his stance on parties during the Bonn process. Supported by then-U.S. ambassador to Afghanistan Zalmay Khalilzad—he was adamant that the inclusion of political parties in the new state's political infrastructure would divide the population and risk a further descent into conflict. Referring to Afghans' bad memories of political parties, Karzai made clear that in his view a no-party democracy—with himself as father of the nation—would be the best way forward. For similar reasons, he also refused to either found or join any party himself, citing the example of George Washington's resistance to party formation when building a political framework for the United States. Analyst and close confidant of Karzai, Ahmed Rashid, writes of attempting to convince him of the potential pitfalls of this stance, calling it the president's "biggest mistake."[10]

One concession was made, however, in the form of the political parties law introduced in 2003. A step in the direction of party development, the law was the first of its kind to be ratified in the country. While parliament had passed a similar piece of legislation during Zahir Shah's reign, the king refrained from signing the document, leaving parties without legal or political status throughout his so-called "decade of democracy" from 1963 to 1973. Even in 2003, however, parallels could be drawn between Karzai's approach and that of the king before him. Although ratified, the law was nonetheless brief, inconclusive, and vague, neglecting to specify a *political* role for parties.[11] Instead, they were left as ill-defined organizations that were permitted to exist as long as they registered with a government agency inside the Ministry of Justice. This lack of an independent registration body rendered the process long, laborious, and subject to government interference.

All of this masked the important party allegiances that many candidates had developed in the not-so-distant past, which continue to shape politics today. At the time of the 2005 parliamentary elections, a number of studies highlighted the real connections between candidates and parties in an attempt to work out the political makeup of the new parliament.[12] However, for a number of candidates interviewed at the time, candidacy for this new institution, albeit based on a familiar model, represented a break from the past. This was reflected in the perceived separation between being a parliamentarian and belonging to a political party. In a study conducted during parliament's first year, legislators referred to the existence of "inside" and "outside" parties, the former indicating the early groupings being made among elected representatives, the latter referring to the often provincially and ethnically based ex-military parties of the war era.[13] This was not to say that the latter did not wield influence within the Wolesi Jirga—they did—but they had not managed to consolidate membership or form formal blocs that could vote in a consistent, dependable manner or mobilize consistently.

Instead, these parties served more as patronage machines that allowed certain key leaders such as Sayyaf and Rabbani to offer resources in exchange for support for their favored candidates for appointments to ministerial or parliamentary office, for example. Rather than relying on political ideology, these affiliations between party members or associates were informal, continued to be based around personal relationships, and were always at risk of breaking apart as a consequence. While there was a tendency for members of these networks to vote together on certain issues (such as over changes to the electoral law), this happened primarily when they were mobilized by a charismatic political leader. This would become a recurring theme as the first parliamentary term progressed.

The inherent contradiction here, of course, is that the only figures who had the political influence to push Karzai to support the development of political parties were figures like Sayyaf and Rabbani, whose power would also have been threatened by the creation of alternative forms of political organization, and would certainly have been undermined by a more concrete institutionalization of the party system. In terms of external pressure, the international community did not seem to view the issue as a top priority. Essentially, with no significant effort or political will to make the radical changes that would have been needed to encourage a culture of peaceful political opposition—such as a strong parliamentary system, and electoral system incorporating a role for parties—the trajectory of Afghanistan's relationship with opposition was unlikely to change. Even if emphasis had been placed on institutional changes during Bonn, centuries of violent reaction to opposition by those in power would probably have taken a considerable time and a more secure space to reverse. Yet the institutional framework developed in the early stages of the international intervention precluded the existence of any space within which to make legitimate, peaceful challenge to the government. This was short-sighted at best, and at worst a recipe for encouraging political disillusionment that would fuel violent insurgency.

CAMPAIGNING IN 2005

While seemingly encouraging local participation and the inclusion of an increasing number of political voices, the way the parliamentary and provincial council polls played out in 2005 would be a continuation of Afghanistan's political history of discouraging opposition.

Elections for the president in 2004 had been hailed internationally as a success. But independent observers operating at the time raised a number of concerns about the next set of polls.[14] First, in the absence of thorough disarmament, a number of eminent commanders were still able to demonstrate a potentially violent threat to voters. Second, there had been little effort to ensure effective candidate vetting, meaning that those candidates with dubious track records were able to campaign in the elections. This, along with the subsequent candidacies of several commanders and ethnic leaders accused of major human rights violations, would send a message of impunity that would be later solidified in law.[15] The fact that none had been formally convicted of such crimes mattered little to most voters, who saw their inclusion as evidence that the strong could still oppress the weak with impunity. Third, no one really knew what the mandate or responsibilities of provincial councils were, since voters were given little sense of what the role of these bodies would be, in part due to the fact that the Provincial Council Law had not been completed by the time of the election.[16]

In hindsight, this was a grave mistake. The weak remit of these bodies meant that they were quickly marginalized as government officials and international actors placed greater emphasis on relationships with centrally appointed provincial and district governors instead. This in turn put more power in the hands of the president, whose ability to use the appointments of governors as valuable bargaining chips further strengthened his authority in relation to parliament. Had significantly more weight and responsibility been assigned to these elected bodies, a more functional interface between the central government and local politics might have developed, but there was no opportunity for this to happen.

Campaigns officially began a month before Election Day, although many candidates complained that their opponents had begun illegally canvassing voters many weeks beforehand. With no official limit on campaign spending, the amounts candidates spent on posters, meals, and the hiring of venues and vehicles varied widely, largely dependent on how much candidates could raise through their connections to parties, commanders, or influential family members. However, the rich and well-connected were not the only ones to spend significant amounts of money on campaigns. In the face of limited resources, female candidates in particular sometimes resorted to unconventional methods of raising funds. One female provincial council candidate we spoke to in Balkh Province in 2006 had sold all her gold jewelry to finance her campaign, and another Wolesi Jirga candidate had sold part of her family's land. Other female candidates exploited less material sources of support, relying instead on the backing of their communities or links to powerful figures to propel them into office. However, what was undeniably remarkable for many was the fact that women were able to compete as candidates at all.

A WOMAN'S PLACE

In the summer months of 2005, the streets of Afghanistan's cities were adorned with the enlarged and ubiquitous colored portraits of women candidates for parliament and the provincial council. In any other country, this might not have been an odd sight, but four years after the fall of the Taliban, the multiple significances of these photographs could not be missed by even the most casual of observers. These women—young, old, Tajik, Pashtun, Hazara, Uzbek—included the wealthy and the middle-class, the conservative and the liberal, the educated and the illiterate. Across the country this scene repeated—women in headscarves of many colors, presenting themselves as new leaders for the new Afghanistan. Each competing for one of the reserved seats for women in the parliament or provincial council, these 582 women candidates were making a clear statement in their campaigns: there is space for us, now, and we will take it.

These women adopted a variety of campaign strategies. Young women candidates had often gone to great lengths to emphasize their youth and beauty: enormous eyes emphasized with kohl and mascara gazed out from their posters with the hint of a smile. Older women highlighted their respectability in the community as teachers, doctors, or admired elders, often registering their names on the official ballot with the prefix of "Ustad" (teacher), "Doctar" or "Bibi" (a term of respectful endearment used for grandmothers). As was the case with their male rivals, their choice of attire in a campaign poster was important—suits and a small *chadar* (scarf) implied a modernist, liberal stance, while a *chapan* (long coat) and fuller shawl indicated a commitment to some of the more conservative values of the country. Some portrayed themselves alone, demonstrating independence and a lack of connection to parties or regional strongmen; others instead chose to include a picture of an ethnic or religious leader in the background. The sheer variety of choices available was reflected in the visually dizzying array of images emblazoned on large banners, plastered to park benches, or staring out from the back windows of passing cars.

Women were more restricted than men in their campaigns, primarily due to the lack of public space available to them for meetings and lunches. As such, they had to be creative—visiting their home villages, talking to groups of women in the largest house available in return for providing lunch; spreading word in the bathhouse; hiring campaign cars with megaphones and distributing hundreds of posters. Officially, no candidate was allowed to run a campaign in a school, but since many women were teachers, some were able to rally the support of other teachers in the staffroom, of older children who would be eligible to vote, and of their parents.

One candidate who was a headmistress in Balkh actively held campaign meetings in her own school, reportedly in spite of UNAMA's attempts to intervene. However, this individual's defiance clearly paid off—even while some of her rivals complained, she went on to win a seat in the Wolesi Jirga. As one of the three female victors in Balkh, she had competed against fifteen others. A relatively well-known woman in Mazar, she had connections to the provincial governor, and her husband was known to have been a member of the prominent Jamiat-i Islami political party. There were even rumors that she

FIGURE 4.2 Campaign posters. (Reprinted by permission of
Farid Ahmad Bayat)

FIGURE 4.3 Female candidate with religious leader Pir Gailani.

herself had carried bombs in saucepans to aid the cause of the mujahideen. It was difficult to determine whether such tales were true, but they certainly did not hurt her campaign in the region—Mazar long since having been a stronghold for Jamiat, and these stories echoed historical tales of women spurring their husbands to jihad in order to protect Islam.

Another successful female candidate in Balkh was a doctor who had studied in Germany and recently returned to Kabul to work for an international NGO. More familiar with Kabul than Balkh, her family had left their rural Pashtun village in the area many years previously and her father had been a member of parliament in the time of Zahir Shah. Returning to her roots by running in her home province instead of Kabul, she was a formidable character with a distinguished elegance of tone and expression. The third parliamentary seat reserved for women in Balkh was won by a student and former radio presenter with connections to a high-ranking family whose menfolk had a history of service as generals in the military. Her modest house was adorned with portraits of the president, and one got the sense that her campaign was undertaken as a form of duty, something expected of her as an educated young talent born into an influential family. As these three women reflect, there was a wide array of backgrounds, ethnicities, and allegiances that would be represented by women in parliament when it assembled, along with the different kinds of influence and agency that would accompany them as new members.

POLITICAL LEANINGS

Initially, candidates in the 2005 elections did not openly position themselves as "pro-government" or "opposition," adopting instead an "independent" approach that many proclaimed was for the benefit of the country. At this point, no one really knew how the new parliament would stand in relation to the different sources of authority prevailing in the country at the time. As it happened, many of the previously competing former commanders opted to join the system and run for election themselves (with the notable exceptions of Mullah Omar and Gulbuddin Hekmatyar). Their decision to do so was by no means a statement of unqualified support for the government, but they were in no hurry to form an overt opposition group at this early stage either.[17]

Election Day itself passed relatively peacefully, although compared to the previous year there were fewer celebrations or street parties. The carnival atmosphere had dissipated, and far fewer voters came to the polls—an estimated 53 percent, compared to nearly 80 percent in 2004—reflecting to some extent people's unease and disappointment with the candidates who had put themselves forward for election. One Mazari family retrospectively discussing thoughts on the elections after an evening meal in 2006 talked about their surprise at having seen the faces of infamous local commanders on the election ballot. Having voted for Karzai the previous year, they were now more wary of choosing between the individuals listed and were suspicious of the connections of those they did not recognize. The family consensus was to avoid voting completely—a sentiment we found mirrored across other parts of the country over the course of that year as we interviewed people.

Others expressed significant concerns about fraud—ballot boxes apparently found in rivers, or stolen from polling centers, opened, and stuffed overnight. The stories abounded; true or not, they demonstrated the considerable divide between local perceptions and the international pronouncement of elections as "free and fair." As one Afghan electoral observer told us in 2006, "Before the elections I was optimistic, but after I saw the violations that were occurring, I was totally disillusioned. The problems in the counting process were seen from below, but not from above, from the international level."

As it turned out, these issues were a justified cause for concern. Of the eleven parliamentary seats available for Balkh Province, most were won by prominent local leaders of the predominant ethnic groups in the area. Jamiat came out strongly, with a margin of over 6,000 votes over the rest of the field: the two highest vote-winners both had connections to the party, as did the woman with the most votes in the province—the local headmistress mentioned above. In spite of the fact that none of these candidates had officially declared their allegiance to the party, their connections and personal histories were well known across the province. As in other provinces the election also demonstrated—violently in some cases—the value attached to a seat in parliament: one leading Hazara candidate was killed before results were announced. Indeed, in spite of the turnout figures proudly documented in international reports, the process was by no means an exercise in promoting high democratic standards. While the elections were in themselves a significant achievement in a challenging, post-conflict environment with little preparation time, the deep underlying cracks in the electoral process would become debilitating fractures in the composition and activities of the new parliament.

A CLOSER LOOK: INSIDE THE HOUSE

In spite of the problems pervading the electoral process itself, the inauguration of Afghanistan's parliament on a cold January morning in 2006 was greeted with a great deal of optimism by Afghan and international observers alike. The change that it appeared to represent was nothing short of monumental. Following the brutal treatment of women during the Mujahideen and Taliban eras, even the alphabetical seating arrangements, in which men and women were allocated places alongside one another, were the source of considerable comment. Just as incredible was the diversity of newly elected parliamentarians that were thrown together in such close proximity: the communist alongside the mujahideen fighter, the commander exchanging pleasantries with the teacher. This was more than just the start of a new era—it was the start of a new set of rules in an entirely different game. Or so it was thought.

At this stage, many were still uncertain about just what this new game would involve. This was reflected in the fact that comparatively few mid-level warlords with reputations for violent crime had run for election. Lacking the kind of prestige, resources, and connections to international governments enjoyed by the most prominent figures, such as Sayyaf and Rabbani, they appeared to have been wary of the unknown and potentially dangerous ramifications of taking public office. For those successful candidates present at the inauguration, however, the general consensus appeared to be that, new game or not, this was a hand worth playing. With the United States and the wider international donor community clearly establishing themselves as the patrons of a new Afghanistan, there was little to lose in (superficially at least) aligning with their agendas and from time to time perhaps exchanging traditional robes for suits and ties.

This is not to undermine or belittle the determination of many elected parliamentarians to take part in building a better future for their country. Indeed, a number of lesser-known legislators spoke in interviews of their pride at being a representative of their province in the national assembly, the institution that would change the face of Afghan politics into a peaceful exchange of views between equals. As one parliamentarian from Helmand commented in early 2007:

> At first we didn't think we could even sit together, after thirty years of war and all being from different provinces with different ideas. We didn't think we could sit with Sayyaf, Rabbani, and other famous men. But it has been very positive. We have been able to sit together and share ideas like brothers. We are like brothers coming together to serve the Afghan people, for national unity, and this is a really positive thing.

But the ability of parliamentarians to play an effective part in bringing about this national unity, and in their being able to form groups that could oppose each other peacefully, was dependent on more than their newfound opportunity to talk to one another. Perhaps just as significant were the actions of the president and those of neighboring countries, of commanders inside and outside the parliament, and the continuing strength and perceived legitimacy of the international actors who had so strongly supported the rapid installation of the parliament in the first place.

STRUCTURES AND DIVISIONS IN PARLIAMENT

In the days following the ceremonious inauguration of parliament, the lower house held internal elections for its Administrative Board. The election resulted in a runoff between Sayyaf, well-known for his pro-Pashtun stance and hard-line, Muslim Brotherhood–inspired religious conservatism, and Qanooni, a Panjshiri Tajik close to the Northern Alliance with links to Jamiat, who had run for president the previous year. Despite the close margin, elections went smoothly and the results—narrowly favoring Qanooni—were not contested. Significantly, the position of second deputy speaker was won by a young woman. Fauzia Kufi, a Badakhshani parliamentarian who was also an ally of Rabbani with rumored connections to Jamiat, was the first woman in Afghan history to be elected to this position.

As Speaker of the House, Qanooni's role was ostensibly that of a facilitator, his formal responsibilities centered on the often arduous task of navigating parliamentary procedure and protocol as he chaired the daily plenary debates. And yet, in his highly selective choice of contributors, and in his impeccable timing—sometimes bringing controversial issues to the floor at the end of a Thursday session just before the beginning of the weekend—he was able to have a substantial impact on the outcomes of debates. Known among parliamentarians (and later by international observers) as "the arsonist and the fireman of the House," the significant informal influence Qanooni was able to generate through his manipulation of parliament's formal processes was widely recognized.

FORMAL PROCESSES

Qanooni's skills in managing the debates in parliament epitomize a political landscape in which informal bargaining and negotiations were central but molded around the formal procedures of the plenary. To better understand how they can be manipulated in practice, it is worth looking briefly at the formal processes and structures that determine how parliament was meant to work, in theory.

The lower house is comprised of up to 249 parliamentarians, each representing a provincial constituency. The number of representatives per constituency is determined by rough populations estimates, ranging from 33 parliamentarians for Kabul Province to just two for the remote southwestern province of Nimroz. Parliament's five key positions of authority are contained within the Administrative Board, for which any parliamentarian can stand in a plenary election. These positions include the speaker (also known as the President of the House), first and second deputy speakers, secretary and deputy secretary—all of which exist as a result of constitutional provision. The position of speaker is elected for an entire parliamentary term (five years) while other positions are held for a period of one year. Elections for the positions of first and second deputy speaker, secretary and deputy sectetary, are held at the beginning of the first session of each year.[18]

Of these positions, the speaker is the most prominent. The position is charged with chairing the daily plenary discussions and the weekly parliamentary leadership committee. However, it became clear after the inauguration of the second parliament that this position can be one of both extreme power and relative weakness, depending on the personality of the incumbent and his ability to manipulate the role. In contrast to Qanooni, the speaker for the second parliament, Abdul Rawoof Ebrahimi, was the product of an arranged compromise of warring parties after their inability to elect Sayyaf or Qanooni as speaker for the second term. A little-known Uzbek parliamentarian, the second-term speaker did not demonstrate the influence or control that his predecessor commanded, underlining quite clearly the personalized nature of authority in the Wolesi Jirga.

Parliamentarians are formally divided into eighteen thematic committees which focus on different aspects of legislation, such as international relations, education, and defense. At the beginning of each five-year term, interested individuals can put themselves forward for specific committee positions, a choice often related to their employment history or area of expertise. They are then voted into committees by an election in the general session. Some committees obviously carry more weight than others—the committee for foreign affairs, for example, is perceived to generate lucrative connections to international actors, and positions within it are thus highly sought after. One parliamentarian described in an interview in 2010 how a meeting where members of his ethnic group had tried to distribute themselves evenly between committees had stalled because too many people had wanted to be in the national security committee—known to be involved in the appointments and dismissals of district governors.

Heads of committees are also elected by the plenary, and join the Administrative Board once a week to discuss the agenda for the forthcoming week. Committees are supposedly apolitical in the sense that they are largely composed of parliamentarians from different ideological and ethnic backgrounds, with the exceptions of the Committee for Women, Youth and Social Affairs—usually made up entirely of female legislators—and the Committee for Kuchi

Affairs—normally given over to Kuchi legislators.[19] Interestingly, at one point during the first parliament a Hazara parliamentarian put himself forward and was elected to the Kuchi committee in an attempt to address some of the land conflicts between the two groups in the central highlands. He described his reasons for joining the committee to us:

> Since my homeland was at the center of the Kuchi land issue, I felt I needed to be working with the Kuchi committee. So, I nominated myself for the committee and was accepted to it. At the time, Qanooni was joking around with me and asking why I was trying to be on the Kuchi committee. I competed for the position of secretary of the committee and won the post. I was keen to resolve some of the tensions between our peoples, since twenty-eight residents in my hometown have been killed as a result of this conflict. So I raised the issue, but nothing happened and finally I resigned from the position. The committee had no mandate or power. I realized that a *wakil-i guzar* [head of a small urban neighborhood] has more power than a parliamentarian, because all power in this country has been distributed between a few people like Karzai, [Vice President Mohammad Karim Khalili, [Uzbek leader Abdul Rashid] Dostum, Sayyaf, Mullah Omar, and Rabbani, but other people are nothing. When the matter of the Kuchi land conflict was supposed to be solved, it was discussed and decided between Khalili and Karzai and no attention was paid to us and our efforts.

This legislator's story highlights a clear difference between the formal roles of the committees—which are to draft, amend, and present legislation on issues related to their field—and the actual power ceded to these groups. Power remains highly dependent both on the personalities within them and the interests of more powerful figures outside. Frustrated with the lack of progress made by the committee, and evidently having spent a good deal of effort to get a seat there in the first place, the parliamentarian went on to explain how, for him, there was little point in trying to influence policy when decisions were made at the top. Among many parliamentarians, this perception of elite control was to become more widespread as time passed, as will be discussed at length in chapter 8.

PARLIAMENTARY GROUPS

In comparison with the thematically divided committees, "parliamentary groups" as featured in the parliamentary rules of procedure were designed as a formal means to encourage the formation of political blocs. These were envisioned as a way to organize the plenary according to ideological groupings and ultimately to form the foundations of issues-based political parties. According to the rules of procedure, groups may form with a minimum of 23 (formerly 21) members, but must not represent a single ethnicity, linguistic group, religious sect, gender, or region.[20] These conditions were invoked to encourage the development of interethnic, ideologically focused blocs. However, in parliament's first term, they actually served to prevent cohesive groups from forming since issues-based ties between parliamentarians were rarely strong enough to overcome divisions of class, ethnicity, or sect.[21]

Four groups had officially registered by 2007: *Esteqlal-i Milli* ("National Independence"), chaired by Sayed Mustafa Kazimi, with 23 members; *Nezarat-i Milli* ("National Monitoring"), chaired by Engineer Mohammad Asem, with 22 members; *Taraqi Khwah* ("Progressive"), chaired by Mohammad Naim Farahi, with 22 members; and "Afghanistan," chaired by Mirwais Yasini, with 41 members.[22] Another, the *Khat-i Sewum* or "Third Line," existed for all intents and purposes as a group, but never formally registered due to a lack of sufficient members. In spite of the initial enthusiasm to form, however, these groups soon dissipated, while others neglected to register at all; two years later, the Third Line group was the only one in the list still meeting. Others had formed but had not managed to gather enough members to register. Incentives to remain in a group were simply not strong enough when there was little to bind groups together ideologically, and when there was always the opportunity for greater individual renown by forming a separate group and making a claim for a leadership position. Representatives also suspected other groups of bribing members to join them, as one parliamentarian stated with some exasperation in an interview in 2007: "we tried to make a group three times but other groups bought our members from us!"[23]

Moreover, there was a significant concern among parliamentarians that groups would be formed only to serve the interests of their particular leader. As one MP from Ghazni described in an interview in 2006,

> One or two people are trying to hijack a group of parliamentarians and I will not join this group until these issues are solved. I do not want it to serve the impractical ambitions of one individual. . . . If parliamentary groups are created and they remain true to their purpose then this is good, but not if they are created to further individual ambitions.

This element of distrust would prove debilitating since it meant that no one could really be sure of the real intentions of the leader of their group. Among the parliamentarians we interviewed, there was a real sense of reluctance to support the personal ambitions of counterparts whose plans for groups and their political positions were not entirely clear.

From another perspective, it was difficult for parliamentarians trying to form groups to convince others to join them without the promise of a leadership position. Describing just such an attempt, a representative from Parwan Province talked about the need to create multiple positions of authority in order to attract more members, or "friends":

> I wanted to be a member of a group but I was supported by 36 legislators, and of these I am trying to make two groups. In order to make two groups however we need 42 legislators. . . . The requirement is for a minimum of 21 people [in a group] but since we want to have all of our friends with us, it is easier to convince them to join us if there is more than one leadership position available.[24]

This statement draws attention to the numerous coexisting sources of power in the early days of the first parliament. The parliamentarian here clearly felt he was not the only viable candidate for a leadership position amongst his supporters, but instead of stepping aside he attempted to create other spaces at the top. However, this kind of informal bargaining had to be molded around the formal rules, in that extra parliamentarians needed to be found to make up the numbers of a second group and the new set of leadership positions that would accompany it.[25] In this sense, the rules discouraged the formation of groups, but at the same time so did many of the political values, practices, and tendencies that individuals brought with them to the Wolesi Jirga. Just as elections function as structuring structures in the Afghan political landscape more broadly, so do these new formal rules in the landscape of the Wolesi Jirga—as they affect but are also affected by informal norms and institutions that pervade the way in which politics plays out in parliament.

This example also demonstrates on a micro level one of the major problems faced by parties throughout Afghanistan's history and across the political spectrum: the continual splintering of groups due to the value placed on leadership positions. The trend toward political fragmentation was reflected in the fact that in 2007—a year after the inauguration of parliament—most of the 40 parliamentarians we interviewed at the time were unwilling or unable to specify which parliamentary group they belonged to, or the specific platform or priorities of that group.[26] In the way it was framed and implemented, the formal mechanism of parliamentary groups was therefore not so much encouraging the formation of new, issues-based blocs as it was reinforcing an existing inclination to diverge.

The Third Line group was something of an exception, in that its members managed to maintain a relatively coherent core group with an identifiable message throughout the early years of the first parliament without being formally registered at all. This group of modernist-leaning liberal legislators was keen to emphasize that it was not pro-government, nor in opposition, but promoting a new, middle ground that would prioritize the needs of constituents by dealing with issues on their own merits. As one member stated in early 2006, "we are neither with fundamentalists nor are we the puppet of the government." Led by the formidable figure of Shukria Barakzai, a Kabuli MP and English-speaking former journalist whose regular outspoken comments on the popular Tolo TV station would make her a household name in cities across the country, the group was made up of several Kabul-based intellectuals representing a variety of ethnic, religious, and political groups. However, while they would quickly become known for their modernist agenda—such as their efforts to promote the raising of women's age of majority to 18 (the same as for boys) instead of 16—even this group was not free from leadership disputes or divisions within its ranks.

Given their "pro-democracy" stance and most members' ability to speak English, Third Line parliamentarians were popular with the international community and built relationships with donors that resulted in frequent trips abroad. However, as emphasizing one's connection with international actors became increasingly risky both as a political strategy and to the personal security of members, the cohesion of the group began to dissolve. In addition, the "Third Line" platform was no longer distinctive, since many other parliamentarians had adopted a similar approach in a bid to retain the appearance of independence and be seen to prioritize constituent interests. As such, the name lost its initial attraction quite quickly, becoming associated with a more general politics of posturing in the minds of Afghan politicians even if it maintained a level of credibility among Western embassies.

Another critical problem was the fact that individual group members had ties to other interest groups and parties, dividing their allegiance and pulling them in different directions. One parliamentarian we interviewed several times during the course of the first parliament began as a fervent member of the Third Line, but as with other members of the group, his affiliation to it gradually waned as the years progressed. Although not overtly, he was also connected to a political party, which he may well have considered more able to generate valuable public support in the upcoming elections. Despite its early fame, the Third Line had never developed a strong popular support network and only really existed as a group within the parliament. Parties, on the other hand, offered a connection to regional and ethnic voters who could be mobilized quickly if needed.

PARTIES AND PARLIAMENTARY GROUPS

Across parliaments worldwide, it is not uncommon for some parliamentarians to be more equal than others, in spite of their formal votes in parliamentary sessions being officially counted as equivalent. Indeed, in the Wolesi Jirga in particular, parliamentarians can exist anywhere on a continuum spanning from the leaders of major parties like Rabbani and Sayyaf to little-known teachers and village elders who had been adept at mobilizing local-level voting blocs. While this influence gap was reflected superficially in the mere comparison of vote counts after the election, it was enhanced and solidified by the existence of blocs of party supporters or affiliates, who often owed their presence in parliament to the financial assistance of their party leaders or fellow legislators.

The 2005 elections propelled significant numbers of members or affiliates of ethnic-based parties from the jihad period into parliament. But parties were generally not able to harness the formal parliamentary group structure as a means to promote their own blocs. With their membership largely determined by common ethnic or regional identities, these parties did not meet the criteria set out in the official rules of procedure—primarily because these rules had been specifically designed to prevent their reemergence. Once again, parties were left with no formal way to solidify their organizational and political identities within parliament. Rather than curtailing their activities, these rules rendered their activities informal, unregulated, and reliant on connections to influential individuals outside parliament.

Rabbani, for example, was able to draw significant support from parliamentarians with existing or previous connections to Jamiat. This support, in turn, may have been extended to the election of Qanooni (also a former Jamiati) as speaker, or to Fauzia Kufi as second deputy speaker. However, Rabbani's continued backing was far from guaranteed, or consistent. Rabbani and Qanooni had clashed during the Bonn process, with Rabbani supporting Karzai's bid for the presidency over Qanooni's. Kufi was known to be close to Qanooni, potentially jeopardizing her constituency with Rabbani supporters whenever the two men were on bad terms. In this way, party leaders' informal dealings and negotiations within parliament were orchestrated to generate a sense of individual power and control over decision-making that could be spontaneous and unpredictable—not a trait conducive to the building of a bloc or formal parliamentary group. As one legislator described in an interview in 2007:

> To be a parliamentarian in our Wolesi Jirga you need a lot of finesse; you
> need to know how to navigate between ethnic, tribal, political, linguistic, and
> personal affiliations. If you are liked by more than 50 percent of the parlia-
> ment then you have achieved a lot. You need to be imaginative and creative.

Forming a bloc of parliamentarians, and particularly when emphasis is placed
on being "liked" (respected or supported) as an individual rather than for the
ideological platform on which you stand, is, of course, easier said than done.

This proved to be a significant problem for influential women in parliament. Kufi, in particular, was disliked by many women legislators, to the
point at which they would boycott events or resources that she claimed
to have acquired from the international community for the parliament.[27]
Sources of this animosity varied, including the way in which she was in
charge of all international assistance to the parliament during her time in
office, and a perceived abuse of this responsibility. Although this state of
affairs came to be through good intentions on the part on internationals
wanting to coordinate assistance, it led to the creation of a distinct monopoly over the international resources that were flooding the legislature at the
time. As one Afghan working in an international agency confirmed, in an
interview in 2006: "Everything goes through Kufi—she coordinates the
trainings and she has stated what kinds of training she thinks the [Wolesi
Jirga] members need."

Along with the convenience of working through a single individual, international efforts to ensure Afghan buy-in had facilitated the rise to prominence of one individual woman, generating a considerable degree of agitation
on the part of other female representatives as a result. This, combined with
her connections to influential members of Jamiat, probably contributed to her
failure to win a second term in her role as second speaker after the first year of
parliament had come to close.

The example also highlights the way in which the 68 women elected as a
result of the reserved seats system did not form a cohesive bloc promoting
an ideologically based stance championing the rights of women in general.
Although the women were numerically a critical mass of almost 30 percent
of parliamentarians, they were divided just as were their male counterparts

along ethnic, regional, and party-based lines, their networks of connections and allegiances unequal and fluid.

* * *

It would be wrong to say that the 2005 parliament did not see the development of some ideologically based groups. Some parties did have core members in parliament that were accountable to the party headquarters; some women were able to push for gender-sensitive legislation. But these groups were not formalized and did not translate directly into "pro-government" or "opposition" blocs. Parliamentarians who stood firmly on one side or the other did exist, but they were few and far between until the 2009 presidential elections.

PRESERVING DISUNITY

Although neither the electoral system nor the parliamentary rules of procedure encouraged easy organization into pro-government and opposition camps, it soon became apparent that broad groupings of parliamentarians did exist within parliament. According to the most comprehensive analysis of the results of the 2005 elections, produced by Andrew Wilder at AREU, it was possible to make a rough division of the new parliamentarians into three groups according to their affiliations, parties, and personal historical allegiances: pro-government, opposition, and unaligned, all with approximately 80 legislators apiece.[28] However, these groups turned out to be a poor basis for systematic or consistent organization. Rather than solidifying as parliament's first five-year term progressed, they remained fluid and indistinct, fragmenting and reforming along complex webs of personal relationships and past affiliations.

As Wilder's analysis rightly predicted, the existence of these apparent divisions between parliamentarians also failed to pose a serious challenge to the government's agenda:

> The fragmented nature of the [Wolesi Jirga] will make forming and maintaining a legislative majority a challenging and time-consuming task, not

to mention a potentially expensive one in an environment with high levels of graft and patronage expectations. Nevertheless, it should still be possible for the government to use its powers of persuasion and patronage to get the backing of a majority of delegates when required.[29]

Indeed, this proved to be the case on several occasions. At least in parliament's first three years, President Karzai was generally able to sway the vote in his favor at key junctures such as the passing of the Shia Personal Status Law (2009). A controversial bill designed to allow Shia groups separate courts for legal affairs concerning controversial family matters, it was widely perceived to have succeeded as a result of a bargain between Karzai and the leader of a prominent Shia sect in return for their support in the presidential elections.[30]

Karzai would find parliament more difficult to manipulate in the run-up to his reelection bid, especially as disappointment mounted over his inability to solve ongoing Hazara-Kuchi land disputes which had resurfaced in the summer of 2009. Nevertheless, the president was able to maintain a broad control over the plenary, even if he had to go to more effort and expense to do so. One representative from Faryab talked in an interview in early 2010 about the perceived difficulty in maintaining a stance against the government:

> There are only a small number of parliamentarians who are against the government because it is difficult to stay in opposition, it needs commitment, and fundamentally it is too costly to be against the government. Because most of the development projects are given to the parliamentarians who support Karzai, unfortunately they are acting only in Karzai's interest. Perhaps 120 or 140 parliamentarians are working for Karzai with their eyes closed, they are completely directed by Karzai.

As discussed in chapter 8, the president would go on to further extend his control over the plenary in the aftermath of the 2010 parliamentary elections.

Implied in the quotation above, the lack of a coherent opposition did not necessarily stem from a lack of oppositional will—indeed, Karzai generated significant criticism and even tangible anger among a proportion of parliamentarians throughout parliament's first term. As one parliamentarian remarked with considerable bitterness in an interview in 2010:

> In spite of our government receiving extensive assistance from different countries, we are still very poor. And the conditions in Afghanistan have gotten worse, both in the parliament and in the country as a whole. I think this is all because of Karzai's mistakes.

Others considered the president psychologically infirm; as parliament's first term drew to a close, an increasing number of legislators openly expressed their doubts in his competence as a leader or in his physical health. Another pro-Karzai parliamentarian in an interview in 2010 described a meeting with the president, expressing concern for his well-being:

> The president is not well, he is ill—he needs a break and a rest. A few days ago I had a meeting with him, and I told him I didn't agree with some of his ideas about the Taliban. He grabbed me by the collar and told me to get out of the room. I asked him to please, relax. He is taking pills for his illness and he is working from 6 a.m. to 11 p.m., which is not good for his health.

Even supporters, then, were forthcoming in relating their concerns. Estimates vary, but toward the end of the parliament's first term some 80 legislators were voicing a strong oppositional stance. The lack of a unified bloc was thus clearly not a result of a lack of anti-Karzai sentiment.

To get a sense of why the inability to form a cohesive group was so persistent, in spite of a significant number of critical voices coming from the parliament, it is useful to return to the electoral system and the way it shaped the political landscape in 2005. Many commentators at the time were highly critical of the system, arguing that SNTV would merely entrench the patron-client structures that already existed and would require no interethnic or intersectarian bonding.[31] Since such small margins were required to win seats, they feared that voting would effectively become an exercise in cementing social bonds at a local level, with members of one's kin group or members of one's ethnicity—in much the same way as it had done in the

1960s in smaller electoral districts. In contrast, other commentators focused more on the system's encompassing contextual problems. As one international analyst noted after a failed attempt to change the electoral system by a group of parliamentarians in 2008: "Yes, the system is bad. SNTV is not a helpful system, but really we need to understand that we're not going to solve Afghanistan's problems and create a stable democracy by merely tweaking institutions. The underlying issues won't be dealt with this way." Yet another perspective came from the few internationals working with political parties, who saw how parties used complaints about the system to justify inactivity. For these observers, an electoral system seemingly hostile to parties should have acted as a self-disciplining tool, forcing them to be more efficient in their selection of candidates and allocation of canvassing areas.

There are valid concerns in each of these perspectives. However, one thing is certain: the SNTV system left wide open the possibility of a fractionalized parliament, similar in fact to its 1969 predecessor in which over 200 individuals effectively stood as their own parties.[32] For a president hoping to solidify control, this represented a clear advantage. Although he was unable to secure easily a legislative majority through a committed bloc of parliamentarians always willing to support his cause, he was never faced with a coherent or strong opposition. Unfortunately, this situation meant that Karzai's relationship with parliament would be continually characterized by his apparent efforts to preserve this disunity. In addition to his refusal to join a political party or declare allegiance to any specific grouping, the president embarked on a series of indirect attempts to foster divisions within parliament. As discussed in chapter 8, perhaps the most dramatic of these would be the introduction of a Special Court (also often referred to as the Special Elections Tribunal) to investigate fraud during the 2010 elections, and its subsequent attempt to eject 62 inaugurated legislators from their seats. Signs of this coming political storm, however, were apparent from the parliament's earliest sessions.

Another point to consider in explaining parliamentary divisions is the general lack of incentive for parliamentarians to declare their political stances outright. In the context of both parliament's informal power struggles and the worsening security situation in the country, it quickly became politically expedient for parliamentarians to keep their alliances ambiguous. This allowed them to conduct their business without worrying about its potential security implications and—perhaps more importantly—to sell the prospect of their support to the highest bidder (usually the government).[33] This preference for a culture of political ambiguity was also facilitated by simple, technical procedures such as the lack of names attached to representatives' plenary votes. Votes in parliament are conducted through a show of red or green cards, the resulting sea of color quickly assessed and noted by members of the Administrative Board. In this process, accurate tallies of votes are rarely recorded, let alone the names of parliamentarians attached to a given card. With no system of accountability, it became very easy for parliamentarians to change their vote from red to green at the last minute, having given their assurances beforehand that they would not do so.

As one representative described in 2010, "parliamentarians decide one thing in their committees, they decide to vote as a bloc, and then when the vote occurs in the plenary people change their minds and form voting allegiances according to their ethnic links instead." Another suggested the changes were more the result of elite bargaining, saying that "the red and green cards are irrelevant—before the voting there is a trade between the leaders. They make the decisions before the voting and then the voting becomes only a sign, a symbol." One young female parliamentarian told us in 2011 about a time when an older male MP had leaned across the seating rows and offered her a piece of chewing gum if she would change her voting card from red to green. This deliberate act of public humiliation emphasized both the disdain with which some of the elder parliamentarians viewed their younger counterparts as well as the joke that internal parliamentary votes had become.

The lack of a committed oppositional leadership was another major barrier to effective opposition. Qanooni was a case in point. A key strongman and Northern Alliance ally, his election to the position of speaker in 2006 represented a victory on the part of "the opposition." However, he also had his relationship with the president to sustain, and began to lose the trust of his former pro-opposition allies. More critically, he was one of many contenders for the informal post of "leader of the opposition"—and with several highly prominent Jamiat commanders either parliamentarians themselves or wielding influence within parliament, any authority he might have had was not solely in his grasp.

Without a clear contender to lead an opposition movement from within the parliament—no doubt fueled by the fact that informal, behind-the-scenes bargaining had in many respects become the body's standard operating procedure—there was no universally trusted figurehead that could unite those unhappy with government policy. This was a key stumbling block for both the former Northern Alliance camp and Pashtun parliamentarians disenchanted with the president, since there were no key individuals who could unite the grievances of both groups and simultaneously convince the house that they were truly "in opposition." Indeed, it was not until the campaign of Dr. Abdullah Abdullah, former Minister of Foreign Affairs and previously a close associate of Ahmed Shah Massoud, challenged the president in the 2009 elections that a serious candidate for the role came forward, and at this point a good deal more parliamentarians in interviews wanted to demonstrate publically their disaffection with the president by declaring themselves "in opposition" (though by no means did they formally affiliate themselves to that effect). However, by this time, most parliamentarians had adopted practices that made the formation of blocs unlikely. Finally, by stepping down from the planned runoff, Abdullah lost much of the support he had generated throughout his campaign and the momentum for opposition, once again, lapsed.[34]

AN AMBIGUOUS TERRAIN

The lack of a consolidated opposition in the Afghan parliament has been often lamented since its 2005 inception—by Afghan parliamentarians themselves, by analysts within civil society, and by international policymakers and practitioners attempting to encourage the development of an organized legislature. But what is often forgotten is the fact that this was also noted by observers of the legislature as far back as 1971.[35] The problem thus has deep historical roots, born at least partially from the Afghan state's long-standing paranoia about any potential challenge to its authority.

However, combining with the events and political processes of the twentieth century are new dynamics that have exacerbated the difficulties in forming coherent opposition. Perhaps most significant among these is the electoral system, which has in turn affected patterns of voting both for and, indirectly, within parliament. The selection of a strong presidential system indirectly enforced the power of ethnic and regional strongmen by strengthening the old rentier state model of patronage. Beginning at Bonn and continuing throughout the international interventions in Afghanistan, this process has consistently reinforced these leaders' ability to manipulate the structures and processes of parliament to their own advantage. Nevertheless, the advantage gained by these figures pales in comparison to that gained by the president himself through his maintenance of a disorganized and disunified parliament that could be easily bought and bent to serve his own purposes. With such strong disincentives in place for either political or ethnic leaders or the president himself to create a viable opposition, the outcome of an entirely dysfunctional legislature, as it had become in 2011, was all but inevitable.

This fundamental failure of political institutionalization at a national level has meant that the greatest advantage that parliamentary and provincial council representatives had to offer their communities was not a voice in government, or a check on state authority, but a link to national-level patronage connections to powerful individuals. This, along with the way parliamentarians were integrated into complex webs of local power structures, greatly complicated both their roles in government and their influence on political issues in their constituencies. The complication of local with national, of formal with informal, was to become tellingly clear in the 2009 provincial council elections.

5

ENGINEERING ELECTIONS LOCALLY

SHER SHAH AND THE DISTRICT SHURA

*T*HE SHOMALI IS *a wide fertile plain that separates Kabul from the Hindu Kush mountains. Watered by a complex system of irrigation channels, the land is valuable and historically has played an important role in national politics. The political and economic significance of the area, however, has also created a good deal of localized tension between the various ethnic groups and tribes that live there.*

The region's local leaders are deeply involved in complex political webs that tie together actors from the very lowest level to concerns of national significance. This plays out in the debates and discussions that characterize the shura in Qara Bagh, a district situated in the heart of the Shomali. The Qara Bagh shura is one of the many district-level decision-making bodies that exist across the country despite the fact that constitutionally-demanded formal elections for district councils have not yet been held. Many of these bodies have been in place in some form or another for years, serving important local functions. Although it has no formal links to the election process, the Qara Bagh shura was still involved in many of the political debates revolving around the elections and other issues in the area. At the center of these discussions in the run-up to the 2009 presidential and provincial council elections was the then head of the council, Sher Shah Oryakhel, along with his brother, the parliamentarian Anwar Khan Oryakhel.

Sher Shah comes from a powerful local family. His father was a parliamen-tarian in the 1960s and their family has land holdings in the area. During the Interim Administration established in the wake of the U.S. invasion, Sher Shah was chosen as a representative to several districts in Kabul and then served as a member of the Constitutional Loya Jirga. During this unsettled period, he was shot by an unknown assailant when walking home at night from a gathering of other Shomali leaders. He survived despite being hit in the leg and the back. As a result of this attack, he was paralyzed from the waist down and spent time in the United States recuperating from his injuries. On returning to Afghanistan, Sher Shah pushed his brother to run for the Wolesi Jirga in 2005 in his place. Meanwhile, he remained active in politics in Qara Bagh, becoming head of the district shura and often serving as a link between his brother and the community. When members of the community spoke of the brothers, they often referred to them as almost a collec-tive political unit, with one Qara Baghi man making the typical comment, "Anwar Khan and his brother have not yet decided whether they will stand for reelection." The brothers also derive a good deal of their support from tribal ties, and while most of their supporters are locally based in Qara Bagh, they can rely on the backing of other members of the Oryakhel tribe across Kabul Province, many of whom lived in Paghman District, some twenty miles to the southwest.

As elsewhere in Afghanistan, people in Qara Bagh try to avoid state involve-ment in local political life, considering officials a hindrance at best and parasitical at worst. As one man explained in a statement typical of provincial attitudes across the country: "The people generally try to solve their problems among themselves and sometimes with the district council; they generally don't want their problems to be solved by the government." However, this summary oversimplifies the complex relationships between local leaders, the council, and government officials that exist in practice.

As the 2009 and 2010 elections played out, parliamentarians and provincial council candidates in Qara Bagh debated their role and the roles of other commu-nity leaders, local officials, and the district shura, particularly in regard to securing development projects for the area. Access to development funds and the government contacts needed to acquire them were rarely isolated from other political issues. In 2009 much of the debate in the area was over the building of a large teacher train-ing institute in the district and a sizable tract of land in the east of the district, which the government had taken control of but the community still claimed as their own, in part because of a United Nations Development Program (UNDP) project planned for the area.

As head of the council, Sher Shah described his job as facilitating many of the discussions around these issues and working to bring additional resources to the community. But in the Shomali Plain, where a large number of actors compete with each other for rich natural resources, there was continued tension and attempts by individuals and groups to undermine each other, leading to regular feuds. As Sher Shah explained, in one of a succession of interviews in 2010:

> *There are some small hands who are working for the destruction of me and my brother . . . people who are not willing to take the key leadership positions in Qara Bagh. Instead they are always starting rumors among the people and telling them to ask: What have Sher Shah and his brother done for Qara Bagh?*

These questions about who could take credit for delivering resources or who should be blamed for not bringing more were at the heart of local political concerns and elections in the district and were much discussed by the district council.

During this period, the council had an unclear relationship to the government.[1] The district governor—the most senior representative of the Kabul administration in Qara Bagh—often claimed in our conversations with him that most of the representatives on the council, who were primarily maliks, were "legal" (and by this he meant simply that they had been approved by him or his predecessor, even though there was no real legal process to do this), but many were "illlegal" (or had not been approved by him or his predecessor, but were still active on the council). The council had its own meeting room in the district government compound, also home to the district governor's office and the district police station. The uneasy relationship between these three groups played out in a discussion in 2009 over whether council members and their bodyguards should be forced to relinquish their weapons before entering the compound to attend council meetings. The chief of police argued that all others except for police and government officials had to surrender their arms, so they should too. Shura members, however, protested, some implying that the police were not actually capable of protecting them. When the district governor quietly refused to back the chief of police, the council members were allowed to continue bringing in their arms.

Within the shura itself, there was a clear, if informal order. Sher Shah headed the meetings, but there were other leaders who challenged his authority by attempting to reshape the weekly agenda, encouraging individuals not to attend or working in other ways to undermine the group's progress. In many instances, this created debates with a similar disjointed, chaotic feel as those in the Wolesi Jirga. While trying to maintain order, Sher Shah was confronted with a series of challenges from his deputy, who on several instances openly tried to restructure the council. More passive forms of resistance came from certain elders who sat toward the back of the meeting room, chatting and catching up on gossip during the various speeches. Such passive resistance could end up completely derailing a council meeting and was an effective tool for leaders who wanted to avoid conflict, but also did not want their rivals gaining any ground either.

This was the case in several of the meetings leading up to the provincial council election in 2009. With 11 different candidates from the area, there was the strong feeling that unless certain candidates were eliminated, they would split the community's vote and few, if any, would be elected. One had been successful in 2005, and it was generally hoped that better organization and participation could allow the district to increase this representation, electing two, or maybe even three, candidates. Based on Qara Bagh's population, economic importance, and strategic location, the idea of sending multiple representatives to parliament did not seem overly ambitious. The key was to ensure that all the votes from the district were concentrated on a select group of candidates instead of being thinly distributed among all 11—clearly some candidates needed to step aside. A special shura meeting was scheduled to address the issue.

Sher Shah and other key council leaders hoped that in addition to the usual district shura members, all the candidates would attend, along with some other important elders from the district. At the last minute, however, a funeral drew many attendees away and only a few of the candidates actually came to the meeting, with most of the more influential candidates conspicuously absent. The meeting began with both Sher Shah and the district governor, who often, but not always, attended the more important shura meetings, giving introductory remarks on the importance of elections and the right to vote. In turn, it was the duty of those at the meeting, they said, to return to their villages and encourage those there to vote as well. The assistant head of the council, and a man Sher Shah had opposed in the past, then dramatically reported that only 30,000 of Qara Bagh's 180,000 residents had applied for voting cards and that this small number was a result of "the weakness of the Qara Bagh district council and the maliks, who were not encouraging people to participate." He was followed by the mullah of one of the large mosques in Qara Bagh, who emphasized that it was everyone's religious duty to vote and that the people should form a coalition around one or two candidates, something that they should all now discuss.

After this well-orchestrated beginning, however, the meeting ran into some problems. An Afghan representative from an international NGO stood to give an update on some recent projects in the area. The man explained that due to some budgetary issues, several road-building projects were behind schedule and would not be completed for months. A number of maliks interrupted him and called him a traitor to the area for failing to deliver the promised projects. While the meeting seemed to have veered wildly from the discussion of the election, the timing of the speech was meaningful. Under such circumstances, the voicing of dissatisfaction over NGO resource delivery led many attendees to interpret the speech as an attack on community leaders—particularly Sher Shah, who was presiding over the meeting. It was not a coincidence that the current political structures in town were being subtly undermined just as the town was preparing for elections. As time passed, the council meeting grew more chaotic and began to break up. When participants started to leave, Sher Shah hastily encouraged all the maliks present to go and sit with their communities and make a decision about who they would vote for. Most important was that the candidate was from Qara Bagh and not the neighboring districts of Istalif or Kalakan.

With this the meeting ended. In the following weeks, there were several other attempts to consolidate community support behind one or two candidates, but none made much progress beyond this chaotic meeting—something that candidates and local leaders alike lamented to us at length.

Despite this, Qara Bagh still fared better than other areas; when the final results were announced, two candidates from the district had secured the necessary votes to join the provincial council—Adel Khan, the incumbent, and Gul Afghan, a new representative. For many this was good news, since having two representatives on the provincial council would hopefully bring more government resources to the district and these representatives could potentially serve as individual links to patronage structures based in Kabul. Despite this, almost as soon as the results were announced, some began to complain that Gul Afghan, not one of the names most frequently mentioned by voters in the days leading up to the election, had certain connections inside the IEC which he had used to his advantage. Far from being satisfied with the situation, these results further fueled local debates over who was responsible for the successes of these candidates, who should be blamed for the failure of others, and whether the results demonstrated the ability of certain leaders to mobilize voters more effectively than their rivals.

A LOCAL PERSPECTIVE OF ELECTIONS IN 2009

Many accounts of elections focus on the way candidates and parties mobilize voters. In the Afghan case, this is only half the story: elections are also opportunities for communities and individuals to manipulate the political system in their favor. This can be as simple as gaining favors from candidates in exchange for support at the polls, but can also include complex negotiations to realign patronage networks linked to Kabul, which at times defy what might otherwise be considered logical alliances based on factors such as tribe, ethnicity, or area of origin.

Most anthropological studies of "tribal politics" in other settings would suggest that during times of conflict alliances would first be based upon first close kin, then more distant relatives, and finally members of the same ethnicity as predicted by models of segmentary opposition.[2] Yet as individuals and communities worked to manipulate the election process, it was often advantageous to look beyond these close bonds, forming new alliances that crossed political lines. Similarly, more recent political science approaches might look at the role of "non-state" (as opposed to state) actors, but as we saw in chapter 1, this dichotomy is rarely so simple in the Afghan context. Instead, elections show the complicated webs of alliances and opposition that Afghans live in and work to manipulate. This chapter focuses on the role of provincial council members and parliamentarians within this local political landscape, in an attempt to better understand how communities and individuals try to take advantage of the election process and their relationships with representatives to serve their own ends.

* * *

Both the Afghan government and the international community began preparing for the presidential elections of 2009 with cautious optimism. While it was clear that the insurgency was gaining ground in the south and east of the country, international diplomats continued to assert that the Karzai government was able to contend with these issues, even though there were rumors that they might support an alternative candidate.[3] Compared to the presidential elections, there was much less international interest in the provincial council campaigns that were occurring simultaneously. However, in many areas across Afghanistan the focus of voter attention on the provincial council elections was intense, in some cases far outstripping interest in the presidential campaigns. Particularly after Karzai had secured the support of Marshal Fahim, Khalili, and Dostum, key representatives of the Tajik, Hazara, and Uzbek communities respectively, many Afghan voters saw the presidential election as a foregone conclusion. Many suggested in conversations with us that most of the 42 candidates were not serious about winning the election, only running to increase their own reputations for future political endeavors or secure financial gains by later backing out of the election in favor of other candidates. By Election Day, the only candidates discussed as having the potential to generate a significant number of votes were President Karzai, Dr. Abdullah, and Ramazan Bashardost (and to a much lesser extent Ashraf Ghani and Mirwais Yasini, who were the only other candidates to earn more than 1 percent of the vote).

In the presidential election, President Karzai failed to secure the 50 percent plus one necessary to win the election outright during the first round of balloting on August 20. This spurred a national crisis, leading to differing arguments from the IEC, ECC, and Supreme Court on how to proceed. Ultimately, it was decided that a second round of voting between Dr. Abdullah and Karzai was necessary, but before this could happen Abdullah rescinded his candidacy, citing the best interests of the country as reasons for doing so.[4]

Much of the debate on the 2009 elections as reported in the national and international media revolved around the staggering amount of fraud, with some 23 percent of votes being declared fraudulent.[5] Lost in much of this dis-

cussion was the fact that the many colorful posters of local provincial council candidates generated more local consternation than did the fraud in the
presidential polls and the way in which Afghan voters were just as distressed
by the outcome of the provincial council elections.

While often separated by outside observers, the presidential and provincial
council campaigns were deeply linked on a local level, and in many instances
provincial council candidates affiliated themselves with presidential candidates. The key candidates, particularly Karzai and Abdullah, set up campaign
offices in most districts, and presidential campaign workers often worked to
promote certain provincial candidates at the same time, in spite of the lack
of any official links between the two.[6] This affiliation rarely had ideological
overtones and was based instead on the patronage networks to which certain
powerful local figures belonged.

In the case of Qara Bagh, this meant the loose formation of two groups:
a pro-Karzai and primarily Pashtun camp, of which Sher Shah and Anwar
Khan were members, and an anti-Karzai group composed mainly of Tajiks,
who opposed the current government (though clearly did not oppose it
enough to join the insurgency), of which Sher Shah's deputy on the district
council was a key member. However, the area's loyalties were by no means as
clearly distributed as this generalization suggests. Distinctions were extremely
difficult to make, and it was common to find alliances that crossed what one
might assume were standard kin-based, ethnic, or party lines. Anthropological political models, such as segmentary opposition, in which an individual
supports close kin or tribe members during periods of conflict but oppose
them in times of peace, were often ineffective at predicting how political loyalties formed. In many cases, allegiances were fluid and shifting, part of the
complex maneuvering, negotiating, and manipulating on the part of both
individuals and groups to use elections to further their own interests. As in
parliament, individuals tended to change sides frequently and use the very
porous nature of political boundaries to their advantage, making it difficult in
practice to isolate either a clear pro- or antigovernment camp.[7]

One of the key issues with an approach to elections that favor rules, procedures, and institutions (as often characterizes international efforts in Afghanistan) over individual and community experiences is that it diverts the gaze of

the viewer away from important political issues beyond simple questions of who won and lost. Particularly in cases where political power and legitimacy are not clearly bounded by the state, political performance over the course of an election cycle can be a crucial factor in reshaping power within the community. In such cases, power and influence may be gained or lost based on how political figures perform during elections, and not simply on whether they secure a position. This is intimately tied to the issue of how communities themselves manipulate elections and use them to further their own agendas. Elections, as political structures, reshape and reformulate local dynamics. Ironically, instead of embedding an area further into a state system, elections can be used by communities to establish new patronage networks to increase their autonomy, or simply as an opportunity to challenge and undermine those in power.

ELECTIONS AND DISPLAYS OF POWER IN LOCAL POLITICS

As the description of the Qara Bagh district council meeting at the beginning of this chapter suggests, campaigns and elections are deeply embedded in other, local political issues. As such, they frequently offer a reflection on questions of honor and relationships between individuals and groups within the community. The council meeting that was supposed to focus on reducing numbers of candidates turned quickly to other issues when the NGO worker stood to give his report. In fact, it was later speculated in our conversations with some who had attended the meeting that Sher Shah's rivals had told the man to time his speech as a means of disrupting the meeting and so make it less likely that the council would successfully eliminate candidates. In general, candidates and elections were always discussed as part of broader local political issues. Questions of how far various representatives were able to deliver resources, represent their communities in Kabul, and tie into national-level patronage networks were considered far more important than their stances on national issues or capacity to influence legislation. This meant that while communities by and large ignored the details of debates within the Wolesi Jirga and provincial councils, they maintained a keen interest in who was taking part in these debates and the selection processes that had brought them there.

Although elections were taking place at the provincial and national levels, they were intimately bound to local-level politics. In fact, it often seemed like the election and campaigns were not even the central point of contention, instead forming a backdrop for the playing out of local political issues, such as feuds between families and individuals. In Qara Bagh, for example, the campaign leaders for Karzai and Abdullah were two former commanders with a long history of enmity. Here, opposition had little to do with the political agendas of Karzai or Abdullah; once one of the commanders decided to support Karzai, it seemed almost inevitable that the other would support Abdullah for fear of losing prestige and influence by not participating in such an important political event. As a result, local sentiment about these two commanders had as much to do with how individuals decided who to vote for as the more commonly cited issues of ethnic or tribal affiliation.

In a separate case, a little-known provincial council candidate in Qara Bagh described in an interview in 2009 how he felt that he had no chance of winning the election, but was running only because his cousin, with whom he had a long-running feud, was also standing as a candidate. He was concerned that if his cousin won a seat in the provincial council, the cousin would benefit politically and this would bring shame on him and put him at a disadvantage in their future dealings. By also running for provincial council, he could therefore exploit the nature of the SNTV system and divide the vote of his community and relatives, making it very unlikely that his cousin would win. He viewed the price of campaigning as small compared to what he could lose if his cousin won a seat and he lost honor. Such a loss would be sure to hurt him in future economic and political struggles, damaging his long-term position in the community.

In other instances, district-wide political disputes were also a major factor in shaping the elections. This was particularly true for candidates who were influential but were viewed more ambivalently by the community due to their roles in this series of local disputes. For example, the equitable distribution of government and international resources in Qara Bagh was a major source of tension. Anwar Khan and Sher Shah, for example, were seen as delivering resources to the community, but only to their own supporters—a factor that encouraged those who had not benefited from the brothers' resource allocation to try and undermine Anwar Khan's reelection campaign for a parliamentary seat in 2010. As one local man described it: "Most of the 17 candidates in Qara Bagh stood against Anwar Khan not in order to win the election, but for political ends aimed at dividing the votes to ensure that no one, and especially not Anwar Khan, would win the election." In allowing any number of candidates to stand, the electoral system thus facilitated the undermining of the campaigns of certain individuals.

As these examples suggest, elections can function as a public measure of political power and the ability (or lack thereof) to mobilize supporters. In Afghanistan, where power is often hidden from view and alliances kept secret, such public displays of influence put politics, which are often masked in formalities and elaborate language, on center stage. And in a system where honor forms an important aspect of political and social life, this can prove problematic. Losing any sort of competition publicly is a serious threat to one's honor. This was evident in the resistance Karzai showed to a runoff after the initial presidential poll in September 2009. A second round of voting seemed to pose little threat to Karzai's actual political power, since no analysts truly felt that Abdullah had a chance of winning it (in the first round Abdullah trailed Karzai by almost 900,000 votes).[8] Instead, it seems likely that Karzai's resistance had more to do with the fact that submitting to an additional round involved accepting the EEC's removal of 1.3 million of Karzai's votes as fraudulent.[9] In turn, accepting another round meant accepting both the ruling of the EEC (which Karzai later attacked in the Afghan press as manipulated by foreigners) and admitting that not all of his support was genuine—something that would be perceived as a loss of face and honor by many in Afghanistan. There have clearly been times in Karzai's presidency when he has cultivated an image of quasi-regal detachment from other political bodies, apparent in his refusal to submit certain ministerial nominees to the Wolesi Jirga and his refusal to join a political party, which might suggest that he was somehow equal to other members of the party.[10] This approach to power, however, means that Karzai's honor is threatened whenever he is held accountable by another government body because this is an admission of the limitations of his authority—something strenuously avoided in Afghan political culture.

HONOR IN LOCAL ELECTIONS

On a local level, the provincial council election results generated similar potential for the candidates involved to lose or gain face. One of the results of this was that nearly every losing candidate attempted to greatly exaggerate levels of fraud. By pointing to the flaws in the system, these candidates were suggesting that had the vote been legitimate, they would probably have won, effectively defending their honor. In other cases, candidates turned to violence to reaffirm their political strength despite having lost the election.

The ability to demonstrate power is important for local communities as well as individuals, since elections allow groups to demonstrate both their size and their political strength. During the 2009 elections, the central polling stations in communities such as Qara Bagh and neighboring Istalif were particularly busy as voters from outlying villages traveled into town instead of voting closer to their home. Some Istalifis living in Kabul even chose to bypass the dozens of polling stations closer to home, driving back out to Istalif specifically to vote in the district center. While the festive atmosphere at such polling stations played a part, this was also an important symbolic display of political loyalty. Most of the main political leaders in town (or at least their representatives) spent a good deal of the day chatting in the bazaar next to the polling station, clearly observing who was voting and who was not. After voting, many came over to pay their respects to these men and display their allegiance as many would have done on a traditional feast day, such as at the end of Ramazan. Such visits and greetings reaffirm political loyalties and are public displays of power for other groups in the area to see.

Beyond these local displays of political allegiance and strength, elections have been used in some instances to compensate for the fact that, as discussed in chapter 1, Afghanistan has never had a reliable national census. With each ethnic group and even the tribes within them tending to overinflate their own size in order to demonstrate strength, the potential political repercussions of a census providing "accurate" data on the relative size of different groups make it unlikely that one will occur soon.[11] As a result, most population figures are speculative, particularly at the district level. For community leaders and local government officials, the tallies from these elections serve as one of the few opportunities to establish something that resembles a population figure. Just as Sher Shah did at the end of the council meeting above, many leaders of communities across Afghanistan made it clear that they were trying to mobilize as many voters as possible. In part, this was to demonstrate to the government and international NGOs that relative to neighboring districts, particularly Istalif and Kalakan, Qara Bagh had a large (and politically active) population. This, they hoped, would lead to an increase in funds or projects planned in the area. These tendencies also help explain why leaders in Qara Bagh were so concerned with how many people in Qara Bagh voted vis-à-vis how many voters in neighboring Istalif voted and why they were not concerned with districts on the far side of the province: these two districts were seen as competing directly for development funds marked for the region, and an increase in projects in Istalif, many assumed, would lead to a decrease of projects in Qara Bagh.

The ability to secure government resources was thus a reflection of political strength; leaders and communities competed not only for the sake of material returns but because securing them was a demonstration of political might. This was a major factor in the establishment of the teacher training institute in Qara Bagh, leading many to talk about it in seemingly overly dramatic terms. As Sher Shah explained,

> There is a big rivalry among the districts in these areas [in the Shomali, north of Kabul] and each district is trying to become stronger and more developed than other areas. Each area is trying to destroy other areas, so they won't become as strong and as developed as their area.

He claimed that the institute was originally supposed to be built in Qara Bagh, but while he was in the United States recuperating from the assassination attempt, there was a move to have it built in Kalakan instead. Sher Shah claimed the governor of Qara Bagh had allowed the move to Kalakan in order to "defame the important figures in Qara Bagh and to show that they are less active than those in Kalakan." While there was certainly an economic incentive for

Qara Bagh to ensure that this project was completed in their area, the material gain probably would have been limited. It seems more important that Sher Shah chose to phrase the problem in terms of honor rather than missed economic opportunity. This rivalry also surfaced in the efforts of the Qara Bagh district council to focus the community's votes as effectively as possible. As Sher Shah said, it would be best if they all voted for one candidate, but if they could not do this, it was at least important that voters did not vote for candidates from neighboring districts. The possibility of a rival district securing a higher voter turnout was again seen as deeply damaging to the honor of the entire community.

In each of these cases, for leaders and voters whether the candidate actually won the elections mattered less than the ability of political actors to perform with honor in the elections. For Karzai, the various political groups in Qara Bagh and the community as a whole, the ability to mobilize supporters and show political strength, was of primary importance. Having a strong reputation allows an individual to avoid engaging in direct violent confrontation since the reputation means that the leader or community is feared. This also makes it important to fiercely guard this reputation when challenged. Honor and reputation have long been central aspects of Afghan political organization, and feature strongly in the current, primarily nontransparent system. Elections in Afghanistan have been far from transparent in the Western sense, but they have offered a few exceptional—if brief—glimpses of clarity. It thus becomes even more important for Karzai and other figures to appear strong and legitimate during such periods of public competition, since they will shape how other actors deal with them in the less transparent situations that follow. These issues of the relationship between honor and elections were in fact so crucial that they were often discussed before the actual ability of representatives to deliver more material resources to a community.

REPRESENTATION AND RESOURCES FOR LOCAL COMMUNITIES

Despite the fact that local political issues and interests can take precedence over elections themselves, elections remain a unique feature of the Afghan political landscape for two reasons. First, as discussed above, is the public discussion during elections of many political issues and judgments about actors which are otherwise dealt with quietly, through rumors and negotiations out of public sight. More significantly, perhaps, is the fact that provincial council and parliamentary elections provide one of the few opportunities for communities to link themselves to both the government and international resources available in Kabul. The models of patronage networks based upon a range of dependent relationships including tribe, ethnicity, and simple economic reciprocity, which can be difficult to access, are suddenly shaken up during elections.

In the unstable economic and political landscape of Afghanistan following the U.S. invasion, government and international resources were difficult for individuals and communities to access in a predictable manner. While the country was flooded with new funds and different types of projects, the distribution of these resources often seemed haphazard to local communities, many of whom felt that they were not receiving their fair proportion. While part of the reason for this relates to the often-cited corruption and ineffectiveness of government officials, much of it also stems from the structure of the government itself.

The highly centralized Afghan constitution and subsequent years of Karzai's consolidation of power have created a state with a strong executive branch. Key local government officials tend to be district governors and chiefs of police who report to executive branch bodies, such as the Ministry of Interior Affairs or the Independent Directorate of Local Governance. While communities and individuals try to use these avenues to secure resources, in reality most communities have limited influence over these officials, who are appointed in Kabul and are rarely native to the areas they govern.[12] Even while certain provincial governors and other regional strongmen have cultivated a good deal of power on their own, they too maintain connections with the center in order to access critical channels for resource distribution.[13] As with other local government officials, these powerful regional players also remain practically inaccessible to local communities, regardless of where the resources they command come from, due to the lack of an institutionalized process that would allow public complaints and petitions to be made formally.

Instead, people rely on relationships, using personal connections of kinship, ethnicity, or simply friendship to access key individuals in the government when needed. For example, having a friend or connections at the Ministry of Education is a helpful way of securing a diploma or entrance at a state university. In some cases, these connections can link communities to the highest levels of government. Residents of Qara Bagh have on several occasions relied on Omar Daudzai, who was Karzai's chief of staff and later became ambassador to Pakistan, to put pressure on other officials or to secure meetings with the president. Daudzai, whose family is from Qara Bagh and whose father was still a teacher at the central high school, had not been an active figure in district politics. However, his connection to national-level networks of power offered a useful informal channel for Qara Bagh's ruling elite to make their voices heard. Particularly when it came to securing land for the teacher training institute mentioned above, it was widely reported that Daudzai's ability to use his connections in the presidential palace to the advantage of the district had helped ensure that it was built in Qara Bagh, as opposed to in a neighboring area.

These connections to government officials and other notables in Kabul were often discreet personal relationships, however, and were difficult to control or regulate. Some communities, such as the Turkmen living in Kaldar, who are much more isolated, have few opportunities to establish such connections. In this context the Wolesi Jirga and provincial council members occupy a particularly important position in the struggle for resources since they offer communities a way to generate for themselves a new—and theoretically accountable—link to Kabul.[14] Most importantly, these positions are links that communities can manipulate through the electoral process. This has helped fuel interest in and competition surrounding provincial council and Wolesi Jirga elections at a local level. Having a parliamentarian or provincial council member from one's community or tribe can be useful, especially for individuals or families with grievances or complaints. Anwar Khan, for example, had open hours weekly at his home, where petitioners could come to visit and raise issues with him. These issues ranged from helping a young man try to secure an extension for his exams from the Ministry of Education to small-scale public works projects for villages. When Anwar Khan was not available, people often brought issues to his brother Sher Shah instead, reinforcing the personal and kinship aspects of such interactions.

While representatives were likely to be able to deliver resources to their communities, unsurprisingly this was not a straightforward or transparent process. The more candidates were able to appear involved in projects supporting the community, the more likely they were to get elected—but *appearing* to be involved was not the same as actually being the person responsible for the procurement of a project. For example, many Qara Bagh residents reflected that Adel Khan had won his seat because he had been involved in a large irrigation project that brought water to the district. But further demonstrating the complex relationship between local political capital and resource delivery, Adel Khan's role in securing funds for the project appears to have been fairly limited. Instead, most described how he had negotiated between landowners over how much water would get allocated to each area. These political negotiations made the project a success, enhanced Adel Khan's reputation in the community, and contributed to his success in both 2005 and later the 2010 elections.

The delivery of resources also led to contests over which representatives should assist communities, and in what capacities. As detailed in chapter 3, the fact that both provincial council members and parliamentarians are elected in province-wide official constituencies on the one hand, but are often seen to represent a specific group or community within that province on the other, creates a certain inherent tension. Voters acknowledged that representatives tended to favor certain groups, but there was clear frustration when it was felt that this went too far. In Paktya, one Ahmad Abad resident described how he felt that only a representative's home district, rather than the official constituency of the province as a whole, benefited from parliamentary patronage:

Around a month ago, Gul Padshah Majidi [a parliamentarian from Zazi district Paktya] brought some sapling trees and said on the radio and television that he had brought these for the youth of the Zazi. Now, this makes us think, why not work to provide such things for people of other districts as well since you are the representative of all the districts of Paktya Province. We have never heard from you and yet you say you are also the representatives of Mangal, Zazi, and Zamkani districts. When he brings anything, he puts his district's name on it.

This complaint is part of a deeper debate in Afghanistan over what a community is and how certain groups organize.

THE RELATIONSHIP BETWEEN ELECTED AND "TRADITIONAL" LEADERSHIP ROLES

Parliamentary elections also demonstrated some of the confusion and tension in Afghanistan over the different types of leadership roles, and particularly the limitations of Western categories such as "state" and "non-state" actors. Despite the fact that Afghans have historically had relatively low expectations of the state and what it should provide, most voters we spoke to felt that the provincial council and Wolesi Jirga members claiming to represent their communities had not provided enough resources for them. Further, it was almost universally stated that elected representatives *should* be providing such resources.[15] This related to the fact that elected representatives and other more "traditional" community leaders, such as maliks and arbabs, are seen by local communities to occupy fairly similar roles, but on different scales.

As anthropologists often point out, "traditional" is often a problematic concept, since "traditions" are often both invented and manipulated. In Afghanistan it can be an even more dangerous term, masking the way that historical practices have evolved and been shaped by what are generally considered very modern practices. Many "traditional" tribal elders, for example, are highly skilled at negotiating with modern organizations such as NGOs and the international press, and they use the seeming timelessness associated with these "traditional" positions to justify what are actually situations that are continuously evolving. Voters expected parliamentarians to simultaneously fulfill "traditional" roles and to serve as a liaison to the government. Parliamentarians should provide government resources for their communities, but they were also expected to provide hospitality for members of the community, hold feasts, attend marriages and funerals, and resolve disputes. In one village in Qara Bagh there was a dispute between two former commanders who both claimed to be malik of their village, a disagreement that divided the community there. Some elders then brought the issue to Anwar Khan, who went to the village with his brother Sher Shah and set up an informal election for all the men in the village at the local mosque. After the votes were counted, one commander was named malik and the other his assistant. The authority of Sher Shah and Anwar Khan allowed the villagers to solve the problem themselves, where other local actors might have been considered too biased.

Sometimes these duties were intertwined, and Anwar Khan was said to often resolve disputes while attending weddings or other social gatherings. In some cases, public expectations of Wolesi Jirga and provincial council officials extended even deeper. For example, one respondent in the Turkmen community of Kaldar (as discussed in chapter 1) described with some bitterness how Ruz Goldi had refused to lend him money to buy medicine for his sick wife. In another, more symbolic case, a candidate outside a polling station in Qara Bagh handed medicine directly to a man who complained of being sick in front of other voters. However, this degree of social and economic integration tended to be more apparent in remote areas such as Kaldar, which often have more deeply integrated and highly dependent social structures.

It was not always clear whether voters saw the role of their elected representatives as any different from that of other informal leaders; this confusion was compounded by some of the language used to describe their positions. For example, the term *wakil* or representative was often used as an honorific to refer to parliamentarians or provincial council members (thus, Ahmad could become "Wakil Ahmad" or was simply referred to as "wakil sahib" or "Mr. Representative"). A wakil was often referred to as *pul*, or bridge, between the people and the government. The confusion was that the term was also used to refer to other figures (though usually more rarely than elected officials). These could include members of district or village shuras, along with other active community leaders.[16] In several historical cases, particularly in Qara Bagh, people discussed individuals who had been known as wakils (e.g., "he is the grandson of Wakil Ahmad") without knowing whether these individuals had been elected during the parliamentary elections in 1964 or 1969, appointed by the king, or were simply men with many connections in Kabul. This further demonstrates how, in many instances, the role that such figures play is more important than the precise or formal position they hold. For example, Sher Shah's father was described as having been a wakil from Qara Bagh for forty years.[17] It would have been impossible for him to be a member of the Wolesi Jirga for this long, since it had only existed for eight years. Instead, the term implies both his status as a parliamentarian in the Wolesi Jirga and his more general role in representing the community at other times. In such cases, Afghans were not interested in whether these local leaders were "state" or "non-state" actors; they were simply interested in the resources that they could provide.

In general, demands made of provincial council members and parliamentarians suggested that they should be accountable to local communities, in line with historical expectations of local leaders. Historically, leadership positions in Afghanistan are inherited by the eldest son, but this transition is not guaranteed; in most areas, it is acknowledged that if the eldest son is not worthy, someone else in the community can be selected in his place. This provides the community with a limited amount of agency and, in the ideal case, makes leaders more responsive to community opinion. The fact that authority is not strictly determined is thus one key reason why concepts such as honor and reputation are so important in the Afghan political system. The emphasis on the equality of all men means that, at least within political rhetoric, there is almost always an emphasis on responsiveness to community needs. Since political authority can come and go, gossip and rumors become important threats to political power, and leaders worked hard to try to stop local gossip from undermining their power.

While in some ways these historical modes of checks and balances appear vastly different from the cold, anonymous ballot box, in reality they function in a very similar way—communities use their representatives to secure resources for them in Kabul, while trying to hold them to account as best they can. Ideally, many felt that elections should function in a similar manner, ensuring that those most responsive to community concerns were the ones selected to represent them. While elections may have been interpreted by some as Western imports, most still embraced the way they theoretically enforced or complemented existing notions of representative governance. This makes attempts to distinguish between state and non-state actors particularly problematic in Afghanistan. In reality, as elections have become integrated into other local political processes, leaders have adapted to these new official positions, which work in a very similar way to their older roles. However, as voters increasingly came to believe that elections were failing to provide the resources that they should (and in some ways making leaders less responsive to communities by allowing them to gain legitimacy from other sources, such as corruption in elections), criticism of both elections and the government they had created grew stronger and stronger.

THE MAGNANIMITY OF CAMPAIGNS

The success of candidates in portraying themselves as able to provide the community with resources was a crucial aspect of almost all campaigns. Candidates attempted to demonstrate a track record of delivering services to a community and their ability to continue delivering in the future. In some cases these attempts were blunt, such as the strategy employed by one particularly bold candidate in Paktya who had a Pashto campaign slogan that read "Staso sawal aw zama jawab," or "Your question and my answer," implying that if constituents needed anything, all they had to do was ask. In most cases, however, candidates employed more subtle methods to directly demonstrate their magnanimity and political connections.

Candidates relied on their patronage networks to offer symbolic demonstrations of how they were able to provide for the community. The most common campaign tactic was the holding of political gatherings, which more closely resembled holiday feasts than campaign rallies in the Western sense. These were often large meetings, where men (and in some cases, though more rarely, women) gathered at someone's house, usually on a Friday, to eat, talk, and listen to speeches about the upcoming elections.[18] These campaign gatherings centered on elaborate meals arranged by local elders. As one voter explained: "[The candidates] give money to elders or maliks for expenses and then the maliks go and buy meat, rice, and cold Pepsi. Then they prepare the food at home and invite people." In the case of presidential campaigns, candidates rarely attended themselves.[19] Instead, campaign workers, usually local elders, organized the gatherings and made speeches in support of the candidates. In 2009 these gatherings were sometimes combined to promote both a presidential candidate and a local provincial council candidate with whom they were informally allied. However, the fact that elections were so intertwined in local politics further complicated how these gatherings were understood. For example, as discussed earlier, the heads of both Karzai's and Abdullah's campaigns for the presidential elections in Qara Bagh were former commanders. As a result, although these gatherings were superficially aimed at gathering support for presidential candidates, they were more significant in demonstrating loyalty to the commanders involved, who were far more influential in the daily politics of the region.

Although this campaign technique had been widespread in the elections of 2004 and 2005, voters in 2009 and 2010 often expressed misgivings about its use. Attending the feast of a local leader has historically been a way to demonstrate political loyalty (for example, the order and timing of visits to certain homes of relatives and community leaders over holidays such as Eid-e Ramazan make clear political statements). When this practice was translated into the election process, some made the assumption (particularly in the first round of parliamentary polls in 2005) that attending would necessarily bind the voter to that candidate. This idea, however, was largely rejected by voters in 2009 and 2010 as something that only "uneducated" voters thought, while the more sophisticated approach was to visit a number of campaign rallies and partake in the feasts of all of them, without committing oneself one way or another. While people often cited the "waste of time and money" involved, many still continued to attend while emphasizing that this did not dictate the candidate for whom they would vote. In other instances, after viewing the high levels of corruption in the previous elections, some voters became more blunt in their demands for resources from various candidates.

As a result, many candidates in 2009 seemed to use much more direct and less symbolic means to augment these rallies in order to demonstrate their ability to deliver resources, though some of these approaches were also received with a good deal of skepticism. One slightly disgruntled voter in Ahmad Aba in Paktya Province outlined his views on local campaigning:

I want to tell you my own observations about an incident when a candidate came to our village, assembled everyone around him, and gave 5,000 Afs (about $100) to the local madrasa. He wanted to show that he was a good man and in the village all the people accepted the sayings of this malik.

Such public displays of generosity were questioned by local villagers like this one both because giving to religious causes for political reasons raised certain moral issues, but also because it was questionable that such displays would actually lead to more resources in the future.

It was difficult for candidates to guarantee that charitable activities would be publically attributed to their own campaigns, as in many cases there were disputes and debates over exactly what resources each candidate had contributed. This made the stories and perceptions about such projects particularly important. One candidate in Qara Bagh had made a contribution to a mosque while it was under construction. His supporters claimed that he had paid for the entire mosque, while some of those opposed to him said he only paid for the paint at the very end of construction, and still others seemed to think that he had paid for the construction, but only a part of it. Thus, the ability to control these descriptions and narratives about resource provision was central to candidates' preelection strategies. Actually providing resources was important, but the way that the individuals *talked* about such acts was ultimately more important in struggles for local influence. In this manner, community members could choose to exert a meaningful check on the power of candidates and local elites by spreading rumors that damaged their campaigns, even when they controlled vast resources.[20]

In some cases, candidates—particularly Wolesi Jirga incumbents in 2010—were very open in their admissions that they had failed to deliver resources effectively to those they were representing, expressing dismay at the elaborate campaign promises made by other candidates (such as Ruz Goldi's comments at the beginning of chapter 1). This often formed part of a more general criticism of the government, and of President Karzai in particular. However, even such regrets fundamentally reinforce the sense that in an ideal world free from insecurity, corruption, and other challenges, representatives would still be responsible for providing such resources. As campaigns gradually focused more on the resources that a candidate would or should be providing to local communities, local leaders and the communities they represented learned to increasingly manipulate the system in order to maximize what they could get out of the various candidates. One of the best ways of doing this was by pledging to vote as a bloc.

VOTING AS A "COMMUNITY"

A great deal rests on communities' ability to convince candidates that they can offer a unified bloc of support, since this can be used as a bargaining chip to secure political influence and material. In contrast with this, voting individually minimizes the potential capital that can be gained by voters during elections because it is more difficult for an individual or small family to hold a politician to account when the time comes to deliver on his or her promises. Local political leaders have therefore tended to emphasize the need to maintain community cohesion when voting, in order to be able to extract as many resources as possible from candidates in return for a bloc of support. Compared with Western models of elections in which voters are in theory meant to make private, individual decisions, voters in all of the areas we studied were encouraged by local leaders to discuss candidates collectively and decide together whom they would support. This, however, was not a simple process, since even defining a "community" in Afghanistan can be a difficult, political task.[21]

Thus far, we have used the term *community* in a straightforward, general sense. This needs to be further problematized. In Afghanistan, where villages or neighborhoods are often not clearly demarcated, the precise definition of a given community can have political implications. This, in part, is because locality is only one of a series of layers of social organization. Thus, in Paktya, certain districts tend to be dominated by particular tribes (the Ahmadzai in Ahmad Aba or Zazi in Zazi), though such areas of influence frequently overlap as populations intermingle. In larger, more diverse Qara Bagh, Pashtun tribes dominate certain villages, while in nontribal Tajik communities it is certain powerful lineages that hold sway. In more isolated rural areas such as

Kaldar, notions of belonging to a wider community are often less important than ties to extended family living in close proximity.

Political identity in Afghanistan can perhaps be conceived of as a series of concentric circles, with the individual and the immediate family at the center, extending outwards via the extended family and the village, followed by lineages or subtribes, with ethnicity as the outermost circle. The circle that an individual might draw upon to invoke solidarity at a given point in time depends on social and political circumstances, with extended family being important for economic cooperation, such as sharing agricultural labor, but with ethnicity becoming more important when an entire ethnic group faces threat from another. While the names of these circles might vary across different areas (with subtribe the dominant unit among Pashtuns, and *manteqa*, or locality, more common among Tajiks), the pattern remains essentially the same countrywide. Evidently, a variety of other factors, including security, business interests, and loyalty to persons outside these circles, such as university classmates or work colleagues in urban areas, can also have an influence on the allegiances an individual chooses to prioritize at a given time, but the presence of these groups in all parts of Afghanistan still shapes how decisions are made collectively. By extension, this affects candidates' efforts to gather votes, along with the strategies groups use in their attempts to extract resources from them.

In many places across Afghanistan the term *qaum* is used to refer to political groupings (though *khel* is used in Pashtun areas as well). Qaum can refer to a social group as small as a family or as large as an ethnicity. The word is often used strategically depending upon what level of political cooperation the speaker wants to emphasize. The variety of uses of the term is not simply a matter of semantics, since qaum membership and other social markers sometimes determine an individual's marriage choices, their rights and access to water and land, and, in the case of representative governance, which individuals should have the right to receive resources from their representatives. Due to the importance of such issues, however, there is an incentive to keep definitions vague. In this way individuals can claim group membership when claiming certain rights, and then back out in an attempt to avoid some of the obligations attached to them. So a representative might claim to represent as wide a community as possible when trying to mobilize voters, convincing people to show solidarity with him because of their shared qaum, but then emphasize a much more limited definition of qaum when actually delivering resources. Qaums at any level do not necessarily vote together (though sometimes they do); more important in shaping politics around elections is how far they are able to maintain *the perception of their potential to do so.* These patterns and forms of organizing are particularly important when we consider how both candidates and local leaders have attempted to manipulate blocs of voters.

During the 2009 presidential election, the most discussed political unit in the national and international press was that of ethnicity, since voting blocs often split along these lines. The ability to pull together blocs of voters along ethnic lines was clearly an important aspect of Karzai's negotiations with Fahim, Dostum, and Khalili in the spring leading up to the election. As one Hazara elder recounted, describing the way in which the two most prominent Hazara leaders in the country, Khalili and Mohaqqeq, had declared their support for Karzai:

> There was an agreement between Karzai, Khalili, and Mohaqqqeq. Karzai bought the elders of our qaum. It is like a family, if you think about the Hazara, Mohaqqeq and Khalili are like the elders of the family. Now all the [Hazara] people are running to vote for Karzai as . . . we vote according to what our leaders say.

In this case, Hazara leaders clearly felt they stood to gain the most through supporting the reelection of Karzai—a Pashtun—as a way to counterbalance the Pashtun-Hazara conflict that has historically dominated relations between the two groups. These leaders were then able to use a political rhetoric that emphasized Hazara unity, often described in kinship terms as in the quote above, to ensure that Hazara communities voted predominantly for Karzai.[22]

In the more locally contested provincial council and Wolesi Jirga elections, communities split into smaller voting blocs. Part of the reason that politics and campaigning around the elections looked so different in the areas we studied was because each organized itself according to different political units. Despite this, these very different appearances, blocs often tended to function in fairly similar ways in political landscapes that historically have been shaped by similar events and processes. Of all the localities studied, the area with the most coherent blocs was Paktya, where local Pashtun tribes and subtribes voted together in large numbers. It was difficult to find voters in Paktya who had not voted for Karzai in both 2004 and 2009; this was equally true in the case of their respective tribal candidates in the provincial council and Wolesi Jirga elections. Similarly, most Turkmen voters in Kaldar claimed to follow similar patterns, supporting Ruz Goldi, the primary Turkmen candidate. By 2010, however, some of this support had weakened, and while few openly expressed any dissent, an increasing number voted for other Turkmen candidates or, in fewer cases, Tajik candidates from other parts of the province who had campaigned in the area.

Partially because politics in Qara Bagh were so tense and fractured, this was also the area of all those we studied where voting blocs—and even the very notion of qaum as a political community—were the most contested. While community leaders like Sher Shah tried to emphasize the unity of the entire district, divisions between the area's Tajiks and Pashtuns remained substantial. Nevertheless, feuds between commanders and other local leaders were often so complicated that political alliances commonly crossed ethnic lines. Instead, voters were more likely to mobilize at a lower level and qaums—usually in this case referring to extended families residing in one village—became the key political units. As elections approached, candidates and local leaders struggled to control these groups and influence how they voted.

Qaums should not be thought of as historical relics from Afghanistan's past that will disappear with increased exposure to elections. In fact, some qaums, particularly in the urban Kabul suburb of Dasht-i Barchi, solidified during elections around very young leaders and members of civil society who used political rhetoric that emphasized Western definitions of democracy and focused on issues like political parties and human rights. While individuals in the urban environment often claimed to have voted for candidates because they were younger or more educated, the vast majority of votes were ultimately still cast along qaum lines. Even among younger candidates, much of the socializing and ritualized visiting remained the same, focusing on family links and patronage networks that tied in with other community leaders. Just as they used websites and media-savvy marketing to campaign, these candidates continued to function in a way that had many parallels with more "traditional" forms of mobilizing communities.

The ambiguous definition of qaum created opportunities for debate over whom certain representatives were representing, and candidates and political brokers often tried to emphasize their representation of the largest political group possible. For example, in the run-up to the elections, most claimed that Anwar Khan represented not just people in Qara Bagh but also members of the Oryakhel tribe in other parts of Kabul Province. This was even more complicated in the case of Dasht-i Barchi, where candidates often hailed from communities of recent immigrants from other provinces such as Ghazni and Wardak. Most of these representatives claimed to work for both their areas of origin and those that had voted for them. Recent internal migration has further complicated the way that these blocs functioned. For example, in the urban center of Dasht-i Barchi, there were some attempts, particularly among younger people, to move beyond historical patterns of social organizing using qaums. Despite this, for many candidates, such modes of organization remained important. Anisa Maqsudi, a candidate who was widely considered to have good access to funds from NGOs, also described how she met with elders of the Jirghai and Borgehai qaums for her native district of Narhor in Ghazni Province who were now living in Kabul in order to secure their support and to ensure that no other candidates from these qaums were planning on running. She then worked to shore up support from members of these qaums by having several roads paved in Dasht-i Barchi, where many of them had migrated.

This case is particularly interesting because it demonstrates how many forms of social organizing can transcend geographic bounds. Running in Kabul, Maqsudi could not actually receive votes from those living in Ghazni, but instead worked to mobilize the large population from her home district who had moved to Kabul. This was facilitated in Dasht-i Barchi (and to a lesser extent in other areas of the city), by the fact that settlement patterns in Kabul and other major Afghan cities tend to lead migrants from the same province to settle together. By paving the roads around her neighborhood in Kabul, Maqsudi was providing a resource for a group of residents who were linked by their shared origins in Narhor. In the Wolesi Jirga, this also created an odd pattern of parliamentarians from Kabul working to deliver resources to their families' home provinces. However, in demonstrating their ability to provide resources, these representatives' intended audience was not so much those living in these provinces, but rather their co-provincials who had moved to Kabul. All of this greatly complicated concepts such as community and constituency during the elections.

Despite the clear logic of voting in blocs, many candidates (and particularly those who were unsuccessful) lamented the practice of bloc voting by other groups, often arguing that this demonstrated ignorance and a lack of education. This was especially true when their complaints were directed at the followers of former warlords. As one failed provincial council candidate complained,

> The people generally vote for those candidates who were warlords in the past and they generally consider ethnicity and their own relationship to the candidate. For example, Rashid Dostum only studied until seventh grade, but most of the northern people are following him because he was a warlord . . . and this is all because 85 percent of our people are illiterate and ignorant.

However, such complaints only serve to demonstrate the potential power of bloc voting, which continues to be based on a political logic that maximizes the resources a political group can secure. Ultimately, multiple layers of political identity greatly impacted the way that elections played out in 2009 and 2010. At the same time, elections reshaped some of these layers and reinforced others, depending in part on how they were manipulated by communities and candidates.

MANIPULATION OF VOTING BLOCS

At the center of the relationship between candidates and (supposed) community voting blocs were a series of community leaders who claimed to be the political brokers that could control these blocs. These figures were impor-tant because they provided a focal point through which groups could reap the benefits of their collective strategies, but they generated many a dispute over exactly who controlled which bloc of votes. As discussed above, in the presi-dential elections, key leaders of ethnic-based political parties such as Khalili and Dostum were the central brokers, negotiating with candidates like Karzai. At a local level, however, it was much less clear who controlled blocs and how these should and would function on Election Day. This led to a series of strat-egies where local leaders manipulated the groups they represented, while the groups themselves also worked to manipulate their leaders and candidates.

In many instances, there were clear attempts by community leaders to broker deals with candidates where votes were exchanged for cash, local resources, or future political influence. Maliks and other tribal leaders in Qara Bagh took phone calls directly from presidential candidates or would receive visits from provincial council candidates. In these, they would attempt to con-vince candidates of their ability to provide votes in exchange for either money or services. In some instances these figures served primarily to link communi-ties with candidates. As one voter in Paktya described,

> Previously, when candidates were making contact with the maliks, the maliks were slaughtering chickens for them and gathering the village peo-ple together in order to say good things about the candidates. And later, when they could not come [due to security], candidates were calling maliks to visit them in Kabul. Relationships were good between maliks and par-liamentarians.

As a result, in some areas elections themselves were seen as beneficial for local leaders on a purely financial level. As one mullah from Paktya explained, "Brother, few people are happy with [elections]; the majority of the people are unhappy with them. . . . Maliks are the ones that are happy with them because they get money to buy votes during them." Others, however, genu-inely felt that these leaders had the community's best interests in mind and were attempting to exchange votes for projects or other resources that would benefit the entire community. Still others were apathetic about the elections themselves, but were eager to exchange their votes either for political favor or money from the local leaders who served as brokers. This sheds light on the way in which representation is perceived in many communities in Afghanistan—not through the discussion of ideological and legislative concerns in parliament but through the provision of tangible resources.

Ambiguity about which candidate a bloc would support and ambiguity about the composition of the bloc itself was often used strategically since it allowed greater space for negotiation. This, in many ways, was a similar process to attempts of parliamentarians to maintain ambiguity in how they were planning on voting in the Wolesi Jirga, as discussed in chapter 4. In maintaining a degree of mystery over who they might vote for, both political blocs and the individuals that claimed to represent them were potentially able to gain rewards from more than one representative. Several elders recounted receiving phone calls and visits from multiple candidates, then waiting to declare who they would vote for until the days just before the casting of ballots in the hopes of driving the price of their votes as high as possible.

Negotiations could be even more complex than this. In one case near Qara Bagh, one malik reported how he had offered the votes of his qaum to a candidate in exchange for the promise of a small-scale irrigation project for the community. At the same time, however, the elder admitted that he personally supported another candidate and that he and his sons would be voting for that man instead. He was cautious in discussing this strategy, since in the previous election an election monitor claimed to have watched his son vote for a candidate other than the one he had publically supported. The malik's family denied that this had happened, but there was still genuine concern over whether balloting was truly secret. Debate over whether certain individuals or groups were following up on proclaimed support with actual votes further complicated the discussions about bloc voting.

As these examples demonstrate, relationships between candidates, communities, and local leaders are far from static and have evolved over the course of recent elections. One of the key complaints of failed candidates during the 2009 elections was that local elders had failed to deliver promised votes. As a result, there were several new attempts to ensure that votes were delivered in the 2010 elections. Among the most interesting were rumors in Paktya that tribal elders were drawing up formal, written contracts with candidates to deliver a set number of votes for a certain price. The money and contract were then given to a moneychanger in the bazaar at Gardez (the provincial capital), who would hold the money in escrow. This system worked because, as part of a technical reform attempting to make voting more transparent, ballots in 2010 were counted and reported at each polling center, rather than sent to the district capital for collection and counting as they had been in previous polls. This meant that the moneychanger could send someone to the polling station and see how many votes the candidate had won. He would then give the elder the money if the requisite votes had been cast, or return it to the candidate if they had not. Here the historical role of the moneychanger had been adapted to the electoral process in a way that reshaped how votes would be bought and sold in upcoming elections.

All of these elements combined to make elections a venue where political relationships between communities, local leaders, and candidates played out in public. Elections gave individuals the ability to manipulate the existing political situation to try and bring additional resources or political favor to their areas. The fact, however, that both the concepts of qaum and community are highly malleable and that leaders had influence, but rarely absolute control, over voters, affected how far communities were able to further their interests. True discontent with the electoral process tended to emerge in those settings where individuals felt that they did not have the opportunity to shape the outcome of these processes.

WHEN BLOC VOTING FAILS

While many approaches to elections focus on whether voters are successful in electing their candidate of choice, the examples above demonstrate how in Afghanistan, elections also serve as means for communities to reshape patronage networks, play out feuds, and display strength. In fact, for most of the people we interviewed, these various adaptations of elections to fit local concerns represented the best chance they had to shape the patronage networks linking their communities to the national government. When these processes worked well, they demonstrated to voters that elections were not simply top-down affairs, and that there was some hope for representative governance capable of responding to local concerns (albeit through service provision rather than the promotion of legislative interests, for example). For many people, it was not necessary to actually have their candidate of choice win a seat in the provincial council or Wolesi Jirga. In some cases, simply feeling that their vote had had some kind of impact on the political landscape was enough. This could be through demonstrating the strength of a certain community (as was the case with many minority ethnic groups in the presidential election of 2004) or securing certain resources in exchange for their vote.

What became increasingly apparent to voters in the 2009 and 2010 elections, however, was that their ability to influence electoral outcomes, choose their representatives, or gain much at all from the process was far from guaranteed. This was manifested in some way in the increasing difficulty that respondents had in predicting the winners before the voting began, and the extent to which winners appeared to be selected through secret negotiation processes among the political elite. More than anything else, these trends heralded a growing dissatisfaction with both the concept of elections and the relationship between citizen and state in Afghanistan.

Voters during the 2009 and 2010 elections expressed their dismay at what they perceived as a growing divide between the ruling elite and average Afghan citizens. Representatives and other leaders were increasingly seen as unresponsive to the daily needs of those they were expected to represent.[23] As one man described:

> Brother, one of our villagers had a problem [with the government] and he spent thirteen days in Kabul because of it. Think about it. We are from the village and we don't have relatives in Kabul and this person had to spend 8,000 Afghanis (about $160) only for hotels and food. Even if a person is very careful and trying to save, still he spends 8,000. . . . [During this time] these parliamentarians would not meet with him. From my point of view, they should meet with us, but they are too proud.

The man went on to describe the situation as similar to the caste system: "[Our leaders] have started working like the Indians, because in India they have three kinds of people: people on the low level, on the middle, and on the high level. We are on the low level." For this man, and other respondents, elections were seen as solidifying and justifying a social order that continued to block out most of the country from important political processes, such as the division of the spoils from the international community, that were taking place in Kabul.

Another of the key sources of frustration for voters was their reliance on political brokers to translate individual votes into group votes and thus real political influence. Some community leaders in this position were viewed positively, but an increasing number were criticized for either failing to deliver resources or for only working for themselves. Community leaders were criticized for being too close to parliamentarians and other high-level officials, and not close enough to their own communities. Increasingly, they were perceived as just another part of an impenetrable political machine. As one voter stated:

> There is a link between parliamentarians and local leaders because they get the votes for them and these candidates succeed. They will be candidates in the upcoming elections so they need to keep a relationship with local leaders. . . . Candidates invite only [local leaders to their homes] and if they go to an area, they only visit these leaders and go to those who will do something for them.

Voters were most satisfied when they felt that they had an understanding of how political processes worked and how decisions were being made. However, the ambiguous role of political brokers, the fact that the SNTV system allowed candidates to win by very small margins, and the growing importance of fraud meant that in certain areas voters had real problems successfully predicting who would win the elections. As one man stated in an area that had 12 candidates, "We can't predict who will win. Maybe no one will win. Maybe all 12 will win." This is striking, because even candidates who were seen as likely to win (because they were highly corrupt and maintained strong political connections) ended up losing in both Qara Bagh and in other areas more generally. These men were well-known figures in the community, and when, for a series of reasons (whether it was their own failure to mobilize votes or fraud committed by others), they failed to win seats in parliament, this highlighted to many the ways in which elections did not reflect local understandings of how politics should work. For voters, this system without logic was often considered worse than a highly corrupt system, since it is so difficult to make political decisions in such an unpredictable landscape. While elections are intended to institutionalize uncertainty, to return to Przeworski's phrase—in this case uncertainty prevailed without the institutionalization necessary to render the process transparent, ultimately making most feel that the system was ineffective, corrupt, and alien to their understandings of local political representation.[24]

In some cases voters explained this unpredictability by pointing to outside political forces either in Kabul or abroad, contributing to many conspiracy theories about who was controlling the election process. It was common to hear statements such as: "Most of the mujahideen and commanders won the last election [2005] because it was all planned by the West." This reflects a growing sense among many that the international community, and the United States in particular, was actually encouraging instability in order to justify their continued presence. Strikingly, in those areas where voters felt that they had the least ability to influence the political process of selecting representation, opinions about elections, democracy, and the current state of affairs in Afghanistan were the most negative.

The variation between local political structures in the areas studied created some sharply different opinions about both the ability of average voters to shape their political world, and the value and function of elections themselves. In Paktya, with generally insecure conditions and strong tribal structures, voters were most negative about their leaders and about their own ability to influence the outcome and results of elections. There was an assumption that tribal leaders controlled the entire voting process, and that through negotiations with influential politicians and powerholders in Kabul, these tribal leaders were the ones making the real decisions about the elections. The results there, which surprised many, created a sense that they were not really participating in the process and that leaders did little to truly represent them.

In contrast with this, while voters in Kaldar knew the least about the election process, they were fairly happy with the way Ruz Goldi had provided them with resources, something he was perceived as continuing to do even after he lost his bid for reelection in 2010. As a result, there were far fewer complaints about the election system, and even those who felt they were not receiving enough resources were still fairly confident about how the system worked and why they had been neglected.

Finally, in Qara Bagh, where political allegiances were more fractious, the opinion of voters about the political system was split. On the one hand, because local leaders were struggling so intently against each other for power, they needed to work harder than leaders in other areas to ensure that communities continued to support them. On the other hand, there was so much bargaining and negotiation taking place that alliances could reform in confusing and nontransparent ways, giving voters a limited view of the important political negotiations that were taking place.

A SENSE OF DISENFRANCHISEMENT

Throughout the research conducted for this book, most voters we interviewed ultimately wanted to feel that they were able to influence the election process and the linked concept of the distribution of resources. Unlike in the West, this does not necessarily demand transparent and free elections. In fact, many tolerated a fairly high degree of manipulation and what were technically "irregularities" in the system, particularly if they felt they could access parliamentarians and influence resource distribution. Voters' satisfaction with the ability to influence elections did not appear to demand that this influence be purely "legitimate." In fact, in areas where votes were bought and sold successfully, and where corruption was more visible, voters we spoke to were much happier with the outcomes of elections in contrast with people in those areas where the general perception was of a ruling elite making the decisions behind closed doors, out of the view of local communities.

Elected representatives were often seen as having similar roles to maliks and other tribal elders, who in an ideal world could be selected and removed by the community and would be responsive to their needs (even if this rarely occurred in practice). In this sense there was no clear difference between state and non-state actors. Ultimately, the demands and expectations that Afghan voters place on the election process come from a certain cultural and political context that does not necessarily conform to the Western perspectives that were so key in the design and setup of the electoral system in Afghanistan. In this way, while elections created a new, albeit loose set of rules for how resources would be distributed, local practices and individuals themselves shaped how elections actually played out in the communities in which they were held. Individuals and communities then took advantage of these structures to rework alliances and attempt to gain resources, often using patterns that did not conform to the simple "tribal politics" of supporting immediate kin during times of conflict that segmentary opposition might suggest. Instead the Afghan approach to elections is neither simply Western, nor "tribal," but a highly local affair that has adapted to changing political circumstances.

As this suggests, elections are not simply top-down affairs; communities and individuals have the ability to manipulate them to create more favorable political circumstances, often in ways that are very different from internationally sponsored processes. Elections are embedded in a series of local political relationships and issues, which are often perceived as far more important than the elections themselves. By contrast, the tendency by international policymakers and academics to view elections in post-conflict settings as be-all and end-all isolated events helps explain some of the challenges the international community has faced in creating meaningful reforms in Afghanistan's political system.

6

THE UNINTENDED CONSEQUENCES
OF INTERNATIONAL SUPPORT

BOOM AND BUST:
THE CHANGING FACE OF FEFA

THE FAUX GRANDEUR *of the building was not out of place in this part of the city. Over the years since the Americans arrived, plots in Karte-e Se had increasingly been bought up for ambitious construction projects by warlords, parliamentarians, and businessmen—sometimes one and the same person. These had begun in the center of town near the embassies, in the exclusive Shirpur and Wazir Akbar Khan districts, but had later moved out west where space was more readily available and marginally cheaper in the early days of the intervention.*

The wide, once tree-lined avenues of this neighborhood still maintained an air of exclusivity, in spite of the way in which a number of buildings visibly retained the scars of war, missing walls or a roof, or peppered with shrapnel holes. Oddly placed next to these remnants of the conflict, gargantuan new homes had been forged out of concrete, their gaudy pillars, high curved walls, and colored glass rearing up out of the dust, only a foot or two between one and the next, to resemble a crowded assortment of wedding cakes in a bakery window. No expense was spared, it seemed, to flaunt wealth and status—and given the extortionate rent it was possible to charge the foreign organizations looking for a base near parliament, at the height of the intervention, the costs could soon be recuperated anyway. How the Free and Fair

Election Foundation of Afghanistan, or FEFA—the country's only independent elections watchdog—was able to afford the monthly payments in this particularly kitsch corner of realty was a story in itself.

FEFA's offices had been situated in this part of southwest Kabul since its formation in 2004, close to both parliament and the offices of the U.S.-based National Democratic Institute (NDI), which had helped establish the organization with technical and financial support. In its first year, FEFA's rented accommodation took the form of rather smart premises. With international actors keen to establish an Afghan organization that could monitor elections and provide the much-needed "local footprint" on the electoral exercise, it had attracted considerable attention and funding, demonstrated by the countless times its name was mentioned in donor reports on the elections. This overnight rise to prominence in donor circles was duly reflected in the offices the organization was able to procure. Well-furnished and spacious, the building had the facilities to host planning meetings and training workshops, along with offices for a number of permanent staff members.

All this would change after the polls in 2005. With elections no longer an immediate concern since there were no polls scheduled until 2009, donor interest in an electoral watchdog waned, and funds became scarce. With salaries and rent no longer supplemented by the projects commissioned by international donors, staff began to leave and the office was forced to move. While still in the same neighborhood, FEFA's second home was of more modest proportions. When we visited in the winter of 2008, the changes that had taken place since the first election were all too obvious—not least in our host's continual apologies for the lack of heating. The building was much smaller—this time a remnant of the old King Zahir Shah's time, with its period wooden doorframes and staircase standing shabby and ill-maintained. Threadbare gray floor carpeting was, unusually, not overlaid with characteristic Afghan rugs or gillims, and furniture was sparse. Evidently beautiful in its time, this house was now a shell of its former state.

Looking back on that time, a founding member of FEFA talked about the difficulties the organization had faced:

[The period from 2006 to 2009] was a critical time for us and it was difficult to stay alive. We lost our professional staff and we thought we might have to

close. In 2008 there was the voter registration process and we applied for funds to monitor this. We got some money through UNDP [United Nations Development Program] for this project. . . . After 2009 the focus was back on us and in 2009 donors funded us, as the election process began again.

On an ensuing visit, we found FEFA had moved once again. This was in the fall of 2010, in the aftermath of parliamentary elections and toward the end of FEFA's latest electoral program. Returning to and perhaps exceeding the grandeur of its first home, the organization was renting a large new building complete with the usual array of pillars and balconies. Furnishing was not excessive or lavish, but this was a notably more expensive setup than the previous location.

The director's polished faux-mahogany desk was covered in colorful booklets produced by the organization over the years, documenting electoral irregularities and legal procedures, that were ready to hand out to guests and prospective donors as samples of the organization's work and potential impact. Glass-fronted cabinets behind were filled with shelves of similar publications in Dari and Pashto, and rolls of posters—presumably duplicates of the ones adorning the walls of the office—promoting good practice in campaigns as well as guides to casting ballots in a series of brightly colored cartoons.

Despite our familiarity with the director, our call to arrange a meeting was answered by an international consultant working alongside him. However, when we arrived, it was also clear that FEFA was once again wrapping up its programs: bar the cleaner, a guard, and a lady bringing tea, few members of the Afghan staff were working full-time in the central office, and the consultant was coming to the end of her contract. Our friend at the organization was understandably concerned: "If after these elections the donors don't fund us, we will lose our good staff and we will have to hire new people. And we can't just hire anyone—we need people with the right experience."

Observing the changing fortunes FEFA had experienced in its few years of existence brought to mind an earlier conversation with an IEC official. Speaking in 2008, he had compared the international community's attention to electoral institutions to a bottle of soda, shaken and bubbling in the months prior to and during elections, but quickly losing its fizz as the cap came off and the excitement died down.

ELECTIONS AS ISOLATED EVENTS (AND THE VOIDS BETWEEN THEM)

I feel like the whole international community—even our organization—didn't pay any attention to the election process. It was like they were just trying to jump over a wall to get to the other side as quickly as possible. . . . After some time, I also lost interest.

—AFGHAN EMPLOYEE OF AN INTERNATIONAL NGO (2006)

In the immediate aftermath of the 2005 elections there was a frenzy of activity among UN and other nonprofit agencies jostling to take part in the strengthening of some of the newly elected institutions (namely, the lower house of parliament) that Bonn had created. Others, however, including the provincial and (yet to be formed) district councils, were overlooked entirely. The international focus on the parliament had also left the recently formed electoral institutions, such as the Independent Elections Commission (IEC) and civil society organizations, like FEFA, isolated and adrift. International priorities had shifted elsewhere, and of course, another election was not due anytime soon. By the time international actors had begun to think seriously about how the second round of elections would be orchestrated, they found themselves working in an environment far removed from the relative calm of 2004 and 2005.

In chapter 1, we started to question basic assumptions about what elections are and what they do in a given political community. In particular, the assumptions that elections automatically confer legitimacy and authority to elected officials and take place on a level playing field where candidates compete as equals are problematic in the Afghan context. Some scholars, including Staffan I. Lindberg, have also recently put forward the claim that elections in and of themselves can promote democratization, leading to the conclusion that "the more elections, the more democratic the regime and society in general."[1] This is based on the presumption that simply conducting competitive elections on a regular basis allows the development of institutions and processes that in turn generate interests and incentives promoting the establishment of democratic society. According to this perspective, the largely technical exercise of holding competitive elections regularly has deeper political ramifications in the form of the interests and incentives created by them. The key assumption here however is that elections will prove, eventually, to have a democratizing influence.

While relatively uncommon in the theory of democratization, this viewpoint—that elections in themselves promote democracy—has been central to the practice of implementing internationally sponsored elections in post-conflict environments. In Afghanistan, the ways in which the international community has promoted elections has demonstrated this through their insistence on holding elections regardless of inadequate voter registration efforts, fraud, and insecurity on the grounds that simply holding elections as one-off, technical events and reaching a quantifiable outcome would somehow trump the problems with the process.[2] Differing from the theories of Lindberg and his colleagues, however, these international efforts have not sought to analyze or incorporate the political interests and incentives generated by the technical administration of elections but instead have remained largely separate from these, viewing elections as isolated events rather than processes or structures that affect and are affected by the landscape in which they take place. International approaches have characterized Afghans as the passive beneficiaries of well-meaning programs, rather than political actors with their own interests and agendas. Further, as time has passed, the prospects of democratization occurring as a result of elections has become less a concern than the need to hold polls simply as a means to maintain a semblance of order and control in an increasingly insecure environment.[3]

CHANGES IN THE POLITICAL ENVIRONMENT SINCE 2005

The political contexts in which elections took place in 2005 and 2009 respectively were remarkably different, given the short time period that had lapsed between them. Perhaps the most notable change was that levels of security had decreased across the country. The number of insurgent-related incidents reported had climbed sharply since the early days of the intervention, and Afghans and internationals working for NGOs increasingly found themselves the target of attacks.[4] Even more telling was the way Afghans were responding—making an increasing number of asylum applications to governments abroad, and leaving home for other, safer parts of Afghanistan. According to figures published by the Brookings Institution, the number of internally displaced persons (IDPs) in the country was climbing rapidly.[5] However, even as late as 2008, donors were reaffirming their commitments to implement the Afghanistan Compact, an international agreement of further assistance to Afghanistan, with little reference to the growing insurgency—reflecting the denial among international policymakers that the country was still, in fact, at war, and a stark lack of acknowledgment of the way in which this would shape the 2009 and 2010 elections.[6]

As 2009 began, the language of war had returned. An acknowledgment of continuing conflict began to spread through Kabul's various embassies, and almost overnight came a renewed focus on stabilization. The newly inaugurated Obama administration allocated $250 million in 2008 and 2009 to provide diplomats specifically to oversee the "nation-building" side of stabilizing Afghanistan.[7] At the same time, however, and somewhat conversely, there was a growing imperative among donors to keep costs down. Since the previous year, the world economy had fallen into a nosedive—and the war in Afghanistan (as it was now openly called) was becoming difficult to justify to indebted home nations. This was further exacerbated by the war's increasing human cost: more and more soldiers were coming home wounded or in body bags, to the understandable dismay and anger of the citizens receiving them. Eight years at war and for what? By all accounts the conflict seemed to be getting worse. As these concerns mounted, following the initial injection of energy through Obama's "civilian surge," signs of donor fatigue began to show among international donor representatives and the policies they pursued.

These conflicting agendas of sending more troops and funds to the country, while simultaneously attempting to demonstrate fiscal restraint, led to an emphasis on stabilization and a rapid handover to the Afghan government. As the focus shifted in this way, great importance was placed, especially by the British and American governments, on a "whole of government" approach in an attempt to streamline defense with foreign policy and aid. In many cases, this resulted in an increasing flow of aid to areas where donor nations' troops were stationed—overwhelmingly the south and east of the country in the case of USAID and the UK's Department for International Development (DFID). Programs run by organizations funded by USAID—including those working on democracy and elections—were thus obliged to align their programs with the priority districts determined by U.S. foreign policy.[8]

Speaking in 2010, a representative of one of these organizations described this shift, highlighting the power dynamics between the donor and recipient agency: "In 2008, USAID said we should stop the work we were doing in the north and west and continue instead in the south and east. We said no, but they said we had to. Parliament work then went to [another organization], and USAID gave us a new area of focus." While not surprising given the pressure for donor governments to produce results and rein in the resources spent to do so, this resulted in the closure of a number of potentially useful democracy programs in other regions and seriously disrupted the work of programs that remained running but were forced to shift either geographic or subject focus. This overall trend in distributing aid based on military priorities substantially blurred the boundaries between combat and development activities, as Suhrke documents,[9] as well as leading to a sense—however unintended—that "safe" areas in the north and west were being penalized for *being* safe.

In terms of domestic politics, the political landscape had also changed dramatically since the first presidential elections. President Karzai had largely failed to deliver the promised services expected by Afghanistan's citizens: while improvements had been made in terms of the number of clinics in remote areas, immunization rates. and the number of children in schools— change had been slow and intangible to many. The honeymoon period was over and, unlike in 2004, public support for his second-round electoral campaign far from given. Fully aware of the dissatisfaction within their own constituencies, the leaders of key ethnic groups in particular would need substantial encouragement before they pledged the support of their bloc to Karzai's cause. In parliament, the ethnicization of debates was becoming more obvious, with renewed tensions over the Kuchi-Hazara land conflict and the Shia Personal Status Law emphasizing growing rifts.

An increasing trend toward religious conservatism was also evident in both the fervent tone of some parliamentarians' speeches and the growing wariness of more liberal-minded legislators to speak up in defense of their views. This was not limited to parliament: the leader of a liberal-oriented political party told us that his home had been burned down by what he suspected were conservative opponents. Another party leader asked us to forward to members of the international community a statement against the Shia Personal Status Law that his and other like-minded, modernist-leaning parties had drawn up, in English, but did not feel able to publish in the domestic press. Extreme statements from political leaders were becoming more common, reflecting some of the polarization of opinion about the intervention and the political changes it had wrought.

A DEEPENING DISTRUST

Central to many of these trends were changing Afghan attitudes toward the ongoing foreign presence in the country. At the beginning of the intervention, many welcomed the international community as a harbinger of long-sought, peaceful change—people who would help rid the country of its oppressors, help establish a new government able to provide services for its citizens, and then leave to allow a sense of normality to set in. In many ways, this was the intent and hope of internationals as well. For foreigners working in the country in the intervention's early years, a *salaam aleikum* to a young mother in a doorway and a handful of sweets for her small son could lead to insistent invites for tea and an hour's conversation, while a daily exchange with a shopkeeper might often turn to the subject of how life had changed for the better, and of his plans to build a new, bigger shop.

While these snippets of interaction and community were to continue over the years, they became more and more rare—and more often than not the preserve of long-staying expats who had developed strong relationships with Afghan friends and colleagues over the years. With organizations enforcing stricter rules on staff movement as the security situation worsened, newcomers were increasingly excluded from these privileged spaces of conversation and camaraderie. However, this was also due to an increasing wariness among

Afghans of the potential perils of fraternizing with foreigners and of what their neighbors might suspect or talk about. Even those with long-standing friendships with internationals became less forthcoming in inviting them home for a meal, a source of great shame in a country that prided itself on its generous and unhindered hospitality. In place of invites to homes and weddings came carry-alls full of *qabuli pilau* and *mantu*—the signature dishes of fine Afghan cuisine—brought in to the workplace for international friends to share amongst themselves. What had become lost—*gum shud*, to use the classic, passive, Dari words—was the sense of trust that had started to develop in the early years—trust of internationals, trust between neighbors, trust of the government, and trust of the electoral system.

This reluctance to put faith in the system and the internationals apparently promoting it was emphasized by the contradictions witnessed and discussed by Afghans on a daily basis: the increased insecurity as a result of troop presence; the talk of democracy but the lack of justice for ordinary citizens; the empowerment of warlords through their dealings with donors; and the continued suffering of the poor and those with no political connections. In the years since 2005, the reasons to doubt the intentions of international actors had accumulated—fast.

Clearly, the changes that had taken place during these years, in terms of the nature of international focus, domestic politics, increasing religious conservatism, and attitudes toward international presence, were going to have an impact on the elections. Assistance shifting to the south and east would lead to politicians emphasizing more strongly the supposed rifts between non-Pashtun and Pashtun groups, using grievances about the distribution of aid to fuel their campaigns. Sensing the need to consolidate voter blocs, leaders resorted to the reraising of old ethnic conflicts as an easy route to reelection. Bolstered by increasing numbers of civilian casualties, intimidations, and night raids carried out by international forces and the declining security that had occurred since the intervention began, religious conservatives were able to claim the moral high ground and consolidate political capital through the condemnation of international efforts of all kinds—including those to support journalists and people accused of converting to Christianity who had been imprisoned without fair trial. These are not the kinds of incentives and interests envisaged by liberal democrats as those that should be promoted by the holding of elections—and yet in the Afghan case they have been inter-twined with the need to generate as many votes as possible for the access to state resources that an elected seat provides.

A LACK OF SUPPORT TO ELECTORAL INSTITUTIONS

One seemingly significant change between the two rounds of elections was the shift in the international approach toward the administration and orchestration of the polls themselves. At first glance, the move from inter-nationally organized elections in 2004 and 2005 to an Afghan-led effort in 2009 and 2010 might appear to be part of a perfectly natural transition toward local ownership. However, when viewed in light of the absence of funding for capacity-building or training of electoral institutions in the interim, this change begins to seem ambitious and unrealistic—an exercise in the absurd, and yet further confirmation of the lack of international effort to situate elections within the local political contexts in which they were actually occurring.

Between 2005 and 2008, very little donor funding was channeled toward building the capacity of electoral institutions or strengthening civic educa-tion programs. During this period, donors did not consider these areas of need urgent enough to merit significant financial support, reflecting the more general approach of the diplomatic community to treat elections as discrete events—a tendency that contrasted sharply with local perceptions of the polls as part of continuous and much deeper political processes. As a result of donors' event-oriented approach, the lull in funding for these activities was apparent as soon as the 2005 elections ended, in spite of the initial establish-ment of a Post-Electoral Strategy Group. One senior IEC official described in an interview in 2008 the consequences of this rather sudden drop-off:

> The international community came in and established institutions with international standards. [But] international support to the IEC stopped after the elections in 2005. There was a lot of equipment bought in 2005, for example many provincial offices were set up and staffed and furnished, and we said they should be kept but UNOPS [United Nations Office for

Project Services] took it all away. Now [in November 2008] we are starting from zero.

Although provincial IEC offices had been established for the first round of elections, facilitating local-level organization of electoral activities and offering a point of contact for Afghans outside Kabul, these were closed after the 2005 polls.

Had these offices continued to exist, they could have administered a number of localized activities in the interim period such as the reregistration of minors turning 18, or civic education in schools. However, with the majority of funding for electoral activity in 2004 and 2005 coming through finite and highly specific donor grants, it was difficult for work to continue. International organizations were slow to issue new funds because elections were not on the immediate horizon and offered no short-term targets for program completion. Seeing elections as individual events as opposed to an integral and cumulative part of a developing democratic politics, international donors considered their responsibilities in this regard complete for at least another three years. During our conversation, the IEC official continued to elaborate on the extent of the problem:

> In the first six months of 2006 [IEC staff] didn't receive any salary from the government. In the end I approached UNDP about this and they gave us money until the government finally started to pay us. We submitted a proposal for the ELECT [Enhancing Legal and Electoral Capacity for Tomorrow] project, which was about the capacity-building of staff. The Asia Foundation supported us, and IFES [International Foundation for Electoral Systems], but we had nothing from the others. The UN did not play their role. Now, once again the international community is excited, in the year before elections, and they have accepted our proposal. They are all coming now. But I have told them that they forgot about us during the nonelection period.

While one or two agencies, including the Asia Foundation, continued to provide in-house capacity-building to the IEC in the interim period, the statement that donors "forgot about" the IEC is for the most part a fair criticism. The fact that IEC staff were forced to approach international donors in person to secure continued funding for electoral institutions in itself demonstrates just how far down the ladder of priorities this had slipped after the completion of a "successful" election. Since the disastrous polls in 2009 and 2010, however, some lessons have been learned on this front—with UNDP starting the ELECT II program (with a budget of $89 million) for capacity-building within the IEC, support to the voter registration system, and assistance in strengthening the electoral infrastructure over two years in advance of the 2014 polls. Whether or not this is a case of too little, too late remains to be seen.

In spite of the distinct lack of interim support to building the capacity of electoral institutions after the 2005 polls, they were now expected to take the lead role themselves: the 2009 elections were to be labeled "Afghan-led." This meant that while electoral institutions would still largely be funded by donors (who would pay the majority of the $223 million tab) and overseen by the UN, they would now be headed by Afghans and the emphasis would be on Afghan implementation. The IEC would take prime responsibility for organizing the polls under the leadership of Azizullah Ludin, a close friend of Karzai and former head of the parliamentary secretariat. In the months before the presidential election, Ludin would betray his loyalties in public on several occasions, stating his disdain for opposition candidates in press interviews.[10] While everyone was aware of his close ties to Karzai, there was nevertheless a shared sense of indignation among internationals working in Kabul that the IEC chairman had voiced his stance in such an open fashion—although for the Afghans we spoke to at the time this was merely an extension of old news.

Another demonstration of how supposedly Afghanized the elections would be was the general lack of international observers: there was less emphasis on international monitoring than in 2005, and in any case the security situation was now so bad that very few internationals were able to work as observation teams outside of Kabul or the other major cities. This was sadly ironic since in spite of growing Afghan hostility to international actors, this was one area where their presence was still considered acceptable due to their perceived lack (as individuals at least) of ethnic bias.

As would become clear later, however, the overall attempt to rebrand the elections as a locally owned process would have little impact on the amount of blame Afghans would bring to bear on the international community for their ensuing failures; it simply meant that the IEC was more forcefully implicated as well. Indeed, international donors would still be accused by many Afghans of working behind the scenes to manipulate and even determine the outcome of the elections. But while conspiracy theories abounded as to the exact role that these foreign hands were playing, such speculation was not entirely groundless. American ambassador Karl Eikenberry's visits to three rival presidential candidates before campaigns began, for example, sent rumors flying around Kabul that the president had fallen out of favor with the Americans and would not be supported by them in the election.[11] The clear, if not always coherent, attempts by international diplomats to steer a process they were simultaneously trying to label as "Afghan-led" thus created a significant amount of confusion (and scope for speculation) about what their role actually was and just how much influence they had.

THE FUNDING OF ELECTORAL AND DEMOCRACY PROGRAMS: SHORT-TERM AND STATISTICS-DRIVEN

For the majority of the intervention years, there was no shortage of intelligent analysis or perceptiveness among the international staff of donors and agencies in Kabul. Bar the views of a few new arrivals, overstated optimism about the onset of democracy in Afghanistan was uncommon. In interviews throughout the inter-election period, many international development practitioners involved in democracy programming would comment on the struggles their own countries had faced in the consolidation of a democratic politics. As one American practitioner articulated in an interview in 2010:

> I've been getting democracy lessons since I was six years old—things like, elections are always good, honest Abe—all this is instilled in us. We have forgotten in this the way that we were set up as a country by slave owners and misogynists. So democracy in Afghanistan? We cannot come in with a "holier-than-thou" perspective teaching values and telling people to

elect liberal democrats. Warlords have constituencies because they fought for people.

In general, internationals in Kabul were under few illusions, and the pervasive sense of realism was often expressed in the typical cliché, "Afghanistan is not Switzerland."

Given the generally high levels of perception and understanding among many working in the country, the disconnect with the actual products of policymaking was all the more stark: in spite of the better judgment of many of their staff, donor agencies continued to fund programs focused on democracy or civil society assistance that generally lasted no more than six to twelve months.[12] While donors demanded comprehensive statistics on the inputs distributed to recipients, there was generally scant focus on the outcomes of assistance programs as the emphasis on security and stabilization edged out the need to ensure sustainability.[13] Evaluations and summary sheets of USAID-funded projects, for example, tended to focus on the number of attendees at workshops or the number of provinces in which they were conducted. One typical example of a quarterly report for USAID, documenting preelection support in 2005, reads as follows:

> In an effort to boost female participation in the upcoming elections, [the contractor] coordinated a candidate registration information session designed solely for women in Kabul in early May. The jointly hosted [session], by [the contractor] and the Afghan Ministry of Women's Affairs, was attended by 550 women from all over the country. More than 300 candidate registration packets were distributed at the event.[14]

No information is given about the content of the session, what the participants might have gained from it, or how they might use the information in their respective provinces. Moreover, there are no details about who the participants were—influential women in positions of authority who might be able to encourage others to participate in election? Students? Women with connections to political parties? How, by whom, and for what reason these women were selected over others is also missing from the report. The simple fact that the workshop took place and that packets were distributed was apparently enough to satisfy USAID's reporting demands. And as one Afghan UN worker commented in an interview, "reports seem to mean everything—the international community is only interested in reports." Whether or not the missing information described were deemed relevant for the donor's internal purposes, as a public document the report gives the impression that such details—the points of contact between international democracy or electoral programs and the political landscape in which they are conducted—are unnecessary. One female parliamentarian reflected on this in an interview in 2007, saying, "Foreign people think like themselves. They do not think like Afghans. They come here, do their job according to quotas and numbers and mandates, tick boxes, and then leave. They do not see the results. Only Afghans see the results."

"Workshops" proved to be a popular choice among donors and international implementing agencies as a medium for transferring knowledge or capacity to Afghan recipients, particularly, but not exclusively, on electoral and democracy-related topics. A typical workshop experience would start with a delay, while organizers waited for an esteemed dignitary of some kind to arrive, after which a short prayer would be given by a participant with a religious background. This would then be followed by a lengthy speech by the aforementioned dignitary, who would often claim credit for organizing the workshop but might also take the opportunity to criticize the excessive number of workshops organized by the international community. The dignitary then typically left to attend some other pressing meeting, and an international consultant or guest speaker would give a powerpoint presentation, followed by questions, tea, and *kulcha* (sweet biscuits with cardamom), group exercises (most often with flipcharts and marker pens), lunch, and a summary given to the few remaining drowsy participants who did not need to be anywhere else that afternoon. The internationals organizing the event would then compile any feedback, write a report on the number of participants (especially women), and send this to the donor funding the event, in the hope of attaining more funds for more workshops.

A caricature, for sure, but one based on similarities across many of the surprisingly similar workshops that we attended ourselves over the years.

While some such events may be genuinely effective vehicles for imparting knowledge, their abundance within international assistance programs in Afghanistan was astonishing. This profusion appears based not so much on any evidence of their effectiveness, but rather on the ease with which they are organized and quantified through numbers of participants and the amount of material distributed. Moreover, they epitomize a key component of international attitudes toward the Afghans with whom they were working during the election years: a kindly but somewhat condescending assumption of workshop participants as grateful beneficiaries, as opposed to political agents with agendas of their own.

* * *

Although individual participants in these events may not have lost sleep over their short-term or short-sighted nature, these characteristics of donor funding can cause a great deal more damage to the local organizations whose existence depends on sustained support from outside.[15] Forced to plan only for the short-term, to move offices frequently, and to let staff go after the end of each six-month funding proposal, their existence is highly unsustainable and their agendas by necessity donor-driven. As one representative of an agency promoting advocacy on human rights issues explained:

> We do not have an alternative [to donor funds]—we cannot raise funds locally as we would probably end up in the hands of this or that warlord. . . . The major problem is that we are often operating on funds allocated to specific projects and thus when the project finishes the money stops—this prevents us from operating as we choose to. We have to operate according to bits and bobs of different projects, meeting deadlines, and every six months we lose our funding and we have to apply again but we lose staff in the meantime. When we get new money, we get new staff but we have to retrain them. There is a real lack of sustainability of funding.

Although funding for these organizations was often trumpeted by donors as democracy-building, or promoting accountability and transparency, it was generally limited and contained to small-scale activity in the capital, and within these limitations, confined even further to agencies with English-speaking staff that had the capacity to respond to Calls for Proposals in a format compatible with bureaucratic requirements. This often resulted in the widespread duplication and repetition of programs with no tangible or long-term effect. Organizations that could potentially have been instrumental to the long-term process of building democratic politics in Afghanistan were often unable to sustain their activities in between short-term donor-funded projects.

FEFA in particular received lump sums from donors around election time to record and report on electoral activities. Having had funding cut significantly between elections, it was a challenge for the organization to find qualified staff in time for new programs to begin. Friends of ours who had worked at the organization in its early days had long since moved on to more stable positions in international NGOs that promised wages far higher than FEFA could hope to match. Given the fluctuations in staffing and funding levels, the organization has produced an impressive number of reports relating to electoral activities to date, including an investigation into campaign financing and a comprehensive assessment of the voter registration process, alongside its standard postelection analyses.[16] Nevertheless, these publications normally signified the end of a project along with its funding, and the follow-up of key findings was thus rarely an option.

As the lack of support for electoral institutions between elections and the short-term nature of donor funding for democracy and election-related programs demonstrate, international promotion of democracy in Afghanistan has been an events-focused affair. But what effect did this have on political change? It is easy to criticize donor approaches for being bureaucratic, short-sighted, and underperforming, but surely this could just mean that democratization might take place more slowly in Afghanistan. Indeed, one might ask: if democratization should be a locally owned and bottom-up process anyway, as many a critic of interventionist democracy promotion might claim, then what does it matter that donor attempts to promote it through elections were insubstantial? In fact, far from remaining neutral, technical events, without the attention to detail needed in terms of monitoring and oversight, accurate voter registration and candidate vetting, for example—all of which are highly politi-cal activities—these became critical vehicles for warlords and commanders to solidify their grasp on access to central resources, and in many ways the inter-national community's focus on isolated elections facilitated these commanders' strengthening grasp on power.

2009: INDECISION AND HASTY PREPARATIONS

Despite having a clear five years' notice of their arrival, international prepara-tions for the 2009 presidential polls felt like a desperate race against time. But if the problem was rooted in years of donor indifference and the lack of planning and capacity-building this produced, it was compounded by the paralyzing indecision that gripped international actors as a new round of elections loomed.

Critical in precipitating this rush was the failure of a core group of UN agencies and donors—UNDP, the United States, the United Kingdom, the European Union and individual European countries, Canada, and others—to decide how the next round of presidential and provincial council elections should be funded and implemented until the very last minute. Although some donors had individually started to map out their contributions at least a year before the elections were due to take place, there were delays between the state-ment of intent to contribute, the actual commitment of funds, and their even-tual release. The process of donor-funding decisions is fraught with delay at the best of times due to the lengthy bureaucratic procedures required to release funds, but in this case the transition from intent to actual delivery was infused with a debilitating uncertainty. This was demonstrated by the way in which the pledging conference for donor contributions to elections was held in Janu-ary 2009, only six months before elections were scheduled to take place. In a vicious cycle of indecision, each donor waited to see what its counterparts (and particularly the United States, with a new president in charge) would do, how much they would commit, and when. It was little wonder, then, that recipient agencies like FEFA were struggling to plan their activities in advance.

On a technical level, donors were wary of how UNDP's basket fund for the ELECT program—the mechanism for coordinating donor funding to the electoral process—would work. One representative of a European donor talked to us about how his agency had pledged fewer funds than initially intended, to wait and see whether or not UNDP would be able to deliver on the services it promised to provide. Others commented for another study conducted in 2011 that they had had real difficulties in dealing with the ELECT program, including disputes over funding and program priorities.[17] But in spite of evident concerns among donors about the capacity of ELECT, by 2009 there was really no other alternative; there was an urgent need for a way to pool donor funds, and no Afghan institution had the means or was considered independent enough to take on this role. As one UN representative described, "The IEC's senior officials are selected by the president, and should be approved by the parliament but this hasn't happened yet. In Afghan reality, there is not a single independent force. The IEC will work for the benefit of the president." Another factor that weighed in UNDP's favor was the nationwide reach of its programming—very few other agencies could boast missions of a similar size and scope.[18] UNDP therefore became the vehicle of choice. But preparations were beginning so late they all but prohibited any serious advanced planning for the process.

Setting up a new Electoral Complaints Commission (ECC) also took time. Disagreements between ELECT, various donors, and the ECC regarding its size and reach into the provinces led to considerable delays before its activities could commence.[19] Although the continuation of an office like the ECC between elections was perhaps not as critical due to its specific role in addressing complaints during the polls themselves, the scramble to reestablish it was nevertheless symptomatic of the entire operation—a rush job starting from scratch in almost every aspect.

Another critical conundrum for international actors concerned security: how could elections be held in the increasing numbers of insecure areas? Unfortunately, these areas were largely in the south and east of the country, home to the majority of its Pashtun inhabitants and the expected support base of President Karzai. If these areas could not be made secure enough to establish polling centers, there would be no escaping the perception among Pashtuns that they were being deliberately disenfranchised by the government and international community, even if it was the insurgency that was driving this instability. Troops were deployed in an effort to stabilize some areas, but this would not prevent violence being used as a political tool by insurgents and candidates alike, as we discuss in the next chapter. The decision to go ahead with the election in spite of increasing insecurity risked the whole exercise being discredited.

The security question was one example of a crossover between the technical challenge of implementing elections and the political landscape in which they were taking place. International actors were distinctly aware of the potential that the elections had to be ethnically destabilizing. As one donor representative calculated in late 2008:

> In the presidential elections next year, obviously security will be the first issue—whether it keeps the Pashtuns in the south and east away from the polls. Karzai needs at least the same turnout from the south and east as last time. If turnout from these regions is 5 to 10 percent less, the vote could go to a second round. If the turnout is more than 10 percent less than last time from these regions, Karzai could well be knocked out. If things went to a second round it could be very interesting. Karzai's popularity has weakened so much since last time. . . . Will the Pashtuns stay at home and not vote, as they are not pro-Karzai enough, and security is so bad that they won't risk it? If the northern ethnicities turn out at around 70 percent, everywhere else around the center at 50 percent, and the south and east at 20 percent—there is no way that Karzai could win.

While this speaker may have underestimated Karzai's political strength, this placing of the election debate firmly within the security and ethnic context was not uncommon among analysts working in donor agencies, demonstrating a willingness to engage at least analytically with the political dynamics of the polls. However, significant as these concerns were, most internationals felt that they paled in comparison to the negative ramifications of the polls not going ahead and the way this would reflect on the state of the international intervention as a whole. Expediency prevailed and, although debilitatingly overdue, the wheels began to turn.

As preparations for the 2009 elections began in earnest, a flood of requests for proposals and terms of reference for electoral programs began to flow from the new temporary top of the donor food chain (UNDP) to donor government agencies and their subsidiaries. Local organizations like FEFA were inundated with program proposals from international agencies suddenly desperate to access data on elections, all keen to claim to have supported the independent elections watchdog or other local civil society organizations in their efforts to promote transparency. Since these organizations had long since been forced to let valuable, trained staff go due to the absence of funding between elections, there was also a scramble to find, train, and hold on to suitable employees. The international funding boost to local agencies involved in elections—many of which, like FEFA, were based near parliament on the west side of town—was also reflected in soaring rent prices in the area, in part a result of the demand for campaign offices for candidates but also no doubt a result of savvy landlords making the most of an obvious spike in international interest in elections. In conversations outside our own homes—a few blocks away from the parliament building—we shared complaints with Afghan neighbors about the way in which monthly payments had risen by 30–40 percent for renters on our residential street in the run-up to the polls.

In the rush to make sure the election happened at all, international donors also managed to overlook one vital component of the upcoming poll that would come to define its controversial aftermath. In their fundamental assumption that the presidential election would function more or less as an election in the West, they had failed to take into account the massive role that fraud and patronage would play across the country at both a local and national level.

THE "SHOCK" OF THE PRESIDENTIAL ELECTION AND ITS AFTERMATH

On August 17, 2009, the eve of the presidential election, we received a phone call from BBC News in London with a request for some commentary on an elections story. Although the journalist who called was familiar, the story they were running was different: the BBC had uncovered "new evidence" that widespread fraud was likely to occur tomorrow. What did we think about this possibility and its likely effect on the election?

The nature of the question, and its timing, reflected the apparent surprise among international actors as fraud allegations began to pour in to the ECC and to international media sources in the weeks after the elections. At issue was the sheer scale of the fraud involved—this was not just a few ballot boxes stuffed here and there, but systematic, organized cheating that seemed to be coming from all directions, especially (according to the presidential office at least) from peripheral, insecure areas. As the pace and number of allegations grew following the initial announcement of results, it became increasingly clear that this apparently unexpected issue, along with the glut of sensationalist stories printed in the international media, threatened to undermine the electoral exercise completely.

Returning to the assumptions that theorists and practitioners often make about elections, perhaps the most starkly inapplicable to the Afghan context in 2009 and 2010 is the presumption of level playing fields on which candidates compete. Evidence to the contrary abounded. First, candidates who could orchestrate ballot stuffing where few observers were present used pervasive insecurity to their advantage; second, this insecurity could also be used as a smokescreen for the intimidation of other candidates; third, without the infrastructure in place to monitor how government resources were being used to further certain campaigns, those with connections to the state were likely to benefit most; and fourth, the ambiguity over voter registration meant that an accurate vote count was unlikely. The process of registering potential voters had already been fraught with irregularities, documented comprehensively, if too diplomatically, by FEFA in its reports published earlier that year.[20] Given the absence of a census, trying to count the number of eligible voters as a percentage of the adult population in a given province with no means of verifying how many people actually lived there was a futile exercise. Whether or not fraud had been officially sanctioned at the top was a valid question, but how high up the ladder it had originated had little bearing on the dealings of local actors who thought they stood to gain significantly by aiding the cause of Karzai or Abdullah through illicit means.

As it also turned out, the issue of security was even more significant than embassy analysts had anticipated. While numerous polling centers were closed in supposedly unstable areas, the criteria for doing so in each case were never made public. Looking back, what is especially puzzling is how international actors could have imagined an election free of fraud (or at least one considered passable by electoral observation missions) given the security and political conditions leading up to the polls.

As the scale of the problem became clear, embassies and donors struggled to come up with an appropriate response. A preliminary statement released by the European Union Election Observation Mission just after the election on August 22 was entitled "Afghan elections take place in a reasonably well-organized manner, amid widespread violence and intimidation," but barely mentioned fraud.[21] Many embassies, including that of the UK, issued cautious statements, but others were quick to congratulate Afghanistan on holding the polls. One American analyst went as far as to imply that the vote had been successful, stating, "The playing field was as level as one could reasonably expect under the circumstances."[22] This begs the question of what would constitute "reasonably level," surely a normative judgment contradicting the apparently absolute terms in which statements about what elections are and do are usually made. It was not until October, when Senator John Kerry paid a visit to the palace and seemingly convinced Karzai to take part in a run-off election with Abdullah Abdullah, that donors finally acknowledged the extent of the fraud that had taken place.

One of the most notable reactions to the post-2009 elections was that of UNAMA, which responded with a clear refusal to consider supporting the parliamentary polls in 2010 if certain reforms were not made to the system and steps taken to curb fraud. The Afghan government did make some effort to show it was taking this threat seriously—a new IEC chairman was appointed (this time a Tajik with former connections to the Northern Alliance and the Jamiat Party) and 6,000 IEC field staff members were prevented from taking part in the 2010 polls.[23] However, these were still essentially token measures and a far cry from the significant reforms that UNAMA had demanded. In spite of this, nothing more was said on the issue, and plans rolled on for the international funding of the next set of elections.

In the meantime, few in the international community appeared to have noticed that 2009 was the year of not one but two elections. Cheating had also been commonplace in the provincial council poll and was causing a good deal of disruption. For example, in Nangarhar, a province where the provincial council had built up an uncharacteristic degree of influence, results were delayed for four months, becoming the subject of widespread public ridicule. However, due to this "other" election's relative inconsequence on the international stage, very little attention was paid by international actors to the way elections were playing out at the local level. Sidelined by the government and by donors since their creation in 2005, provincial councils appeared to have no more significance now in the eyes of internationals than they had done then. As implied in chapter 5, paying more attention to the provincial council polls could have provided a potentially critical insight into the way elections were connected to and affecting the Afghan political landscape, since, in many cases, local communities were far more invested in these more contested elections than they were in distant presidential elections which many simply assumed Karzai would win.

The unexpected debacle of the presidential polls led to a new dilemma: what to do in 2010. Donors were faced with a difficult political climate at home—having funded a fraudulent election in 2009, it would be difficult to justify using recession-hit taxpayer funds to pay for more of the same the following year. Nevertheless, leaving the IEC in the lurch at this point would mean no election at all and the troubling potential for political stalemate. Some analysts suggested holding a Loya Jirga instead of the elections, but this threatened to further complicate the situation and was a risky option, not to mention an unconstitutional one. Furthermore, UNDP's ELECT program was scheduled to last for the whole two-year election period. In spite of their failings in 2009, the path of least resistance therefore appeared to be to continue as originally planned.

However, the events of the period between the two sets of polls would serve to complicate things even further. The most notable was the holding of the London Conference in January 2010. The latest of a long string of conferences, intended as vehicles to present progress but in reality aimed to generate much-needed donor funds, it would by and large be another example of repackaged policy and banal, empty benchmarks to assess future achievement. However, this time around something new would make its way into the post-conference communiqué: the issue of "reintegration and reconciliation." In the space of two years, Afghanistan had moved from "post-conflict" to "at war," and was now apparently planning to negotiate with the Taliban, or "upset brothers" as President Karzai preferred to call them.[24]

This change in foreign policy toward Afghanistan—given weight by the immediate pledge of $5 billion from the Japanese to support the effort at reconciliation and reintegration—would have a substantial impact on a political landscape that had become more ethnically polarized in the wake of the presidential polls. For non-Pashtun ethnic groups who had fought to bring down the Taliban regime a decade earlier, it was a potential disaster. From their perspective, the last thing Afghanistan needed was to welcome back the very insurgents who had plunged the country into darkness and precipitated the American invasion in the first place. Key non-Pashtun leaders made their concern clear by conspicuously not attending the government's Peace Jirga the following year.[25] The Pashtuns we spoke to were divided over the issue. Some saw the move as a welcome step toward peace, and others were more wary, skeptical over whether the government's plan to pay off the insurgent fighters would actually bring them into the fold. One representative of civil society talked about views he had heard on a recent trip to Kandahar: "people were talking about different conspiracy theories, and the main one was that it was just a matter of time before the Talibs took over again and so they should just sit and wait." This resignation to the prospect of the international community leaving the country sooner rather than later, particularly after Obama's declaration on December 1, 2009, of a "pullout" date (or what was seen as such by many Afghans) for July 2011, was far from unusual in the south and east.

In either case, whether people were for or against reconciliation or simply resigned to the fact that the Taliban would regain control, the heightened sense of ethnic identity precipitated by the 2009 elections and new emphasis on reintegration were affecting the way parliamentary candidates were campaigning. As one Afghan political analyst commentated before the parliamentary polls:

> Candidates now are campaigning along ethnic lines even if they are not openly saying this. Everyone from Karzai down denies an ethnic agenda, denies it is important on the surface but acts according to an ethnic agenda. If ethnicity is treated this way, it is not very good for democracy. It makes

democracy further deepen the ethnic tensions. Candidates don't bother to build new constituencies around democratic issues because it is more convenient to mobilize voter blocs around ethnic issues—for example, Pashtun candidates talking about their previous rule of Afghanistan. It is easy to appeal to the collective memory of the people. We need to deal with this if real democratization is to come.

These problems were not a direct result of international policy, of course, and have emerged and reemerged at different points in Afghanistan's history. But they were closely related to the international approach to intervention on elections. The lack of substantive international commitment to delivering on promises of democratization, or at the very least, to ensuring that elections were not just one-off events but part of a broader political process, contributed to the way in which existing powerholders could continue to strengthen their support bases along ethnic lines. Furthermore, the failure to secure (and disarm) Afghanistan in the early years, when resources were being channeled to Iraq, meant that the effects of increasing insecurity added to the weight of ethnic leaders' voices emphasizing the need for ethnic groups to reconsolidate. In this environment, again, the incentives created by forthcoming elections were not of the democratizing kind to which Lindberg speaks, but motivation instead to enforce underlying grievances for leaders' personal gain.

What was also clear was that shift toward reconciliation and reintegration had been decided very quickly: not so long before, two international analysts were disciplined and sent home for allegedly talking with the Taliban, and it was not entirely clear to many Afghans what was prompting this change in policy.[26] However, it was hard not to connect it to the international need for an exit strategy and the imperative to find the most direct route out. Evidently there was a pressing need to find some way to end the war and reverse the growing insecurity plaguing the country. In any case, the timing of the new policy served to heighten the ethnic tensions that had been stoked and rekindled during the 2009 election, not least by the candidates themselves and the bargains they had made with key ethnic leaders. This was to be yet another example of the far-reaching but understated consequences of international policy decisions on elections.

IGNORING POLITICS

Speaking of the international intervention generally, and having described the political realities of working in development in Afghanistan in some depth, a senior representative of a UN agency talked to us in 2006 about her most fundamental concern: "what international aid should be measured against is whether we are perpetrating the weaknesses or setting up a process for the gradual bettering of the system." Recognizing the potential for internationals themselves to extend or contribute to flaws in the system, this self-critical approach was unusual at the time, when technical assistance to the parliament was in full swing following the first elections. However, what the statement did not quite capture was that, beyond perpetuating existing weaknesses, international actors could create new and unintended problems with their activities and approaches.

This chapter has not intended to criticize unnecessarily international actors and their work in Afghanistan. Instead, it has sought to demonstrate how, even with the best intentions in the world, internationally driven programs and policies have been designed separately from the political landscapes in which they would take place. In many ways, this is because the actors involved have not taken the wider political ramifications and impact of their interventions into account. This has been compounded by the tendency to see Afghans as the recipients or beneficiaries of international schemes, and not political agents with their own agendas, loyalties, and concerns.

These unintended consequences ultimately fed into the intervention's growing depletion of legitimacy in the eyes of the Afghan public as it progressed. As Afghans saw how increasing troop presence was matched by increasing insecurity, how development programs consistently fell short of their (admittedly high) expectations, and how the international community appeared once again to be shoring up the position of warlords, they began to express real doubt about the true motivations of this rapidly expanding group of foreigners. These concerns were solidified by the significant role violence played in the parliamentary elections of 2010.

7

VIOLENCE AND VOTING

PACHA KHAN ZADRAN

*P*ACHA KHAN ZADRAN—WARLORD, *tribal leader, parliamentarian, bereaved father—personifies Afghanistan's violent history, weak central state, and fluid forms of authority. A symbol of power among the Zadran tribe, he does not fit into any simple political category, leading to a series of overlapping stories and rumors about who he is, the nature of his relationship with the government, and his role in elections and the political violence that surrounded them.*

As an influential regional leader, Pacha Khan has featured in several news articles, but is often written about in contradicting ways. In 2003 he was described by the New York Times *as "a powerful Afghan warlord" and "a fearsome Pashtun tribesman."[1] Shortly before this, he had been appointed governor of Paktya Province. After reluctant residents denied his men access to the provincial capital of Gardez, in the hope of preventing his accession to the governorship, Zadran told the paper that he would "kill them all, men, women, children, even the chickens."[2] Karzai responded by calling Pacha Khan and his men "a group of bandits," vowing "to take any actions deemed necessary to keep the peace and stability," despite the fact that he had ostensibly been the one who had appointed him governor in the first place.[3] This was followed by sporadic fighting involving Pacha Khan's men across Loya Paktya—encompassing the southeastern provinces of Paktya, Khost, and Paktyka, and historically an area where Pashtun tribes have maintained a more complete grasp on political power than they have in other parts of the Pashtun south. As his forces clashed with those of the new interim government in Kabul and the coalition troops that supported it, one of Pacha Khan's sons was killed in what appeared to be a case of mistaken identity while fighting with American troops.*[4]

An uneasy truce was declared between the two sides and in 2005 Pacha Khan ran for parliament, after apparently shifting closer to the Karzai government. By 2006, on surviving an assassination attempt, the narrative had shifted and the New York Times *ran an article entitled "Afghan Legislator Escapes Suicide Bombing," describing "the politician" as "a former warlord from eastern Afghanistan who was a close ally to American-led coalition troops."*[5]

Pacha Khan's fluid identity in the international press was paralleled in conversations with residents of Paktya, where he is often referred to as a wakil or sometimes as a spin giri *or whitebeard, a traditional term for community elder (despite the fact that his beard is, in fact, very black). As one of the key candidates from the area, his name came up in many political conversations. When it did, many simply shrugged and said that he was a powerful leader. But as conversations progressed, this mask of indifference often gave way to stronger sentiments. Unsurprisingly, members of the Zadran tribe tended (although not without exceptions) to be more positive about Pacha Khan, in contrast with often vehement expressions of contempt by members of other groups. As one woman who lived close to Pacha Khan's home in Paktya said:*

> *I do not accept [Pacha Khan Zadran] as a representative. Because of him our people have been troubled by conflicts which have caused deaths and injuries, including one of my sons. He was ten years old when he was killed in one of these fights. Still I cannot forget him. Since my son was killed, from that time I have had problems with my head—I always get headaches. I do not know who elected Pacha Khan Zadran.*

There were numerous stories that circulated in the province about Pacha Khan's various abuses of power. Perhaps most notoriously many said that he had bulldozed a significant portion of a village near his own home in order to pave a road through the area for his personal use.

By his own account, Pacha Khan is 58 years old and studied in school to sixth grade. During the jihad and civil war period, he primarily sided with the royalists, who hoped to return Zahir Shah to the throne. Due to his tribal connections in an area where tribes often spill across the border into Pakistan along what is often called the Zadran Arc, his influence has increased significantly in recent years despite the death of the king and the marginalization of many former monarchists. This influence has been shaped in part by the growth of the Haqqani network, a primarily tribal and criminal network linked to the Zadranis, based in Pakistan and led by Siraj Haqqani. While the group is not a part of the Taliban, it has frequently been closely allied with them, along with other insurgents and factions of the Pakistani security forces that favor instability in Afghanistan. In fact, it is often rumored that insurgent attacks and bombings in Kabul can only take place with permission from the Haqqanis since their control of the criminal networks and corrupt police in the city is so strong.

Pacha Khan is not himself a member of the Haqqani network, but the network is primarily composed of Zadranis. There has thus been a concern among the international military and the Afghan government that if he breaks with the government as the strongest, non-Haqqani Zadrani, this will mean the defection of essentially all Zadranis. This has led international military forces and the government to cultivate and nurture his allegiance to them, and it was considered a major step when he declared that he would run for Wolesi Jirga in 2005.

In the 2005 election, he campaigned from what was clearly a position of strength as a well-known local leader and won his seat handily. As he recalled in an interview with us after becoming a representative: "I did not want to be a parliamentarian, but people forced me to become a candidate." Although this is a statement often made by candidates in an attempt to suggest that the mantle of leadership had simply been thrust upon them, Pacha Khan plays this role better than most. He is aloof and stern, and not timid around either diplomats or military officials with more polish than he. In a blunt assertion of his authority, the logo on his campaign posters was a lion ("and he looks like a lion!" said one woman from Paktya, commenting on his thick facial hair).

Despite both his political and military power and the continued support of many of the Zadran tribe, Pacha Khan lost his reelection bid in 2010. This was much to the surprise of voters in Paktya, not least Pacha Khan himself. The normally assertive politi-

cian appeared at something of a loss and while being interviewed on an Afghan tele-vision talk show began to rail against the politicians and money changers he implied had rigged the entire election process. In a return to his anti-government tactics circa 2003, Pacha Khan and his supporters set up a series of roadblocks along the major Khost-Kabul highway, stopping traffic, a paralyzing tactic they also employed dur-ing their initial fighting with the Karzai administration.[6] Several people were killed in the confusing struggle between Zadran supporters and police, some of whom were highly sympathetic to the protesters. Pacha Khan made several thinly veiled threats during this period, telling us, "I see conflict and destruction if the IEC announces final results which are the same as the preliminary ones."

Ultimately, however, tensions started to die down and Pacha Khan chose to continue to work with the Karzai government while joining several other former parliamentarians from Paktya who had also lost their reelection bids in peaceful calls for recounts. During this period, Pacha Khan was in close communication with government officials and was said to be negotiating with Karzai through the president's brother-in-law, a close friend of his. Over the years, Pacha Khan has apparently become too integrated into the current political system to break with it willingly—his son was at this point the district governor of Paktya's Waza Zadran District. Despite this, with Pacha Khan, the threat of violence is ever present, and voters in Paktya sit nervously waiting to see if he will pick up his gun and join the insurgency in the mountains.

VIOLENCE, SOVEREIGNTY, AND POLITICAL LEGITIMACY

Although violence and instability have played a contributing role in every Afghan election since 2004, they were a particularly pronounced phenome-non in the country's 2010 parliamentary polls. With 30,000 additional Amer-ican troops flooding into the country as part of the Obama administration's "surge," international troops became more apparent in public spaces and there was an increase in confrontations between insurgents and NATO forces. Counterinsurgency tactics aimed at bringing the people and the government closer together often created more instability as the Taliban responded by increasing its program of targeted assassinations of local leaders. This violence shaped local political struggles and led voters and candidates alike to take into consideration the instability that the threat of violence created while making political decisions.

In the run-up to the elections themselves, much attention was paid to the Taliban's widely publicized threat to cut off voters' fingers and direct attacks against polling stations. Less reported but equally significant, however, was the threat of violence employed by other local actors. Much more than in previous polls, influential figures across the country used violence as a powerful tool to disrupt elections, influence their outcome, or demonstrate political capital. While violence never fully derailed or invalidated elections themselves, the sense of unpredictability and fear it created ultimately allowed individual actors and political groups to manipulate them as part of a wider set of political negotiations in ways that deeply undermined the sovereignty of the state.

For many social theorists violence is at the very root of sovereignty. Violence by the state can publicly assert the sovereignty of the state, while violence by others can significantly undermine it.[7] Violence outside of state control threatens the monopoly of violence that the state assumes in the Weberian notion of the legal-rational state.[8] Increasingly, however, social scientists have looked at the ways in which sovereignty is constantly being debated and reshaped by citizens and, partially as a result, emphasizing that control of violence is not total and never as uncontested as the state often tries to make it seem. This has manifested itself in anthropology in the increased focus on contestations of sovereignty and in political science with increasing attention to the role of non-state actors—a term that we have seen can be problematic in Afghanistan.[9]

Violence—when conceived of as an attempt to do another person harm—can be methodical and formalized, particularly when ordered by a state. But when it takes place outside of the narrow confines of state control, it can create a new situation that is unpredictable. In such situations, violence may reorder society, eliminating predictable social relationships and upsetting the political order in the opposite manner of elections, which in the idealized case are transparent shifts in the political order.[10] Violence upsets many of the predictable patterns that are often studied in politics. The predictability of political, legal, and economic practices are all undermined by violence. Court decisions are meaningless when the state does not have the ability to enforce them; land titles, which should assign ownership of a property to the bearer, are counteracted by the reputations of commanders who seize land and expel residents using force, and even traditional processes of leadership selection in local communities are undermined when one or more of the potential leaders has access to violence that the others do not possess. At the same time, however, political processes may continue despite the threat of violence, but often with those participating in them deeply aware of the threat of violence. In the case of Afghanistan, an awareness of the potential for violence shaped how everyone approached these processes.[11]

The Afghan example is a rather extreme case of a state lacking a monopoly on legitimized violence, but it demonstrates that the assumption that political legitimacy decreases as violence increases is not always correct.[12] It raises important questions about how we understand the role of "non-state" actors, the contestation of sovereignty, and elections. In particular, the way that violence and elections have become so intertwined undermines the simple divide between legitimate and illegitimate violence. To understand the Afghan situation, we must look at how these categories blur: Pacha Khan Zadran was both a state and a non-state actor, and the legitimacy of the violence that he threatened was debated by residents of Paktya. His use of non-state-sanctioned violence did not simply delegitimize him as a government official. In fact, it was difficult to classify some of these attacks as state-sanctioned or non-state sanctioned, since they were carried out by his private militia, but at the same time, his personal relationship with Karzai implied at least some tacit acceptance by the state.

By the elections of 2010, violence pervaded the political system in Afghanistan to such an extent that the possibility of violence was at least an element in most political decisions that were being made. With the Taliban threatening violence against anyone who voted, the very act of voting defied that threat.

What then is the result when elections, designed to be predictable, transparent mechanisms for assigning political power, are deeply connected to violence, which is so often unpredictable? This chapter looks at violence on several levels during the past elections, focusing on the Wolesi Jirga elections of 2010. It considers violence as a means for disrupting elections, violence as a political tool within elections, the way in which both violence and elections become methods for measuring and demonstrating political capital, and, finally, how internationally sponsored elections have allowed violence to remain at the heart of Afghan political processes, further undermining the way in which sovereignty is being constantly debated and reshaped in Afghan politics. Ultimately, the unpredictability and fear created by violence allowed individual actors and political groups to manipulate elections, within a wider set of political negotiations, in ways that undermined the sovereignty of the state.

THE DISRUPTIVE IMPACT OF VIOLENCE

While Taliban and other insurgent threats to attack both polling stations and candidates had the most immediate and public impact on the electoral process, the polls also became a focus for other, more localized forms of violence. The threat of attack damaged the perceived transparency of the elections, limiting the ability of election monitors to carry out their work, and stoking local rumors of fraud and manipulation. At a fundamental level, the potential presence of violence deeply shaped the way that both voters and candidates approached the election process.

Insurgent threats against voters were of course not unique to 2010, but violence was increasingly discussed over the course of Afghanistan's four successive election rounds. More of the people we interviewed and spoke with in 2010 seemed to be taking the threat of violence seriously than they did in 2009. In earlier elections attacks were limited, and there even remain questions about whether the Taliban were actually interested in disrupting them at all. Antonio Giustozzi argues that in 2004 and 2005 the disruption caused by the Taliban was extremely limited compared to their capabilities.[13] In contrast with this, by 2009, and especially by 2010, various Taliban sources made it clear that they were intentionally targeting anyone participating in elections.[14]

In response to this, security measures were increased around polling stations and in some areas they were closed outright—a source of fierce debate in the Afghan media in the run-up to the 2010 elections. Initially, the IEC announced that almost 1,000 fewer polling stations would be open from the year before. In August, however, it announced the closure of another eighty-one stations in Nangarhar Province. The IEC's backtracking furthered the sense that the insurgency was gaining ground by highlighting the growing uncertainty that Afghan security forces would be able to protect polling centers. The ensuing flurry of articles in both the Afghan and international press contributed to the general perception that violence was not only likely, but increasingly probable on a larger scale.

SYMBOLISM AND VIOLENCE

On Election Day itself in 2010, the International Security Assistance Force (ISAF) reported slightly fewer attacks in comparison with 2009.[15] However, it was more the threat of violence in the days leading up to voting that reshaped individual choices than the actual instances of violence that did eventually occur. Although the Taliban and other insurgent groups' ability to launch attacks did not extend over the entire county, the fear that these attacks inspired spread far beyond insurgent areas—a sense that was heightened by news of a rocket attack in Kabul on the morning of voting. Insurgent groups were able to manipulate this fear to their advantage, and in the run-up to the voting threatened to cut off the finger of anyone participating in the elections. The choice was clearly a symbolic one: election regulations required that voters' fingers be dipped in supposedly indelible ink after their ballots were cast, and many (primarily Western) media outlets had used the iconic image of voters holding up their dyed finger as evidence of the voting process in previous polls. This was part of a wider series of public declarations by the Taliban that those aiding in what they viewed as international processes would be cut out of negotiations once international troops left the country.

Despite this, relatively few of the people we talked to appeared to actually decide not to vote based on this threat, with the ineffectiveness of parliament

FIGURE 7.1 Man showing his ink-stained finger.

and corruption of the electoral process much more likely to deter them. However, the threat of violence did color many opinions about the election and contributed to the general sense of frustration that surrounded it. Here was a process that had initially promised to guarantee them political representation, yet not only had it failed to do that, but it had begun contributing to threats of insecurity on a local level. As one mullah told us, "What will I do with parliament, but no finger?"

Attacks also did not need to be successful to have an impact on the elections. In both Gardez and in Qara Bagh, there were failed bomb attacks in 2009 that people were still discussing in 2010 and which clearly shaped debates over the approaching parliamentary poll. In Qara Bagh the bomb was small and removed from the center of town, doing little damage. In Gardez, the bomb exploded prematurely, killing only the would-be bomber, but stories about it still became a central part of discussions about the upcoming elections and whether or not individuals would participate.

This coincides with an understanding of violence as a strategy to shape and disrupt politics. In such cases the prime goal—and indeed the measure of a successful terrorist attack—is not the number of causalities, but the impact that it has on the wider population. This type of violence is meant to give citizens the sense that they are unsafe and can become victims at any moment. In this sense, a "failed" attack that still generates fear and discussion within the local population has not really failed at all, since it has shaped people's attitudes toward future elections and potentially changed how they will act in such situations.

"THEY ARE AFRAID"

Fear of violence also shaped the way that candidates approached the elections. By 2010 the danger of running for a seat in the Wolesi Jirga was already well established. In 2005 seven candidates were killed, joined by a further two parliamentarians soon after the inauguration of parliament.[16] By 2009 a total of ten parliamentarians had been killed.[17] Total casualties for elections in 2010 are difficult to establish, but in the months before the elections that year at least 20 candidates, election officials, and campaigners were kidnapped or killed by the Taliban or other insurgent groups, with another 20 kidnapped by other groups.[18] However, a closer look at some of these cases also demonstrates how the politics of elections and other local political issues can meld together. The role that elections played in these assassinations and kidnappings was never entirely clear. In some cases, especially after the elections, assassinations were clearly part of a wider Taliban strategy to undermine the Afghan government. This strategy was particularly effective in areas that were most opposed to Taliban concessions, as with the May 2011 abduction and killing of the head of the provincial council in Bamiyan Province. However, in other cases it was more likely that local feuds played a role in the killings. This trend suggested to voters that the prestige and resources that came from potentially winning elections was fueling violent conflicts, which may have started for very different reasons.

While candidates complained about security concerns in early elections as well, by 2010 insecurity had greatly curtailed the ability of candidates to campaign and maintain relationships with communities in certain areas. This was true to some extent in all the provinces where we conducted research, but especially in Paktya, where voters often talked with some distain about the failure of candidates and other rich or influential figures to visit poorer, rural areas for fear of kidnap or assassination. As one mullah in Paktya commented in 2010, "They are afraid [to visit regularly]. They say that there are suicide attackers in the areas and are concerned that they will lose their land cruisers and high salaries." Another resident of Ahmad Aba commented:

> Sayed Rahman Ahmadzai's campaign is going very well in Ahmad Aba and when he goes anywhere, a lot of vehicles go with him. One time Sharifa [Zourmati] came here and we appreciated that. Pacha Khan Sahib, however, has not even been seen in Gardez [the provincial capital], how then would it be possible for him to come to Ahmad Aba?

This last statement is particularly revealing of the relationship between the reputation of political figures and violence. In this case it was not just insurgents—who in many ways supported Pacha Khan's inconsistent relationship with the central government—that prevented him from traveling in the area as much as decentralized local groups in conflict with him for other reasons. Rahman Ahmadzai could travel through the community safely since it was composed of fellow Ahmadzais, as could Sharifa Zourmati, a woman who had a reputation of both providing resources and being particularly attuned to the needs of the province as a whole. Although Pacha Khan was one of the candidates with the most access to violence, it was precisely his position as a well-known commander with many long-standing enmities that made him most likely to be targeted himself by one of any number of enemies that he had acquired over years of fighting. In these cases, violence against candidates had much less to do with the insurgency than with the candidate's relationship with local powerholders and their followers.

VIOLENCE AND TRANSPARENCY

Increased insecurity also raised substantial questions concerning the transparency of the election process, as demonstrated by the controversy surrounding one polling station in a small village between Istalif and Qara Bagh in the 2009 election. Following a recent bombing, there was a debate between locals over whether security there was an attempt to protect the station or to limit community oversight. As discussed in chapter 2, one community elder was particularly upset when the police forced everyone who had already voted to leave the vicinity of the polling center on Election Day, following orders from the IEC official in charge. The men angrily gathered in the distance and the elder was eventually able to convince the police to let them back in. This was indicative of compromises reached in many other rural areas as well, where the police and government officials did not have the desire or capacity to provide security, or claim a monopoly on legitimate violence. This then required them to negotiate with the community over what sovereignty actually looked like on a local level.

In other cases, the threat of violence and insecurity spawned rumors that undermined faith in the elections. As one candidate in Paktya explained in 2010:

> In Zourmat District [a highly insecure district west of Gardez], the Taliban announced that no one should vote or go to the district center on Election Day. People obeyed and only those living in the district center, the police, and a few government officials actually voted. Yet, when the ballot boxes arrived in Gardez, they were filled with 6,000 votes.

Here, Taliban and insurgent threats fostered a sense that the voting process was less transparent and more open to manipulation by election officials or other influential figures. While these threats allowed for more fraud to occur, they also simply led to the increase of *accusations* of fraud, which essentially had the same effect in terms of undermining public opinions of the processes.

The growing threat to foreigners in the country also made more formal international monitoring of polling stations much more difficult.[19] By 2010, security concerns had led to a decrease in the number of international observers and agencies that were willing to monitor polling stations, and the monitors who remained in country were usually much more limited in where they were able to travel and observe polling. The sense of insecurity was heightened following the 2009 attack on the Kabul guesthouse housing seventeen internationals working on UNDP's ELECT program, which seemed to suggest that the Taliban were now directly targeting those internationals involved in the election process. The attack killed five foreign UN workers, unsettled much of the international community in Kabul, and led the UN to drastically tighten its security procedures, greatly restricting where its internationals were allowed to live and how they worked.

The connection between monitoring and insecurity was especially important given that, in many cases, insecurity frightened away those who were expected to be watching the polling stations, but not those committing fraud. As one mullah in Paktya in 2010 stated, "I saw with my own eyes that the polling station coordinator himself brought 1,000 fake voting cards and used them and there was no security due to the fear of the Taliban." Even when there were international troops involved in providing security for stations, they were subject to a mixture of curiosity and concern about what their true intentions were. In some cases they were accused of trying to influence the voting, but in others the rumors were even stranger and pointed to a deeper antipathy to their presence: in one instance, some young men told us that American troops were drinking beer on the roof of a local police station during the voting.

By 2010 there was thus a sense that the election process was dangerous on multiple levels: those running for office were likely to be targeted, large political gatherings seemed vulnerable to suicide attacks, and on Election Day itself voters were made to feel at risk. While this fear did not necessarily prevent Afghans from going to the polls, the uncertainty and unpredictability it created deeply shaped the lived experience of participating in the elections. Violence was disruptive, destabilizing, and made political processes even less transparent. Violence, however, was not simply a tool of the Taliban or a way to derail certain political processes. In many instances, it actually served as an effective tool for a much wider array of local actors to increase their political power.

VIOLENCE AS A POLITICAL TOOL IN ELECTIONS

In the Wolesi Jirga election, violence was not simply something that candidates and local leaders were forced to respond to. In many cases, it also created opportunities for them to increase their popular support among local communities, sometimes becoming an indelible part of the election process. The growing instability and prevalence of violence created opportunities to shape elections in ways that would be unthinkable in more stable times.

In some situations, candidates and their followers used violence directly to intimidate voters. In one voting center just north of Qara Bagh, supporters of a local candidate stood near the door of the polling station telling voters to vote for their candidate. When one man defied them, a fight broke out and he was beaten, stabbed, and subsequently hospitalized. Similar stories were frequent in the days following the voting. In most cases, however, violence and the threat of violence were embedded in the politics surrounding the elections in subtler and more complicated ways.

In both 2009 and 2010, instability ostensibly attributed to the insurgency was exploited by actors involved in the election who used violence in an attempt to gain the upper hand in political issues more broadly. In Balkh Province, interviewees explained to us how tensions between candidates and their campaign teams had turned violent during the presidential and provincial council elections of 2009. In one instance in Chimtal District, some of Abdullah's campaign teams were threatened and killed by Karzai campaigners, while ballot boxes from areas that primarily supported Abdullah were burned as they were being taken to be counted at the tallying center. In the latter instance, it was initially stated that the boxes had been burned in an insurgent attack, when in fact they had been burned by supporters of another candidate.

During campaigning in 2010, attacks in the province were also common. For the most part these attacks were once again blamed on the Taliban, but even at this point, insurgent activity was somewhat surprising in Balkh. The area had suffered greatly during the Taliban era in the 1990s, and most communities had little sympathy for the insurgents' cause. Instead, in several instances it was rumored that Governor Atta was actually helping facilitate insurgent attacks. This was a surprising alliance considering Atta's past history of opposition to the Taliban and his strong connections with other Northern Alliance leaders. Discussions with those living in the area, however, suggested that he was using these attacks to force the IEC to close down polling stations in areas where his support was weakest. This meant that votes in peaceful areas where his allies were strongest would count for more, relatively speaking, making it more difficult for those not allied with him to win seats. Whether or not Atta was directly involved in this strategy, over half of the winning parliamentarians from the province turned out to be closely associated with him.[20] This increased the sense among voters that violence could be used to manipulate election results and, on a national scale, put forward the message that exactly who is responsible for violence is often not as important as the perceptions and rumors that follow attacks.

In a political system currently shaped by war, in which individuals are deeply aware of the potential for violence, opportunities to manipulate the system arise that are not present in more stable situations. In Qara Bagh, one Wolesi Jirga candidate, who was a former commander, had long-standing feuds with both the deputy head of the district shura and the governor of a neighboring district. Tensions were heightened when the former commander split from Karzai and his supporters in the area, a move that cost him several key allies. Shortly after the split, the deputy shura head and the district governor apparently approached officials at the Ministry of Interior Affairs, alleging that the former commander had ties to the illegal militant wing of Hizb-i Islami, was carrying illegal weapons, and was potentially in communication with the Taliban. Tipped off by a friend, the candidate managed to avoid the authorities' subsequent attempt to arrest him and went into hiding. There, he spent several days using his contacts to convince officials that he was not, in actual fact, allied with the Taliban. Eventually he was able to convince enough influential people of his innocence to return to his home and continue campaigning. While unable to eliminate him completely, his opponents were nonetheless able not only to prevent him from campaigning for several days but also to create persistent problems for him in the long run.

In these increasingly insecure political conditions, violence thus became a part of many campaign strategies, used to intimidate voters, close polling stations, or distract other candidates from their campaigns. Even those candidates least associated with violence often lamented the fact that they were at a disadvantage to those that did threaten violence. In many instances candidates discussed this frustration in very similar ways to those in which poorer candidates lamented the fact that richer candidates had greater access to campaign funds. This reinforced the fact that violence was simply one of a series of forms of political capital. On a broader level, the extent of leaders' ability to threaten violence also offered a valuable way to bolster this important resource.

VIOLENCE AND POLITICAL LEADERSHIP

In both elections and in politics more generally in Afghanistan, there is a complex relationship between political authority and violence. In particular, the lack of any genuine monopoly on violence by the state means that violence is a necessarily important aspect of how leaders establish their authority. This fact has taken on a particularly strong resonance during election periods, where candidates' ability to threaten violence has deeply shaped voter opinions about them, both positively and negatively.

There are multiple ways of establishing political capital in Afghanistan, from religious reputation, to tribal connections, to the willingness to resort to violence. In some conditions, these forms of authority are clearly distinct. For example, too much economic capital can undermine a leader's claim to be pious and truly religious. Similarly, establishing relationships with NGOs and other international groups might boost a leader's reputation up to a point, but too many of these external connections may make them appear disloyal to their community.[21] Although many leaders tend to favor one type of authority over others when establishing power, they must nonetheless keep these multiple forms of political authority in mind, and are often careful in their attempts to balance them. For example, many politicians will wear suits while in Kabul, but change into *shalwar kemeez*, a traditional costume of loose pants and a tunic, when returning to their home provinces to emphasize their local connections. During campaigning, Wolesi Jirga candidates used a variety of approaches, trying everything from the design of their campaign posters to allusions in their speeches to their religious learning or tribal connections. Tied in with many of these approaches, however, were attempts to remind voters of their willingness to resort to violence.

For certain candidates, a history of violence in their participation in the jihad against the Soviets generated a good deal of political capital. As one voter in Qara Bagh explained after the 2009 election:

Most of the people voted for Anwar Khan because Anwar Khan was a mujahideen in the past, his father used to be a good and effective member of parliament, and three of his brothers were murdered during the Soviet period.

Here the voter references not only his past as a fighter but also the killing of his three brothers as evidence that Anwar Khan and his family were dedicated to Afghanistan and the community of Qara Bagh. The fact that in the same sentence he mentions the role of Anwar Khan's father as a parliamentarian suggests that efficiency as a representative was considered in a similar light to the reputation for violence. In the 2009 presidential election, the candidate (and former parliamentarian) Haji Mullah Rocketi, named for his experience with shoulder-held missiles, used even his name to conjure up positive associations of a violent past.

On a local level, numerous incidents indicated that violence and votes were related forms of displaying political might. In Istalif, the supporters of two feuding local candidates, both armed and in convoys of multiple vehicles, happened to meet in the bazaar. Words were exchanged, tensions grew, and several men fired shots into the air before driving off in opposite directions. The intent of these shots did not appear to be to actually harm anyone, but rather to demonstrate the potential to resort to violence. For Istalifis this was a very public display of the deep connection between the ability to mobilize voters and the ability to threaten violence.

Similarly, on the road between Qara Bagh and Istalif, an area that had been relatively free of insurgent attacks since 2001, three roadside bombs exploded in the days following the announcement of initial results in 2010. Peculiarly, it soon became clear was that these bombs were not actually meant to cause any harm, having been placed quite deep in a ravine below a bridge and detonated late at night when it was unlikely that there would be many passersby. In fact, the bombs had barely cracked the pavement on the bridge above. Instead, the bombs were making a political statement.

While initial rumors about the bombs exaggerated their impact, the context of the situation helped to explain some of the local intrigue. When we conducted follow-up research in the area after the bombing, several respondents noted that the bombs had been laid following the announcement of initial results in an area where there was strong support for Hizb-i Islami, and that in the preliminary returns, candidates from the party (including the former commander, mentioned above) had not fared as well as some had predicted. While some respondents argued that the bombs had been set to target Hizb-i Islami supporters, more felt that the bombs had actually been laid by local residents who wanted to demonstrate that Hizb-i Islami supporters were still a powerful force to be reckoned with in the area. The bombs were meant to send a message to anyone in the area who assumed that the poor showing of Hizb-i Islami in the elections was an actual indication of their diminished power. In this case, the demonstration of violence was being used to compensate for or supplement the ability to mobilize votes.

In many cases, the ability to resort to violence was understandably perceived in a negative light, as with the woman whose son was killed in fighting with Pacha Khan Zadran's men. However, Pacha Khan nonetheless maintained an active following in the region, and in several instances we spoke with voters who claimed to dislike him personally, but admitted they would probably end up voting for him because of his ability to forcefully represent their community. While much of this could be attributed to tribal connections and the desire to vote as a bloc, it is also clear that the violence associated with Pacha Khan Zadran was in some instances considered a positive attribute. In Paktya, where a growing insurgency was increasingly being shaped by Haqqani network fighters coming over the border from Pakistan, the sense was that it might be helpful to have a dangerous and violent man in a position of power and formally representing the government in the province. If the situation worsened, such a figure would be likely to defend his supporters effectively, even if he did display tyrannical tendencies at times. Given the uncertain future of the government in Kabul, it might therefore be better to be on the side of Pacha Khan than to offend him by not voting for him.

In 2010 there also appeared to be a notable increase in the number of former commanders, militia leaders, and other more violent figures running as candidates for parliament compared to the 2005 elections.[22] This was partly due to the perceived declining likelihood of having to answer for crimes committed during the civil war and Taliban periods, which had put many candidates off running in 2005. By 2010 many notable war criminals had risen to high positions in the Karzai administration and worked closely with the American government, not to mention parliament's passing of an amnesty law in 2007 that all but removed prosecution from the agenda.[23]

At a local level, however, votes for such candidates seemed to indicate that the ability to deploy violence was increasingly serving as a political mobilizer. Several candidates in areas that we studied subtly emphasized violence in their campaigns. In one case, an older commander made up campaign posters that used a photo of himself from fifteen years earlier, when he was a young man, that showed him clearly dressed in the military garb associated with those who had fought from the mountains during the jihad. These allusions to violence were further highlighted by the increasing danger associated with campaigning, which seemed to suggest that only those willing to risk violence should run. In these cases, there seemed to be an understanding that for leaders in Afghanistan, the ability to resort to violence, if not desirable, was increasingly seen as at least expected.[24]

This was tied to a broader trend across Afghan politics of former fighters working to solidify their power. One government official in Qara Bagh complained that we should not waste time conducting research in the district shura because it was filled with "former warlords and commanders, who are mostly uneducated with bad backgrounds." He went on to explain how these figures presented a real problem for development in the area since they were interfering with district governance, private organizations, and NGOs as a way to further their own interests. In other cases, technocratic figures formed alliances with former militia leaders, often via kinship ties, as a way to demonstrate their strength. Both Karzai and Ashraf Ghani publically maintained close relationships with their respective brothers, who had much more of a military background and reputation for violence than they did themselves.

On a national level, Karzai was often accused of placing former commanders and those with violent backgrounds into increasingly prominent positions. In some instances the international community successfully pressured him to remove such officials, as in the case of Sher Mohammad Akhunzada, the former governor of Helmand Province. However, in other cases such changes were not made. Perhaps the most obvious case was Karzai's selection of Marshal Fahim to replace Ahmed Zia Massoud as one of his vice presidents in the 2009 election. Both were closely associated with former Panjshiri leader Ahmed Shah Massoud, Ahmed Zia as his brother and Marshal Fahim as a member of his inner circle, and the selection of both was clearly meant to court the Tajik and former Northern Alliance vote. However, beyond their association to Massoud, the similarities between the two figures end. Zia Massoud, while accused of embezzling a large amount of money during the Kabul Bank crisis, was considered by most as a relatively benign figure, who had fought during the jihad but did not distinguish himself, leaving most of the military decisions to his brother. On the other hand, many Afghans closely associated Marshal Fahim with violence. He and his men were accused of numerous crimes and he was widely perceived, even by Northern Alliance supporters, as something of a thug who had a fondness for dogfighting. Although international diplomats placed a considerable amount of pressure on Karzai to select an alternative, and had succeeded in forcing him to do this before the 2004 elections, he clearly considered it more helpful to have this violent figure onside than not. While Karzai's selection of political appointees with unsavory backgrounds may not have been directly related to the increased number of former commanders who were candidates in 2010, these phenomena were perceived by most voters as a part of a wider trend in which association with violence was once again an effective way to establish political power.

In predictable, stable political systems, elections reallocate political power without resorting to violence. By contrast, in violent moments of upheaval where multiple resources, such as government funds and the possibility to link into patronage networks in Kabul, are simultaneously made available, communities can gain by having leaders who are feared and respected by other groups. While most Afghan voters in 2010 did not feel that the political order was on the verge of collapse, the threat of serious upheaval was not far from the minds of many. This made figures like Pacha Khan Zadran, a man with a fearsome reputation if not necessarily an effective legislator, seem more attractive as representatives. Part of this trend was clearly the continued importance of violence as a demonstration of political capital in the struggle for sovereignty.

VIOLENCE UNDERMINING SOVEREIGNTY

Understanding the increasing role of violence in Afghan elections requires a shift in conventional understandings of elections as structural processes defining winners and losers, to focus on the part they play in a broader, more fluid struggle for sovereignty. Instead of being perceived as outside the process, violence was referred to by many people we spoke to as simply another aspect of electoral politics. This is particularly true when considering how violence can be used as a display of political capital, remarkably similar to how communities used voting tallies to bolster perceptions of community size and strength, as discussed in chapter 5. In a political landscape that was in constant flux, often making it difficult to get the measure of opponents, both methods offered a clear opportunity to demonstrate strength.

Elections are about competition, but when they are not transparent and predictable, violence can come to be seen as an acceptable or at least expected part of the process as opposed to an external, illegitimate force. In places where violence is a common everyday occurrence, there is therefore often no conceptual divide between violence and voting. As one woman in Paktya said during an interview in 2010:

> Elections are the beginning of the misfortunes of the people because since the beginning of the campaigns the security situation has deteriorated day by day, prices have jumped, people cannot go from one district to another, and innocent people are being murdered. Elections do not bring any hope for the people.

Particularly as the insurgency spread, many Afghans like this woman saw elections as simply another part of a political landscape that was becoming increasingly violent and volatile.

The presence of violence as an accepted aspect of the current political system in Afghanistan offered a convenient way for some political actors to reassert their political capital despite their failure at the polls. For example, when he lost his seat in the Wolesi Jirga, Pacha Khan Zadran exploited the uncertainty following the elections to make sure that this setback did not decrease his political power. His followers staged several protests, one of which resulted in the deaths of several Afghan National Army soldiers. This was augmented by the rumors that he had negotiated with Karzai to secure an alternative government post in exchange for staying onside. In public, he did little to hide the fact that he was using the threat of joining the insurgency to increase his power. On national television, he claimed that the elections had been decided in Dubai and in the Shahzada Bazaar, referring to the money-changing market in Kabul. This was accompanied by dark threats to reject the current political system entirely and side with the insurgency that he made in discussions with us:

> I said [to the attorney general] if the IEC will not count my votes, I will go to the mountain, and he said to me, we will also go with you. . . . I told Karzai that he should know who his friends are, and who his enemies are. . . . If influential people don't win the election, the government will get weaker day by day.

Since the Afghan government and the international military feared that the strength of the Haqqani network in Afghanistan would increase if Pacha Khan broke with the government, they both seemed willing to make serious concessions to keep him allied with Karzai. Although Pacha Khan lost the election, his violent reputation meant that he did not lose much influence or authority as a result. This was a further demonstration to voters observing this process that elections were not really about whether candidates won or lost, since authority could be grabbed in other ways, such as resorting to backroom negotiations or simply threatening violence.

* * *

Figures such as Pacha Khan Zadran did not simply undermine the election process; at an even more basic level, they caused all Afghans to reconsider their own visions of the state and political authority. Through their actions, they repeatedly demonstrated that the state certainly did not have a monopoly on violence or sovereignty, and that supposedly democratic reallocations of power in the form of elections could easily be renegotiated with the use of force, or at least the threat of it. For many Afghans, further evidence of this manipulation came in the chaotic aftermath of the 2010 elections.

8

"THEY MAKE THEIR ABLUTIONS WITH BOTTLED WATER"

Elites and the Decline of Accountability

THE FLEA AND THE ELEPHANT

"According to the Mullah," said the old man, "three things are unknown: death, doomsday, and the soul. But nowadays people say in this village that four things are unknown—these three, and the results of the provincial council elections."

Speaking at his simple mud brick home in a village two miles to the west of Jalalabad City, this former government driver reflected at length on how the previous year's provincial council polls had been "a mockery of an election," and were still, almost a year later, the subject of public ridicule. This was the reason, he said, why the people of Nangarhar could no longer take elections seriously and were discouraged about voting. "The provincial council, in theory, should be a bridge between the government and the people and should decrease the distance between them. In reality, it increases this distance."

In Nangarhar, the lead-up to the presidential and provincial council polls in August 2009 had taken place without too many irregularities—candidates had campaigned as usual, offering meals to supporters at rallies and buying clothes and turbans for entire villages of people to try to win votes. While would-be councillors' campaigns were more expensive and generated more tension than they had done in 2005, this was not unexpected, given the way in which the provincial council in this province had, unlike most others across the country, grown in prominence over the last four years. What was unprecedented, however, was the four-month delay between the polls themselves and the announcement of results. While results for the provincial council polls in other provinces had been announced relatively promptly, those for Nangarhar, for some reason, appeared problematic.

In conversations in the weeks after speaking with the elderly former government driver, many people across the province used the Pashtun word muamma, *or mystery, to describe the counting process, often alluding to the supposed changes and irregularities it had involved. One young student in the provincial capital Jalalabad described how the process had affected his friends' attitudes toward participating in future:*

> *Last year, the provincial council elections occurred with so much disorder and confusion, and the results were delayed for far too long. It was just a joke election, really. I've heard from many of my classmates that they won't take part in next elections, because it is useless. The members are preselected, elections are just a formality.*

In a similar vein, a computer repairman summed up the sense of disaffection that was echoed throughout the province in interviews with a wide sample of respondents:

> *People know that the government preselects the parliamentarians and provincial council members. If they vote in such elections, which are only conducted to fulfill formalities and show the world that there is democracy in Afghanistan, it means that they themselves dishonor the value of votes.*

The concern with elections being superficial, a façade to impress the outside world rather than a process of any substance, was commonly expressed by the people we interviewed and not dissimilar to the observations made by the woman parliamentarian from Nuristan we had interviewed earlier that had, by this point, become increasingly widespread.

Over lunch one day in an urban district, a local elder joined us for a midday meal, using a well-known proverb to explain his view of the situation. One particularly harsh winter, he said, a flea was experiencing great difficulty in trying to keep warm. Finding no other place to rest, the flea was forced to spend the night inside an elephant's trunk. As morning approached and the sun warmed the air outside, the flea flew out of the trunk and, being a well-mannered creature, thanked the elephant for his trouble. The elephant asked, surprised, "but why are you thanking me?" "Why, for the use of your trunk as a resting place last night!" said the flea. Replied the elephant, laughing: "My dear, I did not even feel you come into or fly out of my nose!"

Chuckling heartily at the joke, the elder continued to extend the metaphor: "Our council is just like the elephant's trunk; the public doesn't know who came into it and when they left it. The actual winners are told they are losers while losers become the winners."

But who was to blame for these changes and delays? In contrast to Paktya Province, where violence had plagued the electoral process in many districts and would have provided at least some reason for an extended or repeated vote-count, Nangarhar was relatively peaceful during the 2009 and 2010 polls. The insurgency was only beginning to grow more serious in the area as fighters were squeezed out of the south following the initial surge, which sent troops primarily to Kandahar and Helmand. Travel was still relatively easy: while at this point we were starting to rely increasingly on UN flights between Kabul and Paktya, instead of risking the drive, traveling by road to Nangarhar was rarely a problem. Clearly insecurity was not the primary reason for the delays in the electoral results.

Some Nangarharis talked at length about how the personal ambition and pride of the candidates themselves was the source of the problem, considered a smokescreen for widespread fraud. Others held the IEC responsible, alleging that the so-called "Independent" Electoral Commission was in cahoots with the government. The suspicion that international interests were somehow involved in changing the results was also common, with fingers primarily pointed at the United Nations. Some pointed to the importance of the area to the coalition as a key artery for supplies over the Khyber Pass. Common across all these conversations, however, was the acute sense that some kind of elite manipulation of the election had produced an outcome far removed from the democratic will of the people of Nangarhar.

This feeling of detachment and removal from the far-off decision-making in Kabul had been the overriding theme of our conversation with the elderly former government driver, back at the beginning of our research in the province. A combination of age and weak eyesight meant that he was unable to work, and his only

son was earning little as a soldier in the army. Under the jovial tones of his recol-
lections, there was an undercurrent of understated suffering: like many of his fellow
Afghans, the old man had experienced great hardship during his 60 years. With life
still proving a day-to-day struggle to find food and to repay creditors, any respite
that old age might have brought to the more fortunate seemed a distant, unattain-
able prospect.

The contrast between the old man's own lifestyle and his perception of the grow-
ing wealth of the province's supposedly elected representatives became evident in his
bitter response to a question about incumbents, specifically whether he thought they
would campaign for their seats again in the upcoming parliamentary elections:

> *Certainly they will nominate themselves, because they have tasted the deli-*
> *cious food, lived in the extravagant buildings, driven the luxury cars, and*
> *experienced the cool weather of our beloved Kabul, alongside devouring the*
> *flesh of Afghans and the needs of the people; how will they not stand for elec-*
> *tion again? And the new candidates will be even more desperate to claim seats*
> *in parliament, because they also want to be like the former parliamentarians.*
> *They also want to live, eat, and drink like them. Until they became parlia-*
> *mentarians, these people were not even able to find water in dirty lakes here,*
> *but today in Kabul they make their ablutions with bottled water; here there*
> *was not even a plastic mat in their home, but there they walk on the carpets*
> *with their shoes on; here people don't listen to them, but there a microphone is*
> *set up to broadcast their voices. Here they are not even given clover to eat, but*
> *there they eat half a chicken and leave the rest. Here they wipe their hands*
> *with their clothes, but there they clean them with tissues. Here, they cannot*
> *even find bread for themselves, but there they eat lamb and beef. How will*
> *they not nominate themselves?*

As the conversation ended, the old man's comments turned toward the subject of
the 2010 parliamentary elections due to take place in a couple of months' time.
What none of us in his small house knew at the time was that these elections
would expand to a national scale the delays and confusion of the Nangarhar
Provincial Council debacle, spreading the growing sense of public alienation
across the entire country.

DECLINING ACCOUNTABILITY

People's sense of distance from an electoral process they increasingly felt was manipulated by unaccountable elites rang loud and clear throughout our conversations with Afghans in 2009 and, to a much greater degree, following elections in 2010. Across rural and urban areas, in districts both secure and insecure and among people of all age groups, there was a growing sense of disaffection with the perceived disconnect between the vote itself on the one hand, and those "voted" into office on the other. This did not necessarily translate into a complete rejection of elections: before the polls in 2010, many still felt that the act of voting was so important that it was worth taking part regardless of known problems in the system and threats of violence by insurgents. However, this determination in the face of an increasingly ambiguous process became a loss of faith in the entire political system for many across all sectors of the population.

It was not just a flawed voting process that contributed to this feeling. For urban residents especially, people we spoke to in the cities of Kabul, Mazar, and Jalalabad, whose access to television and radio broadcasts of current political affairs was significantly greater than their rural compatriots, elections were just part of a long-running story of declining accountability, in part the result of a personalized, presidential system. The aftermath of the presidential elections in 2009 solidified concerns about external interference alongside widespread fraud. In early 2010, the newly reelected president used a presidential decree to change an already flawed electoral law overnight and without warning. Shifts in the proposed timing for the parliamentary elections from spring to September prompted rumors of executive and international manipulation. Standoffs between the parliament and the executive in the spring of 2010 were widely seen by our urban respondents as attempts by parliamentarians to garner the limelight in advance of their reelection campaigns, and as time-wasting tricks on the part of a president whose attempts to shift attention away from his own failings were becoming more and more elaborate. Before the elections, seemingly random or unexplained disqualifications of polling centers across the country in "insecure" areas attracted angry questions from parliamentarians and their constituents, and later the delays in the announcement of final parliamentary results in the fall of 2010 were to be followed by the president's executive decision to create a new institution to investigate fraud—the Special Court—whose authority would undermine that of both the IEC and ECC.

Among other events, these formed a cumulative picture of ambiguity and intrigue that were increasingly perceived by Afghans as vehicles for the political elite to manipulate Afghanistan's democratic process. Together, they suggested a system where the rules appeared to be determined through negotiations at the highest level—a lofty, hazy realm of political bargains to which very few Afghans had any hope of ascending.

2009: BUYING, SELLING, AND BARGAINING

In response to the apparent shock of international actors and the media at the "discovery" of widespread fraud in the 2009 elections, many Afghans shook their heads in disbelief. Had these people not seen the way voter registration was carried out? Had they really held complete faith in a weak electoral commission headed by a close friend of the president? Had they not heard of the violent attacks that had been taking place in the provinces in the run-up to elections, or seen just how many districts were considered too insecure to host polling centers? For local observers and participants in the 2009 elections, fraud, essentially, was inevitable. Most shocking for many was the lack of response by the international community.

Inevitability, however, is different from acceptability: the accounts we heard from voters after the elections were mixed in terms of how they perceived this fraud. Some laughed when they referred to the practice of candidate's representatives cleaning the ink off people's fingers with bleach and sending them back to the polling station for a second vote, a 500 Afghani note in their pocket.[1] Others were quite resigned to accepting cash for votes, particularly for the provincial council election—as one man in Nangarhar told us, "on the morning of the election a man came to my home and asked me who I was going to vote for. I told him as joke that I would give my vote to the candidate who would give me money for it. He immediately gave me 500 Afs. I promised to vote for him and I did."

To some extent, then, and for some people, buying votes was part and parcel of the whole event: this was not just about manipulation by elites, but about how much individual voters could make out of the opportunity. However, others were furious about the scale of fraud—the discovery of stuffed ballot boxes, for example, and hijacking by corrupt officials of entire polling centers. As one village elder described with some vehemence (prompting one of the interview team to express concern over his health), "In a nearby village no one came to the polling station for voting until noon, and then the election officers spilled the ink on the ground and filled all the polling boxes themselves for their favorite candidates."

Nevertheless, as the results for the presidential elections began to flow in, it was the narrative of fraud rather than its actual incidence that became an important strategic tool in the fight for losing candidates to regain their credibility. Accusations of massive-scale fraudulent activity, now plausible given its widespread actual occurrence, were important ways for the largely Tajik anti-Karzai bloc to reassert its power and undermine Karzai's post-election credibility. The strategic nature of such allegations was evident in how quickly formal and informal allegations increased in the weeks after the election. In the days immediately following the polls, the ECC had received only twenty or so reports of fraudulent activity nationwide. As it became apparent that Abdullah had gained fewer votes than Karzai in official preliminary counts announced gradually by the IEC, increasing numbers of allegations were submitted to the ECC, with the number eventually reaching over 2,000. The fact that such a large number of complaints were lodged in the later stages of the counting process and not immediately following the polls indicates an attempt to gain as much political capital as possible through the suggestion that Karzai's victory was illegitimate. This was heightened by Abdullah's appeal to the international community, which eventually helped lead to the proposal for a runoff. For those opposed to Karzai, this was the ultimate achievement: through their successful political maneuvering, they had managed to achieve a point of influence in a new election, in spite of having actually lost the election in terms of number of votes received.

The processes that led to the call for a runoff election involved not just the protestations of Abdullah and his supporters but also the intervention of international diplomats, whose activities were perceived by many Afghans as interference in and manipulation of electoral results.[2] Senator John Kerry's visit to the presidential palace was directly linked by many to Karzai's concession to hold a runoff, and to Abdullah's subsequent decision to step down from the race.[3] Withdrawing was also a savvy strategy since beyond the unlikelihood of Abdullah winning a runoff, by refusing to participate in the second round, he was able to portray himself as taking the higher moral ground, which later allowed him to question the legitimacy of the entire process. Yet even this decision was perceived by some to be the result of pressure from international actors keen to avoid another costly election.

As we found in research conducted after the 2009 elections, people's view of the role played by international actors in the elections was an increasingly negative one. For example, one man following the 2009 elections declared, "I personally know that my vote is useless. Even though I did vote, I am sure that whatever happens is the decision of the foreigners."[4] While far from a new perspective—as Afghan suspicions of the lengthening foreign presence had been accumulating for some time—this still highlights how people were increasingly coming to see a process designed and promised to be people-led as determined by bargaining and manipulation taking place beyond their control or influence.

As Karzai's second term of office began in November 2009, complaints about the international community's role in the elections soon gave way to concerns that the president was not fulfilling the promises he had made to different ethnic groups. In the run-up to his reelection, Karzai had made bargains with the leaders of these groups, exchanging electoral support for ministerial cabinet positions, among other perks. However, by the time parliament was due to take its winter recess, a series of delays and parliamentary rejections of ministerial nominees had left these promises appearing increasingly empty. In addition, they had served to distract parliamentarians from another pressing issue: the revision of the electoral law.

A STRATEGIC MANIPULATIONOF THE LEGAL FRAMEWORK: CHANGES TO THE ELECTORAL LAW

A defining feature of Afghanistan's political system is its emphasis on presidentialism. In part the result of a concern to ensure stability and reduce the risk of ethnic conflict, and in part attempting to resemble the popular, peaceful monarchic regime of Zahir Shah, the presidential system adopted during the Bonn process assigned a great deal of political power to the single person of the president. In choosing this system, implicit assumptions were made by international diplomats and technical experts about where and how aid funds should be allocated, and the direction and end-goals of diplomatic efforts. The reasoning was that a presidential system would be more amenable to external influence and that, perhaps, given Afghanistan's ethnic composition and recent internal conflict, the country was not ready for a political system in which power was more devolved. Once the system was established, however, it was easily molded and reshaped by the Afghan political elite to promote patronage networks that solidified their own interests.

Presidential systems in general have a tendency to personalize leadership and to solidify control in the hands of one individual. As Juan Linz explains, whereas in parliamentary democracies, a prime minister can never address "the people" as an individual, without deference to their elected representatives, a president is in him- or herself an embodiment of the state. Indeed, "[h]e is not only the holder of executive power but also the symbolic head of state and can be removed between elections only by the drastic step of impeachment."[5] This, it is argued, can facilitate among the populace the subtle convergence of perceptions of stability with the persona of the president.

In Afghanistan, a country beset with frequent regime change over the last half century, people's desire for stability has understandably been paramount. A number of voters spoke on Election Day in 2009 of Karzai as the only candidate who could keep the peace and ensure a sense of stability (in spite of the fact that, at this point, the security situation in the country had worsened considerably since he was first elected). Even if the presidential system had delivered on its perceived connection with stability, however, it had also brought with it the considerable risk of the consolidation of executive power. Although some checks against the president's absolute political control were included in the constitution, such as the formation of an elected parliament with the ability to veto a presidential decree with a two-thirds majority, these relied on one critical assumption: the parliament's ability to withstand executive pressure and organize itself. This did not materialize.

* * *

The Afghan electoral law had never been particularly innovative or progressive. While the innate simplicity of the electoral system it espoused allowed high voter turnout in the short-term, this system incorporated no provisions for political development—the expansion of participation through parties, for example. As a whole, the law constituted a jumbled mix of global trends, such as the upholding of the constitutional provision for reserved seats for women, combined with a few superficial concessions to the Afghan context, including the selection of one third of the senate members through executive appointment.[6] Ratified in 2004, the law was designed, largely by international experts keen to implement an impending election, as a prototype: changes could always be made later when there was more time.

Changes, it transpired, would first come in the form of government revisions brought before parliament in spring 2008. Draft proposals included the inclusion of space on the ballot for official party affiliation, and the reduction in size of the largest electoral constituencies. A subcommittee of the legislative affairs committee, headed by Salih Mohammad Registani, a parliamentarian for Panjshir, was tasked with the consideration and amendment of this draft before it was presented to parliament for discussion. This group introduced significant further alterations, primarily calling for a change in the SNTV (Single Non-Transferable Vote) system, discussed in chapter 3. They suggested a parallel SNTV and party list system, in which 100 seats would be reserved for party candidates while the rest would remain free for so-called independent competitors. Experts in international organizations working on elections and legislative capacity-building had advised Registani that 100 seats might be too ambitious given the vehement attachment of many existing legislators to their "independent" status. Further, with 100 seats reserved for parties, 68 for women and ten for Kuchi candidates, few (71) would remain for independent competition. As one international consultant complained to us at the time, "he should have asked for 40 and then accepted 20. He made a mess of the whole thing, really."

As expected, the majority of the proposed changes were flatly rejected by the parliament in the plenary session on April 2 (although a provision was passed to include space for party affiliation on ballot papers). However, this may have had more to do with parliamentarians' concerns about getting reelected than with their views on the structure of the political system as a whole. There were also rumors of executive intervention persuading parliamentarians to vote against the bill. It was also widely known among national and international analysts that the then-chairman of the IEC, Azizullah Ludin, was not only a close ally of the president but also a strong opponent of parties in his own right. According to one international source, the IEC had flatly refused to send invitations to training on voter registration to party representatives, and in general were "trying not to allow parties to compete on a level playing field."

As it turned out, the attempt to change the law in favor of greater party representation was completely overshadowed by a seismic rift in the plenary caused by an entirely separate issue. Article 9 of the electoral law allowed ten reserved seats for Kuchi parliamentarians and considered them to represent a national constituency in its own right, rather than restricting them to certain provinces as was the case for all other candidates. Traditionally a nomadic group, the Kuchis established annual migration routes historically traversed by entire tribes, from the scorching southern plains to the cooler, fertile central highlands. Problematically, however, this often resulted in their grazing sizable herds of cattle on land occupied by others. Tensions lingered particularly from the late nineteenth century when land was reallocated by Abdur Rahman Khan, with many Pashtun Kuchis benefiting at the expense of Hazaras and other smaller minorities.

While many of these conflicts remain simmering under the surface of Afghan politics, much has changed since the days when almost all Kuchis would follow a nomadic or seminomadic existence, and for many Kuchi families the advantages of staying in one location have increasingly outweighed the need to travel.[7] This was certainly the case for one family we interviewed in Kabul in 2006. Contrary to the stereotypes of tents, camels, and girls in brightly colored dresses playing in traveler settlements on the outskirts of the city, the interview took place in a cozy flat in Macroyan, the popular Russian-built apartment blocks toward the center of Kabul, complete with central heating. Some estimates suggest that only around 60 percent of Kuchis now move around the country on a regular basis, as compared to 40 percent who are former pastoralists, now settled, though these figures are difficult to substantiate.[8] This, probably fueled also by tensions over land ownership in the central highlands, prompted a number of Hazara, Tajik, and Uzbek parliamentarians to push for a change in the law to remove the reserved seats enjoyed by Kuchi candidates. The provision of allocated seats meant that the Kuchi family living in Kabul could vote for a Kuchi candidate from any part of the country, whereas a family of Hazara migrants from Ghazni living in Kabul would have to vote for a candidate from Kabul. The electoral law also does not require that Kuchis prove their Kuchi heritage, leading to some candidates campaigning for Kuchi seats whose connections to the minority are tenuous at best. In response to this demand for change, a protracted argument ensued, leading to a plenary vote which favored the continuation of Article 9. This prompted a walkout by those legislators angry at the result of the vote, which eventually turned into a month-long boycott of about 100 representatives that would severely hinder proceedings on the electoral law and legislative affairs in general.

Debates in the legislature considering this issue and further amendments to the law dragged on over the following year and remained unresolved when parliament adjourned for recess in January 2010. At this point, it was too late to make changes in time for the next electoral cycle—or so people thought. A clause in the constitution stipulates that changes may not be made to the electoral law within the last year of the legislative period before the election.[9] While worded in a slightly ambiguous manner, this was widely assumed to prohibit changes at this point, with a parliamentary poll due later the same year. As would become clear, however, there were ways to evade this stipulation.

KARZAI STEPS IN

Parliament's inability to decide on the law before recess somewhat conveniently opened a window for change in the form of a constitutional loophole allowing presidential decrees to be enacted in the absence of a response from parliament after fifteen days.[10] Being on leave for six weeks, there was no way for parliament to prevent a decree made during this time from becoming law. This opened the way for Karzai to make changes to the electoral law as he saw fit. While this still contradicted the requirement that no changes be made to the law within a year of an election, there was no way of establishing which constitutional clause should stand above the other, particularly since the Supreme Court was closely allied with Karzai. This clearly political maneuver sent a stark message to the Afghan population: the constitution was a malleable document that could be configured to the advantage of the president, and parliament, in its disorganized state, could offer no response to such executive manipulation.

Further to this, the president's decreed changes to the law also turned out to be somewhat sensational. Presenting a revised version of the law to his cabinet on February 7, 2010, he proposed a number of additions, including the exclusion of international members from the ECC, and the stipulation that, should there not be enough women in a given province to fill the reserved seats, the IEC should take measures to prevent these seats from remaining empty.[11] Additional criteria were also introduced for those wanting to run as presidential and parliamentary candidates, including the provision that candidates for the presidency should not have suffered from "mental diseases." Changes to campaign deposits were also made, raising the amount of money required to register as a candidate in an attempt to limit the pool of potential competitors.

The first of these measures caused immediate consternation among international actors, for whom the prospect of paying for another potentially fraudulent election was politically untenable, let alone morally abhorrent. One diplomat reportedly compared Karzai's decree to making an obscene hand gesture toward the international community that had incidentally spent millions implementing elections in Afghanistan.[12] As the news came in, it triggered what was fast becoming a characteristic international reaction to Karzai's eccentric and apparently spontaneous political shock tactics. First, tangible shockwaves rippled through the donor community, interrupting dinner parties with urgent messages on BlackBerries vibrating in chorus. This was quickly followed by a series of emergency meetings and consultations between political advisors and ambassadors—then, an attempt to coerce the president into changing his mind or backing down, followed by a swiftly developed prioritization of basic conditions. In this case, the task of negotiation fell to UN officials, who were able to bring about some, but not all, of the desired alterations to the president's version of the law, including new wording that opened the possibility for international involvement at a senior level in the ECC. A similar train of events had characterized international reactions to the Shia Personal Status Law in 2009, in which the rights of Afghan women had been significantly compromised.[13]

The dilemma of how to respond to these situations often left internationals in a no-win position: in this and other scenarios, any deal securing a comedown from the president's original, extreme condition was generally considered better than no deal at all. But in rushing to come up with responses that have likely already been anticipated by the president in the first place, international actors have demonstrated time and again that they are an integral part of the national-level process of elite political bargaining and manipulation. While endeavoring to restrict their involvement in electoral issues to one of technical support, internationals were persistently drawn into the messy politics that surround such processes—whether they liked it or not. And although their interventions were often justified in the name of securing or stabilizing Afghanistan or ensuring smooth elections, in the eyes of ordinary voters they could just as easily have been categorized as "manipulation" as the actions of the president and his cronies. This further consolidated the perception among many Afghans that politics takes place in a contained, impenetrable space.

However, for a number of Afghans, Karzai's move to exclude internationals from the ECC was a worrying sign. Especially in conversations with members of smaller ethnic minorities, people expressed their concern about losing a relatively impartial voice on the commission, whose decisions would not be swayed by ethnic or other internal considerations. As one Hazara parliamentarian told us in early 2010, "In the Complaints Commission, I would prefer there to be international members rather than only Afghans, because internationals don't have ethnic biases in Afghanistan. If they could be present in the commission alongside Afghan members, this would be the best possible outcome." This sentiment was echoed even in more rural areas, where in spite of fiercely criticizing international interference, people often supported the presence of foreign observers as unbiased monitors. While the view of internationals as impartial arbiters was not necessarily consistently voiced across the spectrum of perspectives we gathered during interviews, this was nevertheless one area that many Afghans considered a legitimate space for international assistance.

In many respects, the way in which the president was able to manipulate the system in this manner can again be linked to the constitution and the presidential system it prescribes, because of the sense of legitimacy and absolute authority it confers to the person of the president. As Linz explains,

> The conviction that [the president] possesses independent authority and a popular mandate is likely to imbue a president with a sense of power and mission, even if the plurality that elected him is a slender one. Given such assumptions about his standing and role, he will find the inevitable opposition to his policies far more irksome and demoralizing than would a prime minister, who knows himself to be but the spokesman for a temporary governing coalition rather than the voice of the nation or the tribune of the people.[14]

Such analysis seems to summarize neatly the ways in which Karzai reacted to the controversy surrounding his own reelection in 2009, what he was widely reported to have perceived as personal affronts to his standing as leader. This sense only grew as security concerns limited movement around the country and the media increasingly described Karzai as politically and socially isolated in the presidential palace, which had literally become a military installation.[15]

One of the trends that respondents expressed the most frustration over during this period was that as they increasingly concluded that Karzai was manipulating elections from the highest political levels, more locally a series of commanders and elders were similarly perceived as silencing opposition and solidifying their own patronage networks. For these local leaders, Karzai served as a model for how insecurity could be used as an excuse for increasingly limiting the access of less powerful individuals to political discussion. Across the country, as it became clear that development funds and various other political resources were not being distributed evenly, local commanders became increasingly emboldened in their efforts to exclude ordinary Afghans.

As a result of these trends, in discussions over *destarkhans* and dinner tables in both Afghan and international circles in Kabul, the question turned to motive: What was behind Karzai's latest chess move? Would there be wider repercussions? Among the different theories on what might be behind the president's removal of internationals from the ECC, one view became common: this was a direct retaliation for the embarrassment caused by the international condemnation of widespread fraud in the president's own election six months earlier, and the runoff election that resulted. Whether this was the actual key motivation or not, this was a bad sign for parliamentarians and others who hoped to counterbalance the power of the presidency. Many of these figures were increasingly caught in an executive stranglehold that threatened to stifle their independence as a legislative body and as individual candidates in the upcoming parliamentary elections.

STRATEGIC, AMBIGUOUS TIMING

September 18, 2010: parliamentary Election Day. In Kabul the atmosphere was one of wary uncertainty with rumors of rockets and other attacks. In certain parts of the city, streams of voters began to emerge around 10 a.m., and in some schools and mosques there was soon a steady flow of participants queuing to cast their votes. In other areas, this was more of a trickle, drying up around lunchtime and beginning again, often with a group of women, once the midday meal had been finished and cleared away. At one point in the early morning, distant explosions echoed from the east of the city, but most polling centers remained secure, heavily guarded primarily by national security forces. Throughout the day, the city's windows were rattled almost continuously by the frequent thunder of low-flying Chinooks, providing a sobering soundtrack to the otherwise eerie calm. When voting and conversations in polling centers concluded, the citizens of Kabul returned to their homes and workplaces, one finger blackened, to continue discussions with relatives, friends, and colleagues.

At first glance, a voter turnout of approximately 30 percent of the population (4.2 million)[16] and candidate numbers exceeding 2,500 would seem to indicate a potentially credible, participatory election for Afghanistan's new parliament, especially since the vote was taking place in the shadow of the fraud and violence of 2009's poll. Yet for many Afghans, the parliamentary polls of 2010 ultimately contributed to an increasing sense of alienation from their government. While a number of Kabul residents we talked to had taken part with at least some optimism, the series of events after Election Day would lead to a sense of disillusionment, exacerbated in particular by a series of delays that signaled to many that results were negotiated, and not publicly determined.

From as early as 2008, parliamentarians had been concerned about the timing of the elections and whether or not they should be held simultaneously with the presidential polls in 2009. In a move that clearly demonstrated the hierarchies within parliament, the president met with Speaker Qanooni, the Hazara leader Mohaqqeq, and the powerful ex-mujahideen commander Sayyaf at the end of March 2008 to discuss the issue. As a result, Qanooni was forced to rebut the accusations of some representatives that a secret bargain had been made between the leaders, though according to one report a number of legislators remained deeply suspicious about the matter.[17] Whether or not such a bargain was in place, there was certainly the perception and sometimes a publicly voiced accusation among parliamentarians that electoral timing was being negotiated behind closed doors.

An official schedule for elections was in fact already established by the constitution, determining that presidential and parliamentary elections be held separately on account of their identical-length terms (five years) and their staggered beginning, in 2004 and 2005, respectively. However, there was of course no way to guarantee that this timeline would be followed in practice. Once again the wording in the constitution was odd, stating an approximate date for polls which were impossible in some provinces at the specified time of year due to severe weather conditions.[18]

Furthermore, delays had taken place in the first rounds of both sets of elections, setting a precedent for some flexibility. As it happened, delays occurred once again—this time, largely as a result of international pressure. In December 2009, Karzai had made clear to international actors his intention of holding elections on time, on May 18 of the next year, citing his commitment to upholding the constitution. This raised significant concerns among internationals, given security problems and the prospect of too little time in which to implement much-needed reform. Nevertheless, the IEC duly established a timetable for elections to be held in May and started registering sitting parliamentarians who wanted to run again. However, to the relief of international donors, IEC officials announced in a statement on January 24 that, due to security concerns and a lack of pledged funds, the election would be delayed until September 18. The series of conflicting statements made by the president, the IEC, and international actors over the winter months created a palpable sense of confusion in parliament, with representatives hurrying to register on lists and collect signatures from constituents without actually knowing whether or not this would guarantee them a place as a candidate. While, ultimately, an agreement was made to delay elections until September—intentionally or not, by first appearing to support the constitutionally-determined date, and then supporting a delay—Karzai pulled both the IEC and various international actors into the debate, giving voters and potential candidates the sense that multiple groups were working to manipulate the process.

But if the period before the polls was rife with confusion, it was as nothing compared to their aftermath. To begin with, the actual results of the polls dribbled out in an erratic and highly unpredictable, yet public, fashion. The first unofficial results were released just five days following the polls, based on the accumulated results of counts at individual polling centers. These were posted first on bright pink pages outside the polling centers before certified copies were sent to district counting offices—a new system for 2009 and 2010 introduced by parliament in place of the more centralized approach international experts had pushed for in 2004 and 2005. The IEC was soon

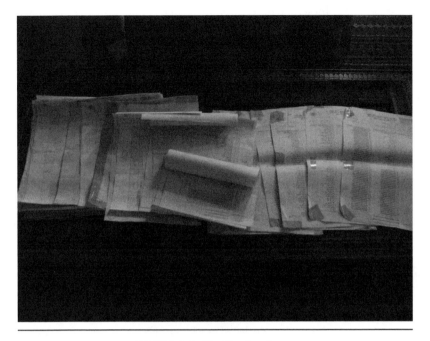

FIGURE 8.1 Certification sheets.

to announce, however, that these were not the official final results, which would be delayed due to complications in the counting process. This confused local communities, which had already seen the pink certification sheets. Such political information, however, was clearly valuable, and in one area we studied a local commander showed us official result sheets that his supporters had torn down from about twenty polling stations in the area. He was threatening to bring these to the IEC if the results were not to his liking, but also implied that if candidates that he supported had won, the potentially manipulated results should be kept from public view. Dealing with such an opaque system, the commander had decided that hiding and controlling the information on the certification sheets was the best initial plan, even if he was unsure how he might eventually use it.

Complicating strategies like these, a month later on October 20, the IEC released the preliminary list of winning candidates but did not certify these as "final." These, and other election-related announcements were made at busy press conferences at the Intercontinental Hotel, a former favorite haunt of international journalists, which would be stormed and briefly held by a group of insurgent figures a few months later. Crowds of national and international press representatives, along with a number of researchers and analysts including ourselves, would typically fill the largest of available conference rooms at the hotel, jostling for space at the front with cameras and microphones poised, only to be kept waiting for what was often a period of up to an hour for the officials to arrive. IEC representatives seemed to relish the media attention, and the announcements were widely broadcast across Afghanistan, adding to interest in the process but also making changes and manipulation all the more public.

At a local level, the rumor mill was in full swing, with different communities speculating over whether the delay would benefit their favored candidates or set them back. Many feared the worst. On November 24, a month after originally planned, the IEC announced its final results, which turned out to replace many of those originally listed as winners. Even these results, however, did not include those from the insecure and ethnically divided province of Ghazni, where the initially announced results indicated that all eleven allocated seats had been won by Hazara candidates. Although there was some speculation that these results would be changed, confirmation was given on December 1 that Hazaras had indeed swept the province.

These time lags between the announcements of different sets of results heightened suspicions among Afghans that the election's outcome was being negotiated at the highest levels. This suspicion was largely confirmed for many closely observing the process by the sometimes dramatic change in vote counts from their original posted figures at polling stations to those that were announced as initial results by the IEC, and again in some cases by the time the final results list came out. As one candidate in Kabul described,

In [one] polling station, in box number 5, I had 21 votes but when the results were announced I had no votes. . . . I complained to the ECC but . . . [t]hey very unpleasantly told me to put on my shoes [to leave] and still my complaint is unresolved. . . . I had observers in some polling stations around our area and they called me frequently to tell me that I had 30 or 20 or 15 votes. But when I saw after the counting that I had no votes from these polling stations, I was really disappointed and I understood that this election was not transparent for candidates like me, because I don't have enough money or influence to monitor the whole counting process.[19]

For many, the delays signified not technical issues with the counting and announcement of votes, but negotiation and political compromise among powerful actors. This sense would become stronger as the process continued, particularly as the delay involving Ghazni rolled on.

In Ghazni, the principal problem lay in the discrepancy between the proportion of Hazara residents in the province—largely thought (although no official statistics exist) to be around 50 percent of the total population, the rest of the province being composed primarily of Pashtuns[20]—and the number of seats gained in the elections—all of them. Analysts at the time produced numerous theories as to why this was the case, although it was generally agreed that intimidation by insurgent groups in Pashtun areas had persuaded many Pashtuns that voting simply was not worth the risk. In Ghazni as a whole, 204 of the 857 proposed polling stations did not actually open on Election Day, the highest proportion (23.8 percent) of closed polling stations in any province.[21] This closure occurred across both Pashtun and Hazara districts, however. Another explanation was that Hazaras were simply more organized in their political campaigning, and that, as was the case in Kabul, community leaders had allocated certain geographic areas to specific candidates in which to collect votes. Under the guidance of their leaders Mohaqqeq and Khalili and in the face of the conflict for land with the Kuchi minority, Hazara voters could have been more disciplined and determined to vote for their own candidates. In either case, the victory of so many Hazara candidates was a considerable problem for Karzai in particular, since it appeared to demonstrate his weakness in supporting his own, Pashtun ethnicity. This was compounded by the fact that Hazara leaders—who had been loyal to Karzai early in his presidency—had increasingly distanced themselves from him, especially since he had failed to deliver on some of his electoral campaign promises to the group. Although the results stood, their delayed announcement had irrevocably stoked a sense that votes were being tweaked to find an appropriate political solution.[22]

THE NON-INAUGURATION OF PARLIAMENT AND POLITICAL LIMBO

In addition to the issues around the announcement of results, the delays to the inauguration of the new parliament particularly offered yet more evidence to parliamentarians and voters alike that the system was being manipulated from the top down, contributing to a more general erosion by elite interference of the fledgling democratic institutions that has been established in the wake of the intervention. Newly certified parliamentarians were already taking part in a UN-sponsored week-long training event at the Intercontinental Hotel when the announcement came from the presidential office on January 19, 2011, that the inauguration—scheduled for the 23rd—would not take place as planned. For many, this last-minute declaration came as a complete surprise. Although the president had declared as early as December that he was creating a "Special Court" to deal with widespread fraud (somewhat ironically given the lack of such an institution following his own election), this generated little concern since it was widely assumed that his ability to enforce such an investigation and act on its findings would be limited. The sudden announcement caused panic at the Intercontinental; training sessions were abandoned as lengthy speeches railing against the president were made by some (if, notably, not all) eminent parliamentarians and political or ethnic leaders. Representatives were divided into discussion groups, and a general consensus to push for inauguration as soon as possible developed. Abdul Rasul Sayyaf was absent during most of these debates, assigning himself the task of mediating with the president, as had been his custom throughout the first parliamentary term (it is possible that this too was a planned move, in the hope that Karzai might in turn be persuaded to back his campaign for the position of first deputy speaker when the parliament had finally convened).

When the announcement was made, the president was in Russia for talks with President Dmitry Medvedev, but returned early to receive angry parliamentarians at the palace. In a typical political move for which Karzai was now becoming known, his initial insistence that the inauguration be delayed by first one and then two months had the intended effect of inciting angry opposition, after which the compromise of a few days' delay seemed a generous, if not apologetic, withdrawal. These negotiations were also heavily laden with political symbolism as representatives were forced to gather at the presidential palace where Karzai essentially "hosted" them, while listening to their grievances, as in previous eras the king had done in the same location. Simply presiding over the negotiations reaffirmed Karzai's dominance in the political system.

While eventually yielding, Karzai did insist on one key condition in allowing the inauguration to proceed: the acceptance by parliamentarians not only of the legitimacy of the Special Court but of the legitimacy of any findings resulting from its investigations. While neither the Special Court nor the delayed inauguration were technically permissible under the constitution, this nevertheless put parliamentarians in a difficult position and one that produced divisions in their ranks. On the one hand, if individual legislators had nothing to fear in terms of fraud allegations, then surely they had no need to worry about the findings of whatever institution the president might whimsically create. On the other hand, it was difficult to know how trustworthy the Special Court would actually be, and in particular whether its findings would be based on objective examination of the evidence at hand, or on other, more politically motivated factors. Furthermore, allowing Karzai to create such an unconstitutional body created a dangerous precedent.

All of these proceedings were reported in the Afghan press, but for many parliamentarians, not to mention the Afghan public, this series of negotiations was confusing, nontransparent, and full of intrigue. What was Sayyaf's role in all of this? Would the Pashtun parliamentarians continue to support Karzai? Were Abdullah or any of the other politicians who had recently spoken out against the administration involved in fermenting opposition? Would voters riot as they had done in Iran eighteen months before, an event often discussed locally? Was this part of a wider conspiracy by the Karzai government and the international community to disband parliament so that new elections could be held in an attempt to foster reconciliation with the

Taliban? Was this the first step in Karzai's attempting to make himself president for life?

Despite all these questions, real facts were difficult to come by. Karzai's office made few statements, which tended to be fairly opaque in any case, while on the other end of the spectrum many lower-level parliamentarians were happy to take advantage of the free publicity and appear on numerous Afghan talk shows. In many of these instances, it was useful for these leaders to appear much more connected than they actually were (as we saw with other local leaders in chapter 5).

Once again typical for Karzai's political actions and decisions, a resolution seemed to come suddenly and without full explanation—it was decided, somehow, that the inauguration would take place on January 26, only three days after it was originally scheduled. For many parliamentarians, this appeared to be the best solution at the time—once they were inaugurated, it would be difficult for Karzai to remove them from office even with the supposed results of the Special Court's investigation in hand. However, the most critical message emerging from this debacle was not the end-result of negotiations, which appeared (and were certainly reported as being) in parliament's favor. Rather, it was the clear demonstration of the president's ability to intervene in, alter, and delay what should have been a constitutionally-determined process. Karzai's use of the inauguration—previously seen as a largely symbolic act—as a bargaining chip made it seem to many in the Afghan public that it was he who truly controlled parliament and could even determine whether or not they met at all. This was posturing at its most effective—a display of presidential power and, following Linz's analysis, perhaps payback for what had been a highly humiliating experience in his own, fraudulent election.

ADDING INSTITUTIONS AND BENDING RULES: ELITE MANIPULATION AT THE VERY TOP

On the surface, Karzai's creation of a Special Court to overrule IEC and ECC decisions was a clear demonstration of authoritarian intervention in reaction to a displeasing electoral result. In some senses, this is exactly what the new institution symbolized, and it was certainly perceived as such by many Afghans at the time. However, it also needs to be considered within a broader context. Looking back at the methods parliamentarians, for example, have used in attempting to overcome difficult situations, boycotts, or deadlock in legislative sessions, there has been an overwhelming tendency to resort to the creation of new committees and subcommittees with the sole purpose of resolving the particular issue at stake. This has appeared as a solution based on consensus and delay—a means to continue with the business of the day while the problem is referred to another, often smaller body for more extended discussion. Although the likelihood of issues actually being solved in this manner is generally slim, in a sense this is often secondary to the more immediate need to overcome deadlock and defer the problem for an indefinite period of time.

Revisiting briefly the case of the 2008 electoral law debacle provides a telling example of this tendency. Here, a new committee was formed to help overcome the boycott of parliament by 100 Hazara, Tajik, and Uzbek parliamentarians, but essentially failed to solve the debate at the heart of the problem. In late March of that year, the government's first draft of revisions to the electoral law was being considered by Registani's subcommittee—charged only with the task of reviewing and amending the law. In the debate following the subcommittee's presentation of the amended version to parliament in early April, tensions rose over the question of Kuchi-allocated seats, ultimately resulting in the mass boycott of parliament. In response, an ad hoc committee headed by another prominent parliamentarian was formed to deal with the contentious issue. According to the parliamentary rules of procedure, the formation of ad hoc committees is permissible as means to "examine special issues" and thus the creation of this group was procedurally legitimate.[23]

However, in spite of discussions with both sides, the new body was unable to come to a resolution through its examination of the issue. By the end of the month, the head of the new committee had resigned and his committee was dissolved, only to be replaced by another committee, this time made up of eight parliamentarians selected by Speaker Qanooni. This was apparently instigated by Qanooni alone and was explicitly formed to *negotiate* between the two groups, taking on a new role entirely. Some progress was made as a result—the committee developed a series of concessions to the boy-cotting parliamentarians that were then agreed by a group of ten legislators from each side, along with parliament's Administrative Board. These concessions—which included the requirement of an apology from a leading Kuchi parliamentarian who had made ethnically divisive comments—resolved the boycott, bringing the disaffected parliamentarians back to their seats on May 11. But while these efforts had succeeded in ending legislative deadlock, they had not come close to dealing with the issue at hand, the actual electoral law, and it was suggested that another, bigger committee be formed to consider the issue in more depth.

Many of the problems associated with these negotiations further demonstrate some of the issues produced by the lack of parties or other clear groupings in parliament as described in chapter 4. Negotiations were largely a process of securing support for a series of key personalities who would have to negotiate with lesser political figures to ensure enough support to overcome the deadlock. The ability of parliamentarians to easily switch sides made securing a lasting compromise less likely and in the long run weakened their position.

In this light, it is possible to view Karzai's creation of the Special Court as an attempt to overcome an immediate problem and defer its ramifications to a later date—essentially, to buy more time for negotiation and compromise. However, negotiation and compromise normally tend to prioritize mediation between groups and reaching a political settlement, over and above the actual causes of the tension. In the case of the Special Court, there were no constraints or considerations of this kind—as an executive-appointed body, decisions regarding the leadership, authority structures, or longevity of the body appeared to be arbitrarily determined by the president and the president alone.

The Special Court was instrumental in solidifying Karzai's political power and minimizing any potential opposition, not least because it undermined in no uncertain terms the authority, legitimacy, and independence of existing bodies such as the IEC and ECC. According to some, this translated into a direct attempt on the president's part to counter the perceived electoral successes of non-Pashtun candidates. Other popular suggestions for motivations behind this move included the need for Karzai to regain face following embarrassment at the hands of the country's electoral institutions and their international backers during his own elections. Indeed, this was in some way supported by his violent and abrupt stance toward electoral officials, who were threatened with arrest when they refused to recognize the authority of the new court while their offices were being raided by the government. Whatever the actual reasons for the president's creation of the new court, the message it sent to the Afghan people was one of presidential, authoritarian rule overriding democratic institutions—even if the commitment of these institutions to democratic values could itself be questioned at times.

Also important is the way the establishment of this court continued and escalated a precedent that had already been set over other issues: once again, the president's political maneuvering seemed to deliberately provoke the international community in Kabul, but cost him little in terms of the repercussions that followed. While statements were made reaffirming international actors' (for example UNAMA's) continued support for the IEC and the decisions it made in announcing final results, there was little that the international community was able or willing to do to intervene. This was consistent with the declining will among international actors to become further involved in internal political affairs after yet another election debacle and in the context of a planned drawdown of troops, despite the fact that elections had been internationally funded. However, it also emphasized that elections could more generally serve as a convenient means for international actors to wash their hands of internal politics, the argument being that if elections take place, they demonstrate the will of the people and it would therefore be undemocratic to interfere.

Yet somewhat paradoxically, this desire to be rid of politics came at a time when a political settlement to reintegrate insurgent groups and facilitate a foreign military withdrawal was a topic of urgent discussion. In this context, the undermining of parliament's authority at the hands of the Special Court appeared even more drastic—with its influence so publicly curtailed, there would be little incentive for insurgents to compete in upcoming elections, making it more likely that they would be assuaged via the distribution of governorships, ministerial posts, and other appointed positions. This possibility would represent yet further erosion of the strength of the country's democratic institutions through political negotiation among elites.

THE RETURN OF THE SPECIAL COURT AND A CONSTITUTIONAL CRISIS

During the investigations of the Special Court, very little information was available publicly about the nature or procedures involved, contributing to the sense of secrecy and ambiguity surrounding this newly formed body. Some felt that following negotiations between Karzai and key members of parliament the court would be disbanded or simply forgotten. However, on June 23, 2011, almost five months after the inauguration of parliament, came the court's abrupt and unexpected announcement that 62 parliamentarians had been found guilty of fraudulent activity and would be disqualified, to be replaced with previously unsuccessful candidates.

This prompted widespread outrage among parliamentarians that was not limited to those on the "disqualified" list. As one representative stated angrily in an interview with the international media, "if the Special Court is not absolved, we will call our constituencies to the streets and the president will bear responsibility for what might happen."[24] Veiled threats like this one were accompanied by more stark warnings from other unseated parliamentarians calling for the impeachment of the president on the grounds that he was not able to conduct his responsibilities in a sound manner. These remarks themselves sparked angry reactions from pro-Karzai parliamentarians, leading to a physically violent argument between two female members who eventually had to be restrained by their colleagues. This embarrassing, televised display further undermined the legislature in the eyes of an incredulous public hearing and watching news reports on the event and, in the case of younger Afghans in Kabul, following the story on YouTube.

It quickly became clear that the court's judgment did not represent a straightforward attempt by the president to bolster his support in parliament—at least not on ethnic grounds—as some had quickly assumed. The 62 legislators listed for removal were not a group solely comprised of non-

Pashtun ethnic minorities, nor did their replacements include significantly more Pashtun members. While the court provided evidence on the fraudulent activities of some parliamentarians listed for removal, other representatives with campaigns widely perceived as fraud-ridden were not on the list. Likewise, certain candidates enjoying seemingly widespread support whose electoral failure had come as something of a surprise—Pacha Khan Zadran among them—were not put forward for reinclusion.[25] Pacha Khan himself appeared surprised by the decision and had previously suggested that a deal was in the works that would have restored his position as a parliamentarian. The way the investigations had been conducted and results eventually generated remained a mystery, again highlighting that for the president and his allies making decisions at the top, outcome appeared to trump process.

Even among parliamentarians who were explicitly supportive of an agreed, consensual settlement between the executive and legislative branches, the degree of uncertainty involved in the process was troubling. As one female member of parliament described in an interview with the Afghan press,

> If fraud is prevented, that is a good thing because people will believe rule of law exists. But one questions the manner in which it has been done. Even if the debate over the legality of the Special Court was settled, why are they announcing the results four months [sic] after the parliament opened?[26]

Suspicions remained high among parliamentarians, who were concerned that the whole incident had left the way open for Karzai to make strategic use of similarly ambiguous processes in future. What was ultimately clear was that the furor caused by the court's announcement had served to further weaken and undermine the ability of parliament to stand as a cohesive bloc against the president.

After a month of what appeared to be unmanageable chaos in legislative-executive relations, meetings were held between senior parliamentarians, including the new speaker, and the president, who apparently promised a resolution within days. Referring to the issue as merely "a part of the evolution of democracy," he explained: "We have some problems in the parliament which [can] be resolved. Each democracy undergoes these stages. . . . It has been ten years since we started and countries with even century-old democracies still tackle . . . such sort of problems."[27] Even in the tone of his statements, Karzai had once again strategically outmaneuvered parliament. By asking for patience and stressing the need for reconciliation, he contrasted sharply with some of the shrill, panicked statements of the parliamentarians, who often appeared on nightly news forecasting doom for the Afghan government.

This contrast was even more acute when the president released his final statement on the issue on August 10. This was perhaps more ambiguous than any document he had ever previously signed, because it did not specifically say whether or not the final decisions of the Special Court would be upheld or not. In avoiding direct endorsement of the Special Court's ruling, it seemed to emphasize the powers of the IEC, but in doing so it prompted numerous different, even opposing, interpretations.[28] To observers, this seemed like another attempt to buy more time and compromise, but in the incomprehensibly vague language of the statement Karzai was once more showing himself a master of strategic ambiguity—keeping his cards concealed and emphasizing his right as president to determine the rules as he saw fit.

These slowdown tactics also kept parliamentarians in a state of limbo, weakening their coherence as a group with each passing day as increasing numbers found reasons to compromise. Indeed, for some legislators the crisis represented an opportunity that could be exploited for substantial individual gain: the longer the state of uncertainty and unresolved tensions between the legislature and executive, the more space for deal-making and negotiation there was, and thus more time to forge (or reforge) lucrative political allegiances. This behavior, also seen in previous confrontations between parliament and the executive, was indicative of a broader trend among some parliamentarians of adopting political positions to extract concessions of one kind or another. Several parliamentarians we talked to in the course of 2009–2010 referred to the practice of promising a party leader or strongman to vote for a parliamentary bill (and so to display a green card in the plenary) but also promising a red vote to another, having extracted fees from both. This was a particularly frequent occurrence in the protracted and delayed elections for internal positions within parliament once it had been inaugurated in 2010, with parliamentarians reportedly selling their votes to potential candidates for $5,000 each.[29] These instances, of parliamentarians making the most of the uncertain environment by bargaining, demonstrate how electoral mismanagement, delays, and ambiguity have reshaped and defined bargaining in Afghanistan's political landscape.

In general, however, the benefits secured in such transactions are not the kind that trickle down to the broader Afghan public, because they remain within the pockets of elite politicians, contributing more to the foreign education of family members, new cars, and the extension of parliamentarians' own patronage networks at the local level. As the old man in Nangarhar bitterly recounted in the narrative at the start of this chapter, the fortunes of elected representatives appeared to change dramatically overnight, compelling them to forget the impoverished existence they had once led in their home provinces and exchange their former lifestyles for luxury in Kabul. The advantages for parliamentarians in maintaining an ambiguous status quo, in order to increase opportunities for bargaining and vote-selling, thus fundamentally contradict the assumption that, in case of a crisis, resolving the problem is always the principal goal. In perpetuating stalemates for their own benefit, Afghan powerholders also further the perception that they have the power to manipulate the system. Particularly in the postsurge political environment, which is rich in resources coming in from international donors, the pervasive ambiguity with regard to finding a political settlement and troop drawdown has ensured that funds have continued to flow and leaders continue to enrich themselves while simultaneously solidifying their own local political networks.

*   *   *

The extent to which the elections of 2009 and 2010 perpetuated political posturing and performance as political norms at the national level in Afghanistan is astonishing. More than simply a process of establishing a representative government, they were a stage on which the bargains and negotiations taking place between elites played out, effectively excluding the will of the people. Moreover, they showed just how much of a malleable process an election could be if one had enough political and economic resources. While some curtailment of fraud and adherence to electoral principles and time-schedules did indeed take place, particularly in terms of the conduct of the IEC and its management of elections in 2010, there was nevertheless the perception among Afghans that electoral processes could be manipulated and bent to fit the advantage of powerful individuals. Returning to the concept of structuring structures, the Afghan political landscape was reshaped in important ways during these processes, as voters discovered their own lack of agency and as perceptions of the function of elections began to change.

This was partly the result of a constitution that was faulty from the outset, most notably in its lack of institutional provisions for the curbing of executive power in a presidential system. More importantly, it stemmed from Karzai's successive, unilateral attempts to change procedures or institutions, either through the bending of constitutional provisions or through disregarding them entirely. Without an authoritative international body positioned to take serious issue with Karzai's abuse of constitutional procedure, there was little recourse for anybody wanting to question his authority to make arbitrary changes at whim.

Regardless of who or what was to blame, the fallout from the 2010 elections also made a deep impression on many of the Afghans we spoke to from across the social spectrum. Critically, the events that followed the polls substantially furthered the de-legitimization of a process which even on the eve of Election Day was still considered by many as a worthy and useful exercise. Characterized by ambiguity, insecurity, and manipulation, they also left an indelible imprint on the Afghan political landscape itself. More than a simple missed opportunity, the aftermath of elections in 2010 established clear precedents and reshaped politics in such a way that left most Afghans with less political agency than they did before the electoral processes began. In stark contrast with an essentialist argument that would suggest that Afghans were somehow unfit or unprepared for democracy, Afghan politics, which has incorporated many democratic characteristics over the years, became less democratic through elections due to a deliberate undermining of these processes by the ruling elite and a complacent international community. This purposeful disruption of democratic practices was not inevitable, but those that stood to gain the most were able to easily push aside the complaints of the real losers in this process—the Afghan people.

9

INTERNATIONAL INTERVENTION AND ASPIRATIONS OF REPRESENTATIVE GOVERNANCE

O VER A DECADE after the initial U.S. invasion, it is clear that many in the West are ready to close the chapter on the troubled international intervention in Afghanistan. But as this chapter closes and another, much less likely to be influenced by the international community, begins, it is difficult to tell what the story of the past decade in Afghanistan is and what can be learned from it. Despite the ways that some may try to simplify it, Afghanistan is not the story of the triumph of radical Islam, nor is it the failure of internationally protected human rights, elections, or other "democratic" approaches. As we try to determine what exactly the future holds for intervention in post-conflict scenarios, Afghanistan does not fit easily into any categories.

Clearly something went wrong. The Taliban from whom most diplomats, development workers, and Afghans themselves initially imagined "liberating" the country now appear likely to be a part of some power-sharing government. So what brought about this turnaround? Was it a problem with the narcotics industry? Terrorism? A creaky, inflexible development industry? Corruption? A rentier economy? An international community that was never fully committed? There are no clear answers. But if, as many believed following the collapse of the Berlin Wall, the world's future will be one of increased democratization, the continued opening of markets, and representative, responsive governments, then the example of Afghanistan suggests that achieving this is bound to be more of a fumbling affair than initially imagined, particularly (but not exclusively) if the international community has a significant role to play in these shifts. What does this mean, then, if anything, for how we think about international intervention more generally?

Compared with other priorities, such as education, agricultural development, or counternarcotics, it is striking both how much money went into Afghanistan's four rounds of post-2001 elections, and how quickly and quietly they have been forgotten by the international community. As the analysis in this book suggests, for many Afghans, elections did not create a government that would represent them, and instead solidified the power of the elite, making access to channels of power less accessible. As the dust from the 2010 elections settled, they were left with little hope that future elections would make the situation better and a general sense that they were likely to make things worse. To push the metaphor of the political landscape to its extremes, the international community promised Afghans a leveling process, while sponsoring elections that allowed elites to create new peaks only scalable by the most powerful.

For us, this project began primarily as an attempt to simply tell the story of Afghanistan's 2009 and 2010 elections. In particular, we tried to reconcile the enthusiasm and political excitement that the elections seemed to generate initially among both Afghans we know and those we interviewed with the lack of interest, political will, and capacity displayed by many members of the international community in the country. However, as we attempted to begin describing how some of the many voters and candidates we spoke with talked about the elections, it became increasingly clear that the stories they told often jarred with the way elections are typically analyzed as technical, one-off events. Few talked about the elections of 2009 and 2010 without also discussing the elections of 2004 and 2005. Similarly, there was not a clear conceptual divide in the minds of voters between various informal leaders such as mullahs and other elders on the one hand, and government officials on the other. Instead, all of these figures and the various forms of political power they wielded took their places on a continuum, struggling to define power in modern Afghanistan in a way that would most benefit them.

Ultimately, reflecting on elections in Afghanistan has led us to draw certain conclusions about the political future of the country itself, about the relationship between the international community and elections there, and more generally about the underexamined way in which elections have become a part of the formula for international intervention.

AN UNCERTAIN FUTURE

As we have argued, the failure of elections in Afghanistan to create a representative government is not at all due to a lack of political contestation and debate. This is not the story of a strong dictator or a single party dominating elections or even a rejection of the idea of democracy; it is, in fact, far more complex and interesting than that. The presidential and legislative elections in Afghanistan to date have in fact been extremely competitive, with a wide range of leaders from various ethnic groups and regions across the country taking part. Despite this, however, there has been a growing sense among Afghans we interviewed that even with many faces to choose from, candidates and parliamentarians alike have still been subject to the strict rules of patronage shaping the broader political landscape of the country. The concentration of political and economic resources into the hands of a small political elite has created a system in which, while the names and faces may change somewhat, particularly as Karzai shuffles leaders through a revolving set of political positions, the systemic concentration of these resources remains the same. Certain elite patronage networks have negotiated control of government and international resources, creating power structures which in turn reshape other structures, such as how elections are conducted, to highlight the emphasis of this book, but also reshaping how development funds are allocated and government positions are assigned. This concentration of resources has allowed elites to make it much more difficult for others to access political power.

At the local level, the initial enthusiasm of many voters took some time to fade, descending gradually into disillusionment over the course of seven years and four rounds of elections. To begin with, the colorful campaigns, the great number of candidates, and the public nature of what were usually private political conversations convinced many that the international community had successfully ushered in a new period of political stability. However, as tales of corruption grew and Karzai succeeded in paralyzing parliament, it became clear that despite the often highly local nature of elections, there was little voters and local leaders could do to actually influence their outcome.

Well aware that he was not strong enough to be a dictator, Karzai himself kept several key potential enemies (particularly his vice presidents) close to him, cultivating his own patronage networks and allowing only a select few others to do so. However, he has been careful to ensure that even these competing networks still rely on his presence as the democratically elected head of state to keep the international dollars that pay for the vast majority of resources in the country flowing. This solidification of the state as a series of mutually reinforcing patronage networks that may compete for resources, but rarely challenge each other directly, has created a structure of governance that on the surface appears weak, but has deep, underlying roots that are difficult to challenge.[1]

Simultaneously, Karzai has done well in balancing calls to follow the new democratic rules of elections with his efforts to undermine those same rules. His rapidly changing positions and rather savvy use of both Afghan and international media (sometimes sending contradictory messages in both) has forced both supporters and opponents to struggle constantly to position and reposition themselves politically. The question, however, is how will these patronage structures maintain themselves as international funds to the country begin to dry up? Will their leaders rely on violence, as during the civil war? Or will we see a return to the fundamentalist and isolationist rhetoric of the Taliban?

The direction the path leads from here will be shaped by the way in which the powerful individuals and networks that have used the past four elections and decade of intervention to further their influence respond to the dwindling of resources. Leaders like Pacha Khan Zadran and Ruz Goldi have decided that allying themselves with the state, albeit cautiously, is in their best interests and may continue to do so or may break with the government. Somewhat ironically, elections may continue to be held regularly, not due to their role in creating the institutions of democratic governance or even due to international pressure, but because elites have now seen that they can continue to use elections to further their own political agendas. On the one hand, ordinary Afghans may perceive them as increasingly farcical affairs while having become too disenfranchised to advocate for real reform. On the other, the ruling elite has no incentive to reform a system that so clearly benefits them. As we have seen with debate over the electoral law and Karzai's Special Court, debates over how to hold elections may occur using the language of reform, but in reality these are unlikely to create real change and serve as a means for further masking the ways in which the political elite are monopolizing access to political resources.

THE FATE OF SOVEREIGNTY

Elections since 2001 have also highlighted serious problems of sovereignty and with Afghanistan's future as a nation-state. In his recent work, Thomas Barfield argues convincingly that a constant expanding of popular understanding of both who should lead Afghanistan and who should participate in national-level politics underlies much of Afghanistan's recent history.[2] In the eighteenth century, struggles over control of the country were confined to the ruling Durrani dynasty, with all other groups expecting leadership to come exclusively from this small ruling elite. Over the intervening 200 years, however, understandings of which groups were entitled to political authority expanded to the point where, during the civil war, practically all involved were competing for a share.

In recent decades, the picture has become even more muddled. While many still believe the old adage that only a member of the Pashtun majority can rule the country, there are increasing demands from other ethnic groups that they too be represented at the national level in important postings, if not the actual presidency. Particularly in the years following the initial U.S.-led invasion, members of the Northern Alliance who were the most closely allied with invading American troops tended to benefit the most politically from the initial occupation. Since then, Karzai has worked to roll back some of the inroads that primarily Tajik leaders from the Northern Alliance have made, but many of these figures still dominate the political scene in Kabul.

This has greatly complicated negotiations with the Taliban, since groups like the former Northern Alliance do not want to see the power that they accumulated in recent years sacrificed to the Pashtuns involved in the insurgency. As the Afghan government negotiates to integrate the Taliban into government structures, if Tajik, Hazara, and other minority groups begin to withdraw their support, the fragility of the current truce may become much more apparent.

Beyond questions of ethnic identity there are questions about what type of person should lead Afghanistan that are perhaps even more troubling. Should Afghanistan be led by technocrats? Former warlords? Tribal leaders? The youth who have been educated abroad? The wide range of candidates in the parliamentary elections of 2010 demonstrates that the Afghan public is far from decided or unified on such issues, and Karzai and the rest of the ruling elite have taken advantage of this paralysis. Equally worrying, the current tendency of national politics to revolve around patronage networks and alliances that rarely have any ideological underpinnings has meant that serious debates over the role and nature of Afghanistan government and its leadership—what is the place of Islam in the state? would Afghanistan be better served by a federalist system that grants greater power to the provinces?—have simply not taken place.

While the Constitutional Loya Jirga and Bonn Conference, among other events, were meant to address some of these issues, it is clear that for the most part ordinary Afghans, in particular, feel that they have had little say in the shape or character of the government that they live under. Little wonder, then, that some are willing to join an insurgency against it. Indicative of this, despite thirty years of fighting, there have been no real attempts by Afghan leaders or members of the international community to begin any real sort of reconciliation process. National holidays have been established for former mujahideen, some of whom are hailed by many Afghans as national heroes, while others are cursed as war criminals. With the country's last king dead, there are few nationalist symbols to hold the country together, despite the fact that there is still a strong sense of Afghan-ness and no popular desire to partition the country. During the Bonn process there was a brief opportunity during which suggestions were made to bring back Zahir Shah as a symbolic head of state. This had the potential to support Afghan nationalism and could have done much to promote the idea of an Afghan nation as an imaged community that transcended ethnic divides. In the rush to usher in a brave new democratic order, however, the king was shoved rudely aside, and the potential symbolic importance overshadowed by Western ideological convictions.[3]

Reflecting some of the deliberations at Bonn, Afghanistan should be a proud, free country, those interviewed said, but few could agree on what that country should look like. Elections seem like an ideal opportunity for voters to take part in this debate, but as this book has demonstrated, they have clearly failed to live up to this potential. At the same time, both national figures like Karzai and a host of local leaders have exploited this ambiguity, mixing rhetoric that includes nationalism, Islam, and democracy to simultaneously be everything to everyone and, too often, nothing to anyone.

All this has deeply complicated the relationship between the citizen and the state, and has reshaped historical patterns. While citizens in the past have had low expectations for service delivery, the influx of international cash for development and state-building left many understandably wanting more—only to watch a small cabal of elites enrich themselves while little in their own lives changed. Many, having lived in Iran or Pakistan as refugees, have increased demands over the types of services that a state should provide. Particularly in light of the amount of the resources coming into the country over the past decade, many are appalled that more has not reached local communities. The sense that government officials have unfairly benefited from the international presence without being responsive to the needs of most citizens has undermined their own claims to sovereignty. It is, for example, difficult to imagine Afghans as eager to pay further taxes anytime in the near future to a state that appears so unresponsive, distant, and parasitical. Elections and other political processes have simply failed to generate any sort of political contract between citizens and the state. In this context, the continued presence of international actors only serves to highlight the fact that recent elections have not created sovereignty in the manner envisioned by most Western politicians.

ELECTIONS AND THE INTERNATIONAL
COMMUNITY IN AFGHANISTAN

Despite the caution expressed in this book about holding elections in unstable, post-conflict settings, we, and most of the Afghan voters we spoke with, still believe in the primary goal of elections: to allow popular participation in the political process. The greater problem is when elections promise to deliver participation, but fail to allow individuals to shape meaningfully the way power is distributed, or worse, allow certain powerful figures in the ruling elite to further consolidate their power in ways that close off political processes to the average voter. While international diplomats and the media point to local and national-level corruption and conflict as marring the electoral process, not enough has been done to question how the international community's technical and intellectual approaches to elections have also seriously inhibited the growth of legitimately democratic processes. When promoting elections in post-conflict settings, the international community puts far too much emphasis on form while little is done to ensure these processes play out in a fair manner.

In the wider story of post-2001 Afghanistan, elections are perceived by many Afghans to be one of a series of unkept promises made by the international community: the promise that certain human rights would be protected, the promise of a transparent political system, the promise of economic opportunity, and the promise of security. The result has been confusion and dismay over when and how the international community has chosen to exert its influence in the country. For example, when Karzai's Special Court threatened to strip 62 parliamentarians of their seats in a bid to further solidify his grasp on power, Ambassador Eikenberry said that the Americans would not intervene because this was a domestic issue. At the same time, American troops were raiding the homes of Afghans who were supporting an insurgency fueled in part by the corrupt ineffectiveness of the very government they were supporting. For many Afghans, it is difficult to see how one of these is a "domestic" issue and the other is not.

The international community's fluctuating levels of interest in the country meant that the initial light footprint approach did little more than set up mechanisms which elite Afghan actors were then left to use to their own advantage. When this failed to bring stability to the country, diplomats and military officials put pressure on the Afghan government to reform while continuing to carry out military operations in the country. However, this only complicated the issue, undermining Afghan state sovereignty while giving Karzai and others a convenient excuse for their failure to deliver on so many of their initial promises.

Elections have accentuated the contradictions inherent in the international promotion of post-conflict democratization in Afghanistan, showing it to be superficial and lacking in substance. With an all-encompassing but often weakly defined role, UNAMA has been generally unable and unwilling to intervene in political matters, or to put due pressure on the president when necessary. Instead, countries, particularly the United States, have tended to approach Karzai individually and have not demonstrated the political will to support UNAMA in taking on more of a role in this regard. This has resulted in a tangle of mixed messages that have clearly demonstrated the international effort's weakness and lack of coordination in its attempt to foster a democratic politics in Afghanistan. The reluctance of international actors to support the development of the political parties vital to a functional parliamentary system is just one example of a more general avoidance of political engagement.

Much of the confusion that Afghans have expressed over the role of the international community in elections can be tied directly to its ambiguous, fractious, and at times contradictory goals. Western diplomats have brought their own biases about the sovereign nature of states and how they should function to the decision-making table. In multiple conversations at Western embassies, we have heard the argument, "well that cannot happen; it violates the constitution," a statement that we have rarely heard from Afghan voters themselves. For them, the eight-year-old constitution—which established the seventh government in the past thirty years—simply does not have the same sacred quality that such documents have in other countries. In the Afghan political landscape, there is always the threat that things could shift dramatically, and Afghans make their political choices accordingly.

Even within the international community there is clearly a difference between the approaches taken by members of the European Union, an institution which has itself raised serious questions about sovereignty for its member states, and the American government, with its rich mythology about Americans as the chosen people spreading across the tabula rasa of the North American continent. Without delving too deeply into how political mythology might shape the way that we all make decisions, it is important to note that the political histories and values brought by internationals to discussions about governance and elections in Afghanistan are simply not the same as those of the Afghans actually participating in such processes, who see sovereignty as a much more contestable notion.

Not only is the international community a far from unified group, but even within the agencies of its individual members, most notably the United States, there has been significant change and debate over the role they should be playing in Afghanistan. At times, it has seemed that the Department of State perceives Afghanistan as a state-building project, while simultaneously the military views it as a counterinsurgency operation. At the same time, some NGOs view the intervention as ideally human rights–based, others as a development project, and so on.

While counterinsurgency and state-building do not need to clash (and indeed are seen as two sides of the same coin in the stabilization discourse), the way they have been implemented in Afghanistan has often been far from complementary. Thus, while many at the U.S. embassy emphasize the sovereignty of the Afghan constitution and the need to hold elections in a timely and legal manner, USAID projects assisted by the military are holding all-male elections for their own, entirely extra-constitutional version of district councils. While these could charitably be seen as prototypes for future, legal district council elections, in reality no serious work has been done to this end, and the current USAID-sponsored councils seem to directly contradict Afghan law, as many officials pointed out to us. Such activities continue to set dangerous precedents that are ultimately likely to destabilize the country and restrict access to political power as international troops begin the inevitable drawdown process.

These local misadventures have been accompanied by similarly troubling precedents set by the international community in general and the UN in particular in the case of national-level elections. The fact that the international community has both fully financed recent elections and clearly stepped in to manipulate them at certain points (at least in the eyes of many Afghans) has left voters unsure how the process will work in the future and made many leaders bolder in their manipulation of the system. Even while declaring that the election process was an Afghan domestic issue, Senator Kerry was seen on Afghan television, spending the day with the president as he attempted to resolve the issue of widespread fraud in the 2009 polls. While some in the West would argue that this was simply informal diplomacy, in the world of backroom Afghan political dealings, the lesson for many Afghans watching on local news broadcasts was simple: the international community had a particular vision of what they wanted the Afghan state to look like and they were going to work to make sure it adhered to that vision.

Such expectations included some of the underlining, and often unarticulated, assumptions about the post–Cold War world order and the place of elections, democracy, and representative governance within that order. The optimistic message for many in Afghanistan, and indeed much of the world, is that America and other Western countries demand a world that is democratic, tolerant, responsive to its citizens, relies on free-market capitalism, and respects human rights; more cynically, it can be pointed out, intervention appears to occur only when states do not conform to the political and economic structures that the Western world has established. Following the collapse of the Berlin Wall and the rapid democratization of Eastern Europe, one could be forgiven for thinking such a dream seemed realizable. The lesson from Afghanistan, and an increasing number of places, such as Somalia, where international intervention failed to deliver on its initial promises, is that sometimes this multitude of goals is not attainable in the short run. By promoting democracy, human rights, and development all at the same time in an unstable political setting, these combined projects now seem overly ambitious. In fact, in the Afghan case, by trying to do too much, too fast, the international community seems to have consistently undermined its own projects, ultimately meaning that even less has been attained.

All of this raises some troubling moral questions as we go forward: when the international community chooses to intervene, to what extent will they take responsibility for the repercussions of their actions? What happens when elections allow undemocratic leaders to come to power? What happens when development funds lead to local violent conflicts? These worrying questions could have long-term effects as the international community begins its hasty retreat from Afghanistan.

A BROADER LOOK AT INTERVENTION AND ELECTIONS

Elections in Afghanistan might seem like something of an extreme example when considering how elections are promoted by international actors globally. As discussed throughout this book, in the Afghan case there are countless political figures, many with weapons and other resources, and authority that often comes from overlapping, contested histories, making sovereignty particularly an unbounded and elusive concept. Elections become a forum in which these issues play out, leading to the high levels of conflict, corruption, and violence seen and experienced in 2009 and 2010.

There is a tendency among those who live and work in Afghanistan to consider these and other traits entirely unique in the global context. While many of the characteristics of the Afghan political landscape that we have described throughout this book are indeed specific to the country's social and political history—demanding context-specific analysis—there are nevertheless lessons to be learned from the international approach to promoting elections within this landscape. In many other cases, elections have been promoted quickly in the aftermath of violent conflict or social upheaval (for example, as in Bosnia Herzegovina, Iraq, Egypt, or East Timor).

The question of when to hold elections in postwar states has become an increasingly common feature of recent debates on state-building.[4] By any logical account, post-conflict environments are perhaps among the least conducive to implementing legitimate elections—resources are depleted, populations terribly scarred by the atrocities of war, and political playing fields rarely level platforms on which to stage competitions for power and influence. Nevertheless, the promotion of rapid elections in the aftermath of conflict has become a trend among international actors as part of a peace-building agenda developed in the wake of several civil wars in the 1990s. In theory, early elections present a way to avoid a power vacuum in the aftermath of conflict that could otherwise be filled by predatory strongmen. Holding elections quickly can allow a new government to be found and installed before other means of power-grabbing can take place, thus theoretically ensuring that the will of the people can determine a country's leadership. This is related to the assumption that a war-weary population that has been subject to the will of dictatorial leaders or violent commanders is one ready to express clear preferences in favor of a national peace.

Additionally, the push for quick elections often embodies a desire on the part of the international community to categorize and label states according to existing systems and structures. In the Afghan case, conducting elections contributed to making the otherwise unwieldy and complex country more legible to international institutions and donors, who could then categorize it as an "emerging democracy" on the basis that its leaders were legitimately selected by popular will.

Elections also serve as a means to measure "progress" according to international standards. They function as markers that international politicians can use to demonstrate tangible successes for voters at home, but also allow valuable statistics to be collected that had been previously unavailable. In Afghanistan, undertakings such as the registration of voters—including the attempt to render Afghan names into a Western format of "first name, surname" to fit the ballots;[5] the attempt to confine sources of sovereignty to a few critical positions of authority within a state administration to make interaction easier; and the attempted measurement of popular support through the quantifiable number of votes gained per candidate—all formed part of the need to simplify, albeit falsely, the complexities of a postwar context for the benefit of an alien (and often confused) international community.

Contrary to some of these assumptions, however, about the ability of elections to help "fix" a fragile, failed, postwar or postrevolutionary state, assigning more political power and international legitimacy through elections to a state structure that is perceived by many citizens as predatory and corrupt can have disastrous effects. Complex developments since the revolution in Egypt in 2011 have meant that elections have not been equated by the voting public with automatic legitimacy for those elected to office. Even if elections in other countries are less entangled with the complex web of local political issues that exist in Afghanistan, however—and this is not to say that they are—they take place within these countries' own idiosyncratic political landscapes and are never purely isolated, bounded events. No matter where elections take place, they are necessarily caught up in local histories, local customs, and local understandings of how politics should and do work. Elections may be idealized as universally generalizable and transferable institutions by politicians and political scientists alike, but as structuring structures, they will always shape and be shaped by the contours of the landscape in which they take place. As lived experiences, elections are fundamentally intertwined with both the deep undercurrents of history and with how individuals and groups make decisions: this is how they really matter.

This book makes an appeal for greater caution in international approaches to elections in post-conflict situations—whether intervention has been military, aid-focused, concentrated on electoral support, or a mixture of all three. Interventions are often shaped more by the political agendas and voting patterns of intervening nations than the concerns of the recipient country, as demonstrated by the West's deep interest in oil-producing, resource-rich, or politically strategic nations (such as Iraq and, more recently, Libya) and its scant involvement in equally turbulent but less "internationally significant" states (such as Somalia, Myanmar, Mali, and perhaps Syria). In particular, this means that the rhetoric employed in such circumstances is almost always aimed more at promoting the intervention both to domestic voters and to other diplomats than at shaping the intervention itself.

Elections give the international community the opportunity to wash their hands of messy political situations that are very much a part of their own creation. After an internationally sponsored election, complicated political landscapes can be seen and labeled as "domestic" issues, no longer the concern of international actors, unless a threat to international security is perceived to be present. In countries as diverse as Iraq, Bosnia, and East Timor, it has been clear that although international actors were unhappy with the impact of warfare, repressive tendencies of authoritarian regimes, or both, they were also uninterested in spending significant resources to support these countries politically in the future. Under such conditions, the rhetoric of democratization provides some useful escape mechanisms. By sponsoring elections, the international community is providing a venue for "the people" to choose the government. If that government then turns out to be oppressive or ineffective, the international community can claim that it cannot take responsibility for fixing the problem, since this would undermine popular sovereignty rather than the self-imposed authority of an anti-Western dictator. This "pick-and-mix" approach to intervention demonstrates the fluidity with which justifications for international assistance can be formulated.

It is becoming increasingly clear that there is a divide between the rhetoric that Western states use to describe the post–Cold War world order and their true goals in navigating it. States, as with rational individuals, always tend to have their own best interests at heart, but the current Western tendency to offer promises of participation and representation without substantive political support for such concepts threatens to expand the gulf between Western countries, where such promises are kept, and so-called developing countries, particularly in the Muslim world, where they are not. The rhetoric of democratization promises fairer access to political and economic resources, but in many cases the process itself fails to deliver these changes.

* * *

The research in this book suggests that when intervening in post-conflict situations, the international community needs to move away from a checklist approach that dictates which steps should be taken in what order to ensure stability. What it needs to do instead is listen more closely, both to history and to the people of the countries they are working in. Representative governance is something worth struggling for and working toward, but there are many paths leading to it, and each country should be able to determine its own, as has been done in most Western countries.

This does not necessarily preclude a role for international actors, should their assistance be requested in a democratizing state. On a policy level, this means a more integrated approach where election officials work more closely with diplomats and development workers, and where elections are not simply viewed as a one-off, technical achievement. More importantly, however, the study of elections needs to be reshaped and reinvigorated, particularly when it comes to elections in non-Western contexts. For some reason, academics are comfortable when discussing the irregularities, personalities, and political nuances that shape elections in their own countries (for example, in the United States' disputed election of 2000), but such nuances escape us once we begin to look abroad. Elections demand a more holistic, ethnographic approach.

Instead of assuming that certain processes like elections or democratization projects will lead to inevitable outcomes, this means understanding the political landscape of a given country and how individual citizens may be helped to navigate this terrain before rushing into elections. Instead of importing Western definitions of political values, it means attempting to understand what equality, freedom, and rights mean within a local context. Instead of the international community claiming to be involved only in the technical aspects of state-building, this means being upfront about the biases and political goals of all involved. Instead of creating bureaucratic divides during interventions, it means communicating more between projects aimed at development, governance, and human rights.

This suggests that more research on elections in post-conflict contexts needs to be conducted using ethnographic techniques. Current approaches rely too much on lifeless "hard" data such as turnout figures, which may suggest certain trends but do not answer important questions such as: Why are people voting? How do they understand the election process and how is this going to change the way that they make political decisions in the future? The standard reliance on quantitative statistics has technical implications as well, with many international policymakers and politicians judging the success of intervention and democratization based upon simple criteria such as whether elections were held, and whether "enough" people participated. Programs that encourage democratization should not be aimed at simply getting more people to vote, but should encourage local political dialogues and the formation of different types of political organization, which could help individuals to become more involved in local political processes. Such programs could actually help to address inequalities in the political landscape and allow for greater equality in access to political and economic resources—an equality that could be considered a real measure of success in democratization. Looking beyond these simple questions will allow the international community to encourage real improvements in how democracy and governance are actually experienced.

* * *

It is, perhaps, too late to undo many of the mistakes made in the early years following the American invasion in Afghanistan in terms of how both state-building and democratization projects were approached. However, there is still much to learn from these experiences. The failure of elections to promote representative governance in Afghanistan should not be dismissed as some sort of anomaly. As this book describes, there is no evidence to suggest that the Afghan context is somehow "unready" or "ill-suited" for elections or democracy. In fact, forms of responsive local governance have deep roots in Afghan culture—they just do not always take the form that many international actors are likely to identify with. However, as bungled elections and other democratization programs continue to allow the political elite to further distance themselves from the population and solidify their own power, we see that representative democratic governance can be both fragile and elusive. Tyranny and greed always threaten to undermine both representation and liberty. If the world is truly to be a place where governments represent their citizens through democratic political processes such as elections, it is essential that we work to understand the grit and detail of these processes, without losing ourselves in the seductive haze of democratization.

NOTES

DEMOCRACY DERAILED?

1. See, for example, Roland Paris (2004), *At War's End: Building Peace After Civil Conflict*.
2. We ourselves were not immune to the cautious optimism of Afghans turning out at polling stations even at this point and wrote a piece pointing, in part, to some of the positive aspects of the elections of 2009, with the subtitle "Why Afghanistan's 2009 Elections Were (and Were Not) a Disaster" (Coburn and Larson 2009).

1. UNDERSTANDING ELECTIONS IN AFGHANISTAN

1. Due to the reserved seats system, in which a certain number of seats per province are reserved for female candidates, some women in the province won seats with fewer votes than Ruz Goldi.
2. The Northern Alliance was a combined group of ethnic leaders and their followers, primarily from the Tajik, Uzbek, Turkmen, and Hazara groups living in the north and west of Afghanistan, who fought against the Taliban in the late 1990s and early 2000s. This group gained power after the initial U.S.-led invasion relied on them heavily for support, rewarding many figures in the Northern Alliance with weapons, cash, or political positions.
3. Robert A. Dahl (1998), *On Democracy*, 95; Adam Przeworski (1999), "Minimalist Conception of Democracy: A Defense," in Ian Shapiro and Casiano Hacker-Cordón, eds., *Democracy's Value*, 50–51. Significant debate exists as to whether choosing rulers through competitive elections defines democracy, with those of the minimalist school such as Joseph Schumpeter suggesting that this is the case (Schumpeter 1942, *Capitalism, Socialism, and Democracy*). Dahl expands on this definition through his influential concept of "polyarchy," which functions as an actual political system that can be achieved through institutional

design as opposed to the idealized state of democracy (Dahl 1971, *Polyarchy: Participation and Opposition*, 8) and calls for greater acknowledgment of the need for frequent elections, among other qualifications (1998:95). Larry Diamond argues that minimalist conceptions do not take into account the potential for systematic marginalization and exclusion of certain people groups under otherwise competitive elections (Diamond 1999, *Developing Democracy: Toward Consolidation*, 9). "Electoral democracy," for Diamond, falls short in capturing the nature of democratic politics.

4. Dahl (1998:93).

5. See, for example, John S. Dryzek (1990), *Discursive Democracy: Politics, Policy and Political Science*; John S. Dryzek and Leslie Holmes (2002), *Post-Communist Democratization: Political Discourses Across Thirteen Countries*; and John Parkinson (2006), *Deliberating in the Real World: Problems of Legitimacy in Deliberate Democracy*.

6. Adam Przeworski (1988), "Democracy as a Contingent Outcome of Conflicts," in J. Elster and R. Slagstad, eds., *Constitutionalism and Democracy*, 63.

7. See in particular Max Weber (1919), "Politics as a Vocation," Lecture to the Free Students' Union, Munich University.

8. Roger Mac Ginty (2011), *International Peacebuilding and Local Resistance: Hybrid Forms of Peace*, 91–114.

9. This being the case, Afghanistan is often labeled a "fragile state"—in other words, a state that does not conform to a Weberian model, lacking political legitimacy, sovereignty, and the will or ability to meet the needs of its citizens. No universally agreed definition of a fragile state exists, however, with different scholars and donors emphasizing different aspects of fragility. See, for example, Department for International Development (DFID) (2005), "Why We Need to Work More Effectively in Fragile States," 7; Francis Stewart and Graham Brown (2009), "Fragile States," CRISE Working Paper No. 51, 2; and Louise Andersen, Bjørn Møller, and Finn Stepputat, eds. (2007), *Fragile States and Insecure People? Violence, Security and Statehood in the Twenty-First Century*, 8–9. We have trouble with the term "fragile state" because it implies that a given state simply lacks some of the characteristics of a "full" state (hence the perceived need to "fix" or "build" it)—rather than have a different set of characteristics of its own.

10. For anthropologists thinking about elections, see for example Kimberley A. Coles (2004), "Election Day: The Construction of Democracy Through Technique," *Cultural Anthropology* 19.4: 551–80; or for a study that touches less directly on some of the issues that elections raise, see Michael Herzfeld (1992), *The Social Production of Indifference: Exploring the Symbolic Roots of Western Bureaucracy*.

11. Approaches such as that noted by Clifford Geertz (1973) in *The Interpretation of Cultures*, in the chapter titled "The Integrative Revolution," outline ways of moving anthropology more toward the study of modern political trends using what have been more "traditional" anthropological terms, but despite being applied in other directions, few studies have used this approach to focus on elections.

12. A more holistic approach is increasingly taken in some political science analyses of democracy, which situate elections within broader historical and social processes (see, for

example, Charles Tilly [2007], *Democracy*). This, however, is still not the norm and still tends to treat elections as singular events.

13. Bourdieu defines *habitus* as "systems of durable, transposable dispositions, structured structures predisposed to function as structuring structures, that is, as principles which generate and organize practices and representation that can be objectively adapted to their outcomes without presupposing a conscious aiming at ends or an express mastery of the operations necessary in order to attain them." Bourdieu (1990), *The Logic of Practice*, 53.

14. David Kertzer (1989), *Ritual, Politics, and Power*, 4–5.

15. For example, the widely popular *Afghan Star* is a television game show (beginning in 2005) based upon *American Idol* during which viewers can text their support for certain performers, choosing which ones make it into the next round. The show serves as an interesting microcosm of larger political issues in Afghanistan, such as the participation of women and tensions between different ethnic groups, though the portrayal of this in the documentary film *Afghan Star* (2009) may be slightly overdrawn.

16. In all Afghan elections since 2004, candidates have been assigned symbols on the ballot, alongside their names and candidate numbers, in order that they might be identified in spite of high levels of illiteracy among voters. Since the parliamentary election in 2005, candidates have been required to pick three symbols blindly from a bag and are then allowed to choose their preferred symbol from these three.

17. For the first of these claims, see Staffan I. Lindberg (2009), "Introduction. Democratization by Elections: A New Mode of Transition," in Staffan I. Lindberg, ed., *Democratization by Elections: A New Mode of Transition*, 6; also Dahl (1998:95). For the second, see Terry Lynn Karl (1990), "Dilemmas of Democratization in Latin America," *Comparative Politics* 23.1; and Diamond (1999:9).

18. Evelyne Huber, Dietrich Rueschemeyer, and John D. Stephens (1997), "The Paradoxes of Contemporary Democracy: Formal, Participatory, and Social Dimensions," *Comparative Politics* 29.3: 323–42; and Diamond (1999).

19. Gabriel A. Almond (1956), "Comparative Political Systems," *Journal of Politics* 18.3: 391–409; Abend Lijphart (1968), "Typologies of Democratic Systems," *Comparative Political Studies* 1.1: 3–44; Giovanni Sartori (1976), *Parties and Party Systems: A Framework for Analysis*; and Markku Laakso and Rein Taagepera (1979), "Effective Number of Parties: A Measure with Application to West Europe," *Comparative Political Studies* 12.1: 2–27.

20. Bernard Manin (1997), *The Principles of Representative Government*; Ian Budge (1996), *The New Challenge of Direct Democracy*; and Dahl (1998:91–95). Theoretical conceptions of the way in which the state interacts with citizens are explored in depth in John S. Dryzek and Patrick Dunleavy (2009), *Theories of the Democratic State*.

21. Aihwa Ong, quoted in Julia Paley (2002), "Towards an Anthropology of Democracy," *Annual Review of Anthropology* 31: 471. For a collection of essays on the subject, looking in particular at the complex relationships between democracy and values such as equality, freedom, and development, see Ian Shapiro and Casiano Hacker-Cordón, eds. (1999), *Democracy's Value*.

22. For more on distinctions between constitutional, substantive, procedural, and process-oriented definitions, see Tilly (2007:7); for an exposition of the many subtypes of democracy

that have emerged in recent scholarship, see David Collier and Steven Levitsky (1997), "Democracy with Adjectives: Conceptual Innovation in Comparative Research," *World Politics* 49.3: 430–51.

23. For more on one set of definitions of democratization and "de-democratization," see Tilly (2007:11–14).

24. Fareed Zakaria (November–December 1997), "The Rise of Illiberal Democracy," *Foreign Affairs* 76.6: 22–43.

25. For more on this see Anna Larson (2009), "Toward an Afghan Democracy? Exploring Perceptions of Democratisation in Afghanistan."

26. Simon Chesterman (2004), *You, the People: The United Nations, Transitional Administration and State-building.*

27. For more on arguments for and against the liberal peace thesis, see Michael E. Brown, Sean M. Lynn Jones, and Steven E. Miller (1996), *Debating the Democratic Peace.*

28. Chesterman (2004:206).

29. Lindberg (2009:9).

30. See Chesterman (2004: ch. 7).

31. Edward D. Mansfield and Jack Snyder (1995), "Democratization and the Danger of War," *International Security* 20.1: 5–38.

32. This tension has been explored by Robert H. Jackson in his discussion of "negative sovereignty" in quasi-states (1996), *Quasi States: Sovereignty, International Relations and the Third World*, 8.

33. Stephen D. Krasner (2009), *Power, the State, and Sovereignty: Essays on International Relations.*

34. See Thomas Blom Hansen and Finn Stepputat (2005), "Introduction," in Hansen and Stepputat, eds., *Sovereign Bodies: Citizens, Migrants, and States in the Postcolonial World.* This is followed by a range of useful case studies. In the Afghan context see Noah Coburn (2011a), *Bazaar Politics: Power and Pottery in an Afghan Market Town.*

35. See Michel Foucault (1991), "Governmentality," in G. Burchell, C. Gordon, and P. Miller, eds., *The Foucault Effect: Studies in Governmentality*; and John Keane (1996), *Reflections on Violence.*

36. See Paley (2002).

37. In many instances this is to take James Scott's concept of weapons of the weak to the extreme. James C. Scott (1987), *Weapons of the Weak: Everyday Forms of Peasant Resistance.*

38. For more on center and periphery, see Thomas Barfield (2010), *Afghanistan: A Cultural and Political History.* For some of the tensions associated with individualism in Afghan political culture, see David B. Edwards (1996), *Heroes of the Age: Moral Fault Lines on the Afghan Frontier.*

39. For more on these processes and related issues, see Thomas Barfield, Nemat Nojumi, and J. Alex Their (2006), "The Clash of Two Goods: State and Non-State Dispute Resolution in Afghanistan"; Stephen Carter and Kate Clark (May 2010), "'Snakes and Scorpions': Justice and Stability in Afghanistan"; and Noah Coburn (2011b), "The International Community and the 'Shura' Strategy' in Afghanistan," in Peter Albrecht, Helene Maria Kyed, Deborah Isser, Erica Harper, eds., *Perspectives on Involving Non-State and Customary Actors in Justice and Security Reform.*

40. See Noah Coburn and Shahmahmood Miakhel (September 2010), "Many Shuras Do Not a Government Make: International Community Engagement with Local Councils in Afghanistan."

41. See Sarah Ladbury (2010), "Helmand Justice Mapping Study." Final Report for the Department of International Development.

42. See, for example, William Reno (1995), *Corruption and State Politics in Sierra Leone*. In the Afghan context, see Antonio Giustozzi (2009), *Empires of Mud: Wars and Warlords in Afghanistan*.

43. For more on the blurred distinctions between state officials and warlords in Afghanistan, see Mac Ginty (2011: ch. 4).

44. This issue is discussed more fully in chapter 4, including some of the issues with the concept of "tradition" in Afghanistan.

45. Olivier Roy (1994), *The Failure of Political Islam*, 148.

46. See Louis Dupree (1980 [1973]), *Afghanistan*, ch. 22; and Barfield (2010, esp. 53–54).

47. The leader of the Hizb-i Islami militant group, formerly supported by the United States during the Soviet-Afghan War but now considered by the U.S. government to be a terrorist.

48. For more on Pakistan's interference in Afghan politics, see Olivier Roy (2003), "Afghanistan: Internal Politics and Socio-Economic Dynamics and Groupings."

49. See Barfield (2010), esp. ch. 4 and 5.

50. As discussed by Thomas Barfield, the dichotomy between these two groups historically runs deep in Afghanistan and can separate groups more forcefully than the divisions of ethnicity or qaum, for example, Barfield (2010: ch. 1). *Qaum* is a term used for a solidarity group, ranging from the immediate family to an entire ethnic group. The flexibility of the term is one of the things that makes it useful for mobilizing at various levels. The Pasthun term *khel*, which translates more directly as tribe, is used similarly in some areas, but tends to be a more fixed term. For more see Coburn (2011a: ch. 3). Chapter 4 in this work will also explore how the flexibility of the concept of qaum made it useful for mobilizing voters.

51. We also looked at the technical aspects of elections, which were often discussed in interviews with diplomats working in Afghanistan, and we will refer to some of these processes throughout the work, but they were never the starting point of our research or analysis.

52. Other more general quantitative polls do demonstrate some interesting social and political trends in Afghanistan, but still have some serious methodological limitations. See, for example, The Asia Foundation (TAF) (2010), "Afghanistan in 2010: A Survey of the Afghan People."

2. OF BALLOTS AND BOUNDARIES: A BRIEF HISTORY OF POLITICAL PARTICIPATION IN AFGHANISTAN

1. Amin Saikal (2004), *Modern Afghanistan: A History of Struggle and Survival*, 115–16. After this, elections were supposed to take place every three years, but stopped after 1952.

2. Daoud's regime as president marked an end to the nascent pluralism that was beginning to take root under the king (albeit slowly), in part through his brutal suppression of opposition.

Interestingly, when Daoud had been prime minister under Zahir Shah (1953–1963), he had encouraged the gradual development of reform and pluralism (Louis Dupree [1963], "Afghanistan's Slow March to Democracy: Reflections on Kabul's Municipal Balloting." *American Universities Field Staff Reports* 7.1, South Asia Series: 12–13). In his later 1977 constitution, Daoud would include the holding of elections in "the traditional manner," i.e., by acclamation, not selection. See also Louis Dupree (1978), "Toward Representative Government in Afghanistan, Part II: Steps Six Through Nine—And Beyond?" *American Universities Field Staff Reports* 22.14, South Asia Series.

3. Dupree estimates that total population figures in 1960 were around 10–12 million, although no official census had been conducted at this point (Louis Dupree [1960], "A Note on Afghanistan," *American Universities Field Staff Reports* 4.8, South Asia Series: 13). This compares with current estimates of around 24.5 million, although again, a full official census has not been conducted (Islamic Republic of Afghanistan Central Statistics Organization [CSO] [2010], "Estimated Population of Afghanistan 2010/2011").

4. Dupree (1963:3).

5. Dupree (1963:1).

6. Dupree (1963:3).

7. Dupree (1963:1).

8. Louis Dupree (1971), "Afghanistan Continues Its Experiment in Democracy: The Thirteenth Parliament Is Elected," *American Universities Field Staff Reports* 15.3, South Asia Series: 6.

9. Dupree (1971:6).

10. The Chronology is adapted from Larson (2009:8).

11. Thomas Ruttig (2006), "Islamists, Leftists and a Void in the Center: Afghanistan's Political Parties and Where They Come From, 1902–2006," 6.

12. International Crisis Group (ICG) (2005), "Political Parties in Afghanistan," *Asia Report 39*: 2; Dupree (1963:12).

13. For more detailed accounts of these histories, see Barnett R. Rubin (2002), *The Fragmentation of Afghanistan: State Formation and Collapse in the International System*; Saikal (2004); and Barfield (2010).

14. Dupree talks about young civil servants wanting to take part in decision-making and to openly criticize their government in 1963, but also about a concern within the service more generally about the ramifications of speaking out in public against the regime—for which only some years earlier people had been imprisoned (Dupree 1963:13).

15. Rubin (2002:181).

16. Barfield (2010).

17. Dupree (1963:7).

18. As with all invented traditions, however, the fact that they are recognized as important events by communities across Afghanistan is in itself meaningful. Embodied in the loya jirga are elements of accountability and participation, which, even if only superficially demonstrated at these elite gatherings, reflect characteristics embedded in Afghanistan's political landscape at the local level. Barfield (2010:295).

19. Ali Wardak (2002), "*Jirga*: Power and Traditional Conflict Resolution in Afghanistan," in John Strawson, ed., *Law After Ground Zero*. The term *shura* is also used, particularly in Dari-speaking areas, to signify more fixed-membership local councils. In some areas *jirga* and *shura* are used interchangeably. In others, *jirga*s is reserved for ad hoc meetings resolving a specific issue. For more, see Noah Coburn (2011c), "The Politics of Informal Dispute Resolution and Continued Instability in Afghanistan."

20. Dupree (1963:2).

21. For more on the tension between community and individual equality, particularly among the Pashtuns, see Edwards (1996).

22. Other terms, such as *alqadar* and *arbab*, are used in specific regions in Afghanistan, and in some cases these positions have slight local nuances. In general, however, all of these positions, in their ideal forms, are meant to serve as representatives from the community to the central authorities and to be responsive to community needs on some level. While some argue there are fixed differences between these types of positions, in reality this is not the case.

23. Dupree (1963:2).

24. For more on this, see Coburn (2011b).

25. Chris Johnson and Jolyon Leslie (2004), *Afghanistan: The Mirage of Peace*, 41–42.

26. Most people we spoke with in local areas stated that local bodies such as shuras were rarely open to all, since women were not allowed to sit on them; but in many cases, both women and men pointed out that women were represented, if not included, since their male family members were duty-bound to speak on their behalf.

27. Dupree (1963).

3. ELECTING THE PEACE? AFGHANISTAN'S FAST-TRACK DEMOCRACY

1. This was very much premised in the conceptual link between fragile states and the existence and propagation of extra-state terrorist organizations. For one donor's perspective on this relationship, see DFID (2005).

2. For the speech in its entirety, see Donald Rumsfeld (February 14, 2003), "Beyond Nation Building," 11th Annual Salute to Freedom, Intrepid Sea-Air-Space Museum, New York City, Department of Defense.

3. Francis Fukuyama (January/February 2004), "Nation-building 101," *The Atlantic.*

4. Astri Suhrke (2011), *When More Is Less: The International Project in Afghanistan*, 10.

5. For more on counterinsurgency theory, see David J. Kilcullen (2010), *Counterinsurgency.*

6. Barnett Rubin considers these kinds of compromises to have been inevitable given the international (and particularly U.S.) unwillingness to engage in removing or disenfranchising warlords by force. Rubin (2007), "Peace Building and State-Building in Afghanistan: Constructing Sovereignty for Whose Security?" in Mark T. Berger, ed., *From Nation-Building to State-Building*, 176.

7. The rentier state dynamic created by aid dependence was not new to Afghanistan post-2001, but had formed a critical characteristic of the state's relationship both to international actors

and to its own citizens throughout Zahir Shah's reign and earlier. In order to keep regional strongmen aligned with the state, Afghan leaders have found themselves needing to distribute vast sums of politically aligned aid to these individuals. In this way, the general population has been largely excluded from any direct means of holding its government to account.

8. Mac Ginty (2011:92).

9. Chesterman (2004:219).

10. James Dobbins, Seth G. Jones, Keith Crane, and Beth Cole DeGrasse (2007), *The Beginner's Guide to Nation Building*, 197.

11. Barfield (2010:295).

12. International Crisis Group (ICG) (2003), "Afghanistan: The Constitutional Loya Jirga," *Afghanistan Briefing*, 1.

13. ICG (2002), "The Loya Jirga: One Small Step Forward?" *Asia Report* 17: 13.

14. Anna Larson (2011a), "Assessing Democracy Assistance: Afghanistan," 18.

15. Suhrke (2011:41).

16. Ashraf Ghani and Clare Lockhart (2008), *Fixing Failed States*, 77.

17. Dobbins et al. (2007:208).

18. ICG (2004), "Afghanistan: From Presidential to Parliamentary Elections," *Asia Report* 88: 11; Ghani and Lockhart (2008:77–78).

19. Chesterman (2004:205).

20. Ghani and Lockhart (2008:78).

21. Free and Fair Election Foundation of Afghanistan (FEFA) (2009b), "Observation Report from the Fourth Phase of the Voter Registration (VR) Process," 5.

22. Elections for district councils are scheduled in the constitution to take place every three years, but the first of these has not taken place to date for several reasons. Most commonly mentioned are the fact that district boundaries in some areas are still in dispute, and the fact that voters are not currently registered by district but by province, meaning that the entire voter registration process would need to take place again before elections could be held. Furthermore, allowing the counting of voters by district would generate figures that could more accurately represent the ethnic composition of Afghanistan. This kind of information is highly political and the source of considerable dispute in the country. It is feared that data like this would contribute to emphasizing ethnic tensions. As will be discussed more fully in later chapters, more local elections would increase local involvement in elections, something that many political elite in Kabul, including President Karzai, see as undermining their political positions.

23. Government of Afghanistan (2010), "Electoral Law," revised.

24. Though there was some local variance here, and in Balkh there was a rather low number of candidates relative to the population than there were in other provinces.

25. ICG (2005), "Political Parties in Afghanistan," 6.

26. See, for example, the difference between parliamentary candidates Mohammad Sarwar and Sayed Ahmad Shah of Balkh Province in 2005 (results of the Balkh Wolesi Jirga elections are published on the website of the Independent Election Commission, at www.iec .org.af).

27. International Institute for Democracy and Electoral Assistance (IDEA) (2011), "Voter Turnout Data for Afghanistan."

28. Deniz Kandiyoti (2005), "The Politics of Gender and Reconstruction in Afghanistan," 6.

29. For more, see Anna Larson (2012), "Collective Identities, Institutions, Security and State-Building in Afghanistan," in Susan Franceschet, Mona Lena Krook, and Jennifer M. Piscopo, eds., *The Impact of Gender Quotas*.

30. Carlotta Gall (June 26, 2002), "Afghan Women in Political Spotlight," *New York Times*.

31. Drude Dahlerup and Anja Taarup Nordland (2004), "Gender Quotas: A Key to Equality? A Case Study of Iraq and Afghanistan," *European Political Science* 3: 91–98.

32. United Nations (1995), "Beijing Declaration and Platform for Action: Fourth World Conference on Women."

33. See Drude Dahlerup (2002), "Increasing Women's Political Representation: New Trends in Gender Quotas," in *Women in Parliament: Beyond Numbers, A Revised Edition*; Anne Phillips (1995), *The Politics of Presence: The Political Representation of Gender, Ethnicity and Race*; Irene Tinker (2004), "Quotas for Women in Elected Legislatures: Do They Really Empower Women?" *Women's Studies International Forum* 27: 531–46. Systematic research on the impact and effects of quotas remains limited to date—on this subject, see Franceschet, Krook, and Piscopo (2012).

4. A HOUSE OF SAND: THE FALLOUT OF THE 2005 PARLIAMENTARY ELECTION

1. ICG (2003:1); Barnett Rubin (2004), "Constructing a Constitution for Afghanistan," *Journal of Democracy* 15.3: 11.

2. Ahmed Rashid (2008), *Descent into Chaos: Pakistan, Afghanistan and the Threat to Global Security*, 256.

3. The political scientist E. E. Schattschneider famously noted in 1942 that "Political parties created modern democracy and modern democracy is unthinkable save in terms of the parties" (quoted in Scott Mainwaring and Mariano Torcal [2005], "Party System Institutionalization and Party System Theory: After the Third Wave of Democratization," paper prepared for the 2005 Annual Meeting of the American Political Science Association, Washington, DC). This opinion has been echoed in much of the literature on parties since, by authors such as Giovanni Sartori (1968), "Representational Systems," in *The International Encyclopedia of the Social Sciences* 13: 470–75; Russell J. Dalton (1985), "Political Parties and Political Representation: Party Supporters and Party Elites in Nine Nations," *Comparative Political Studies* 18.3: 276–99; Herbert Kitschelt (2000), "Linkages between Citizens and Politicians in Democratic Politics," *Comparative Political Studies* 33.6–7: 845–79; Martin Seymour Lipset (2000), "The Indispensability of Political Parties," *Journal of Democracy* 11.1: 48–55; and Mainwaring and Torcal (2005). Parties are considered by these authors as a key means through which citizens' interests can be substantively represented.

4. See, for example, Freedom House (2010), "Checklist Questions and Guidelines: Political Rights Checklist"), a comprehensive framework determining levels of freedom in a given

country, in which questions B1 and B2 imply that the right and ability to organize in parties or "other competitive political groupings" is considered by Freedom House to be a key component of a country's combined score for political rights. In Tatu Vanhanen's academic model for measuring levels of democracy, party competition in elections is put forward as a central criterion. See Tatu Vanhanen (2000), "A New Dataset for Measuring Democracy: 1810–1998," *Journal of Peace Studies* 37.2: 251–65.

5. For more on Northern Ireland's parliamentary system, see John McGarry and Brendan O'Leary (Spring 2006), "Consociational Theory, Northern Ireland's Conflict, and Its Agreement 2: What Critics of Consociation Can Learn from Northern Ireland," *Government and Opposition* 4.2: 249–77. For consociationalist theory, see Lijphart (1968:3–44).

6. There are several good histories of Afghanistan during this period. This section draws particularly from Dupree (1963, 1971); M. G. Weinbaum (1972), "Afghanistan: Nonparty Parliamentary Democracy," *Journal of Developing Areas* 7.1: 57–74; Rubin (2002); Rashid (2008); and Barfield (2010).

7. See Saikal (2004: ch. 4 and 5).

8. For more on Afghanistan's rentier economy at this time, see Saikal (2004: ch. 5); Jonathan Goodhand (April 2005), "Frontiers and Wars: The Opium Economy in Afghanistan," *Journal of Agrarian Change* 5.2: 196. Rubin (2002) also includes an enlightening appendix of Afghan government expenditure from 1952 to 1988, which demonstrates the extent to which the Afghan state was reliant on foreign aid during these years.

9. For more on this, see Roy (1994:147–67).

10. Rashid (2008:258).

11. Government of Afghanistan (2003), "Political Parties Law." This law was updated in 2008, but few substantive changes were made to allow a more political role for parties; changes instead concerned technical issues such as the number of signatures required for a party to register. This approach, of Karzai making certain concessions to parliament but leaving the exact legal ramifications vague, has become common in his dealings with parliament, such as his establishment of the special elections court in 2010. By negotiating an uneasy balance, Karzai has been able to defuse political opposition without actually establishing legal precedents that might bind him in the future.

12. See, for example, Andrew Wilder (2005), "A House Divided? Analysing the 2005 Afghan Elections," and National Democratic Institute (NDI) (2006), "The September 2005 Parliamentary and Provincial Council Elections in Afghanistan."

13. Anna Wordsworth (2007), "A Matter of Interests: Gender and the Politics of Presence in Afghanistan's Wolesi Jirga," 20.

14. ICG (2004); Andrew Reynolds, Lucy Jones, and Andrew Wilder (2005), "A Guide to Parliamentary Elections in Afghanistan."

15. The "Amnesty Law" (officially titled the National Reconciliation, General Amnesty and National Stability Law) was passed by parliament in 2007 and published in the *Official Gazette* in December 2009. It provides immunity from prosecution for any parties involved in "hostilities" provided that they renounce violence: "All political factions and hostile parties who were involved in one way or another in hostilities before establishing of the Interim Administra-

tion shall be included in the reconciliation and general amnesty program for the purpose of reconciliation among different segments of society, strengthening of peace and stability, and starting of new life in the contemporary political history of Afghanistan, and enjoy all their legal rights and shall not be legally and judicially prosecuted" (Article 3, unofficial English translation). Government of Afghanistan (2009), "National Reconciliation, General Amnesty and National Stability Law": *Official Gazette* 1387.965 (2009). Cited in Sari Kouvo (February 22, 2010), "After 2 Years in Legal Limbo: A First Glance at the Approved 'Amnesty Law.'"

16. Wilder (2005:41).

17. Although at Bonn there had been clear divides between royalists supporting the king (the "Rome group"), Northern Alliance members, and the Iran-supported "Cyprus group," the government that was formed as a result of the Bonn process was a mixture of all three, with Karzai's first cabinet including a number of non-Pashtun leaders. Partly as a result of this, at this point "pro-government" and "opposition" stances among successful parliamentary candidates were not strongly ethnically delineated and were subject to change during this period (Wilder 2005:4–11).

18. National Assembly of Afghanistan (2006), "Rules of Procedures of the Wolesi Jirga," Chapter 3, Rule 9.

19. The Kuchis are a traditionally nomadic group generally of Pashtun origin, for whom ten seats are reserved in the Wolesi Jirga as a consideration for their national rather than geographically defined constituency. Their annual migration across the country takes them across Afghanistan's central highlands—largely occupied by settled Hazaras. This has led to persistent and often deadly conflict over land use between the two groups.

20. National Assembly of Afghanistan (2006: Rule 13).

21. ICG (2006), "Afghanistan's New Legislature: Making Democracy Work," *Asia Report* 116; Wordsworth (2007).

22. M. Hassan Wafaey and Anna Larson (2010:9), "The *Wolesi Jirga* in 2010: Pre-election Politics and the Appearance of Opposition."

23. Wordsworth (2007:31).

24. At the time of interview the required number of parliamentarians to form a parliamentary group was 21. It has since been changed to 23.

25. In the end, no second leader was found but the group survived as one unit and persisted throughout the first parliament. However, it appeared to exist primarily as a club for former mujahideen commanders with connections to Hizb-i Islami, working to further the influence of its members within the government. As such, it drew on an existing interest group that already had a significant amount of influence across disparate regions of the country to develop a new platform of sorts within the legislature.

26. Wordsworth (2007:22).

27. Wordsworth (2007:18–19).

28. Wilder (2005:4).

29. Wilder (2005:4).

30. Lauren Oates (2009), "A Closer Look: The Policy and Lawmaking Process behind the Shiite Personal Status Law," 11.

31. For a summary of these arguments, see Andrew Reynolds and Andrew Wilder (2005), "Free, Fair or Flawed: Challenges for Legitimate Elections in Afghanistan."
32. Weinbaum (1972:62).
33. For more on political ambiguity in parliament, see Anna Larson (2010), "The *Wolesi Jirga* in Flux: Elections and Instability 1."
34. Wafaey and Larson (2010).
35. Weinbaum (1972).

5. ENGINEERING ELECTIONS LOCALLY

1. Since district council elections have not been held, no district councils are constitutional in the strict sense of the term. However, most districts have some sort of council which generally has some relationship with the district governor or the government more widely. More recently, USAID funded a private contractor to produce similar councils in certain districts, oftentimes overlapping with councils that already existed, adding to local political confusion. For more on this, see Coburn and Miakhel (September 2010).
2. For a classic description of segmentary opposition, see E. E. Evans-Pritchard (1969 [1940]), *The Nuer: A Description of the Modes of Livelihood and Political Institutions of a Nilotic People.*
3. In the spring of 2009, there were rumors in Kabul that newly appointed American envoy Richard Holbrooke was not supporting Karzai, instead favoring former chair of the World Bank and presidential candidate Ashraf Ghani, who many Afghans complained had "escaped" (*gerkht*) abroad during the Soviet and Taliban periods.
4. Carlotta Gall and Jeff Zeleny (November 1, 2009), "Out of Race, Karzai Rival Is Harsh Critic of Election," *New York Times.*
5. Or approximately 1.3 million votes. For a breakdown by candidate and other statistics, see Archie Tse (October 20, 2009), "Audit Finds Almost a Quarter of Afghan Vote Fraudulent," *New York Times.*
6. Lesser known presidential candidates tended to only set up campaign offices in the regions where they had roots.
7. It is also important to note that in a place like Qara Bagh in 2009, where there was a limited but growing insurgent presence, those who were "antigovernment" were still far more invested in the political system than those insurgents who were truly antigovernment in the sense that they were interested in attempting to completely overthrow the current system.
8. See the Independent Election Commission's website, at www.iec.org.af.
9. Tse (2009).
10. This is discussed more thoroughly in chapter 8.
11. For example, the percentage of the population that is Pashtun can vary widely from around 40 to well over 50 percent and is deeply tied in the minds of many to the fact that Afghanistan has been ruled almost exclusively by Pashtuns for the past 250 years.
12. Historically, Afghan leaders have assigned governors and district governors from other areas than where they are posted to ensure that their loyalty is primarily to the regime in Kabul and not to the people they are supposedly serving.

13. The exceptions to this are figures like Mohammad Atta, the governor of Balkh, who has become so powerful on his own that some claim he runs Balkh Province independently from the control of the central government.

14. If the district and village council elections that the constitution calls for are ever held, theoretically members of these councils will also be elected by local communities.

15. A corollary to this is that while it is difficult to measure resources actually provided, most felt that communities who had more parliamentarian representatives were receiving more resources from the Afghan government and the international community. As one man succinctly explained, "People will vote for candidates from their own area because, if that candidate wins, more services will be provided in their area."

16. Further confusing things, *wakil* is also the term commonly used for attorney.

17. This history of the application of the term *wakil* is another example of how elections fit into previous local understandings of political processes and were not placed onto a *tabla rasa* as discussions by the international community sometimes suggest.

18. In Kabul and other large cities these gatherings were often held at hotels or large restaurants.

19. In the districts where we focused, only Qara Bagh (fairly close to Kabul, with a large population) was visited by Abdullah. Karzai did not visit any of the districts studied, though he did travel to Gardez in Paktya.

20. This process is similar to the concepts of "weapons of the weak," as outlined by James Scott (1987).

21. For a more thorough discussion of this issue, see Coburn and Larson (2009).

22. There were, of course, limits to this and Ramazan Basherdost also secured a good number of votes in Hazara areas. The fact, however, that more people did not vote for fellow Hazara Basherdost suggests the ability of Hazara leaders to control the Hazara voting bloc.

23. There is of course the issue of whether these relationships have actually become more distant, or whether many are simply idealizing the past when they describe the breakdown in these responsive ties. The key for most, however, was the *perception* of an increased distance between leaders and communities, and this in turn has begun to shape how people make political decisions (as evidenced by the decline in voter turnout, for example).

24. Przeworski (1988:63).

6. THE UNINTENDED CONSEQUENCES OF INTERNATIONAL SUPPORT

1. Lindberg (2009:9).

2. In bringing the international community into the spotlight as a protagonist in this chapter, we should emphasize that we use the term *community* to describe international actors purely for simplicity's sake. We do not mean to imply a sense of cohesion or coherence between the forty-eight different countries and their representatives in Afghanistan, whose mandates range from security provision to public health to legislative capacity-building, to a mixture of these. The divisions between multilateral and bilateral donors, their aid agencies, international and national NGOs and private contractors are highly significant,

with many programs that overlap or even run counter to one another. However, the idea of the international community as a collective remains pertinent, especially since very few Afghans outside a small Kabul-based elite distinguish between different sectors of the international assistance machine. This in itself is important to consider when examining the broader political implications of international efforts.

3. Astri Suhrke makes a similar observation about the international imperative to promote the impression of "winnability," comparing the international project in Afghanistan with U.S. military approaches in Vietnam. Suhrke (2011:4).

4. The Aid Worker Security Database, cited in Lydia Poole (2011), "Afghanistan: Tracking Major Resource Flows 2002–2010."

5. Brookings states that the number of IDPs in Afghanistan had more than doubled over three years, from 150,000 in 2008 to 329,000 in 2010, while the number of Afghans seeking asylum overseas rose steadily from 2005 to 2009. Ian S. Livingston, Heather L. Messera, and Michael O'Hanlon (2010), "Afghanistan Index: Tracking Variables of Reconstruction and Security in post 9/11 Afghanistan," 17.

6. See, for example, the communiqué from the International Conference in Support of Afghanistan held in Paris in 2008, "Declaration of the International Conference in Support of Afghanistan, Issued Under the Authority of the Three Co-chairs: The President of the French Republic, The President of the Islamic Republic of Afghanistan, The Secretary-General of the United Nations" (June 12, 2008). Published in Civil-Military Fusion Center (CFC) (2012), "Afghanistan Agreements: A Collection of Official Texts from 2001–2011," 42–45.

7. Rashid (2008:415).

8. For more on this, see Larson (2011a:7–8).

9. Suhrke (2011:6–17).

10. See Rahim Faiez and Jason Straziuso (June 13, 2009), "Afghan Ballots to have 41 Candidates for President" (Associated Press); Human Rights Watch (August 18, 2009), "Afghanistan: Human Rights Concerns in Run-Up to Elections."

11. For more on this subject, see Martine Van Bijlert (2009), "How to Win an Afghan Election"; and Haseeb Humayoon (2010), "The Re-election of Hamid Karzai."

12. In retrospective memoirs, many diplomats working at the time in Kabul have made similar points. For a particularly lucid account, see Ronald Neumann (2009), *The Other War: Winning and Losing in Afghanistan*. Other accounts include Chris Alexander (2011), *The Long Way Back: Afghanistan's Quest for Peace*; Kai Eide (2012), *Power Struggle Over Afghanistan: An Inside Look at What Went Wrong—And What We Can Do to Repair the Damage*.

13. This is coming to light more generally as donors and troops prepare to depart: a recent World Bank report suggests that Afghanistan's aid inflow (15.7 billion in 2010), used in part to pay for public service delivery both on and off budget, matches its current GDP and is unsustainable. World Bank (2011), "Transition in Afghanistan: Looking Beyond 2014. Executive Summary," 1.

14. International Republican Institute (IRI) (2005), "CEPPS/IRI Afghanistan Quarterly Report April–June 2005."

15. For more on this, see Larson (2011a:12). AIHRC (Afghanistan Independent Human Rights Commission) is one exception, with donors having pushed to get its funding included in the government's annual budget.

16. See, for example, FEFA (2009a), "FEFA's Brief Report on the First Phase of Voter Registration Process"; FEFA (2009b), "Observation Report from the Fourth Phase of the Voter Registration (VR) Process"; FEFA (2010), "Monitoring Campaign Finance in the 2010 Wolesi Jirga Elections"; and FEFA (2011), "Afghanistan Parliamentary Observation Mission 2010: Final Report."

17. Larson (2011a:3–4).

18. This is also related to the size of UNDP's budget—the organization spent $768 million in 2010 and was by far the largest donor excluding the United States. About 16 percent of this total was spent by ELECT (UNDP [2011], "Afghanistan Annual Report 2010," 24). See also Larson (2011a:4) for a breakdown of donor spending on democracy assistance more generally.

19. For a detailed report of these issues, see Electoral Complaints Commission (ECC) (April 2010), "Final Report: 2009 Presidential and Provincial Council Elections," 22–23.

20. See, for example, FEFA (2009a); FEFA (2009b).

21. European Union Election Observation Mission (2009), "Islamic Republic of Afghanistan, Presidential and Provincial Council Elections 2009: Preliminary Statement."

22. James Dobbins, as reported in Robert Burns (August 21, 2009), "Obama Lauds Afghan Vote, Warns of More Violence" (Associated Press).

23. Kenneth Katzman (September 20, 2012), "Afghanistan: Politics, Elections and Government Performance," 28.

24. Michael Semple (2011), "The Taliban Movement and Prospects for Reconciliation in Afghanistan," 1.

25. For more on this, see *The Economist* (June 10, 2010), "Reconciliation in Afghanistan: Outside the Tent."

26. British Broadcasting Company (BBC) (December 27, 2007), "Diplomats Expelled by Afghanistan."

7. VIOLENCE AND VOTING

1. Carlotta Gall (January 19, 2003), "Threats and Responses: Afghanistan; Warlord Is Said to Be Ready to End Standoff with Kabul," *New York Times*.

2. Barry Berak (April 29, 2002), "A Nation Challenged: A Warlord Takes His Revenge on a City, Launching an Attack that Kills 25," *New York Times*.

3. Ian Fisher (March 24, 2003), "U.S. Returns 18 Guantanamo Detainees to Afghanistan," *New York Times*.

4. Gall (January 19, 2003).

5. Abdul Waheed Wafa (December 23, 2006), "Afghan Legislator Escapes Suicide Bombing," *New York Times*.

6. Ian Fisher (August 6, 2002), "Warlord Pushes for Control of a Corner of Afghanistan," *New York Time*.

7. See, for example, Michel Foucault (1991), "Governmentality"; Michel Foucault (1995), *Discipline and Punishment: The Birth of the Prison*; and Charles Tilly (1985), "War Making and State Making as Organised Crime," in Peter B. Evans, Dietrich Rueschemeyer, and Theda Skocpol, eds., *Bringing the State Back In*.

8. For more on the assumption that violence undermines political power, see Hannah Arendt (1969), *On Violence*.

9. See Hansen and Stepputat (2005); Tilly (2007) refers to "autonomous power centers" as networks existing separately from public politics, although these can sometimes function within state structures (p. 76). In the Afghan case, Giustozzi (2009) is particularly representative of the shift toward a focus on non-state players.

10. In other instances, violence is used to reinforce a certain social and political order, especially when used to oppress certain classes or groups; in the case of insurgency in Afghanistan, however, it is more relevant to focus on attempts by the insurgents to upend the current political order.

11. See, for example, Coburn (2011a: ch. 9).

12. See Keane's response (1996) to Arendt (1969) in particular.

13. Antonio Giustozzi (2007), *Koran, Kalashnikov, and Laptop: The Neo-Taliban Insurgency in Afghanistan, 2002–2007*, 114.

14. Ben Farmer (September 17, 2010), "Afghans Face a Blizzard of Threats Ahead of Saturday's Parliamentary Elections," *The (London) Telegraph*.

15. Jon Boone (September 23, 2010), "Afghan Elections 'More Violent' Than Last Year's Presidential Poll," *The Guardian* (London).

16. Wilder (2005:16).

17. American Free Press (AFP). March 19, 2009. "Bomb Kills Anti-Taliban Afghan MP."

18. Farmer (September 17, 2010).

19. The decrease in international monitors was certainly also shaped by the decrease in international interest in the Wolesi Jirga elections of 2010 in comparison with the presidential election of 2009.

20. Six out of a total of 11 parliamentarians elected in Balkh in 2010 are known to have connections with Atta, the Jamiat Party to which he is loosely affiliated, or both.

21. For more on some of these tensions, see Coburn (2011a: ch. 5).

22. Doing a precise measure of the number of commanders and former warlords who were candidates was, of course, difficult, since such categories are blurry, as discussed above in the section on non-state actors. However, most voters agreed that the number of candidates with violent pasts increased in several areas and this was a trend in each of the research areas.

23. Kouvo (February 22, 2010).

24. Among a few groups, noticeably in younger, urban areas, the exact opposite seemed to be occurring, with voters mobilizing around young, educated candidates who had no role in the civil war. Such candidates, however, appeared to be less successful as a group in 2010 than they were in 2005. More importantly, this galvanizing of candidates around two poles, one associated with the fighting of the 1980s and 1990s, and the others turning from that past, only further demonstrates the increasing importance of violence in organizing politics.

8. "THEY MAKE THEIR ABLUTIONS WITH BOTTLED WATER": ELITES AND THE DECLINE OF ACCOUNTABILITY

1. Reports of rates paid per vote varied, but in Kabul in 2009, 500 Afghanis or approximately $10 was a commonly cited figure for the amount voters were receiving per vote.

2. Noah Coburn (2009), "Losing Legitimacy? Some Afghan Views on the Government, the International Community and the 2009 Elections."

3. Abdullah publically cited "the country's best interest" as the main reason for not participating. British Broadcasting Company (November 1, 2009), "Abdullah Pulls Out of Afghan Vote."

4. Coburn (2009:6).

5. Juan Linz (1990), "The Perils of Presidentialism," *Journal of Democracy* 1.1: 51–69.

6. Government of Afghanistan (2004), "Electoral Law," Chapter 6, Part 1, Article 23, and Chapter 6, Part 2, Article 24, respectively.

7. This trend is not entirely new, and nomads have often balanced migration with more permanent settlements. For studies of Afghan nomads and settlement patterns, see Thomas Barfield (1981), *The Central Asian Arabs of Afghanistan: Pastoral Nomadism in Transition*; and Gorm Pedersen (1994), *Nomads in Transition: A Century of Change Among the Zala Khan Khel*.

8. Frauke De Weijer (2007), "Afghanistan's Kuchi Pastoralists: Change and Adaptation," *Nomadic Peoples* 1.1: 9.

9. Constitution of Afghanistan, Article 109.

10. Constitution of Afghanistan, Article 94.

11. Government of Afghanistan (2010), Articles 61 and 23.

12. Reported in Jon Boone (February 22, 2010), "Hamid Karzai Takes Control of Afghanistan Electoral Watchdog," *The Guardian* (London).

13. Oates (2009).

14. Linz (1990:56).

15. See, for example, Elizabeth Rubin (August 4, 2009), "Karzai in His Labyrinth," *New York Times*.

16. This figure, released by the IEC, does not include disqualified ballots. Also, it is calculated on the number of ballots cast, as opposed to actual turnout. For more detailed analysis, see Martine Van Bijlert (September 20, 2010), "Afghanistan's Elections: Let's Talk Turnout," *Foreign Policy*.

17. Afghanistan Parliamentary Assistance Project (APAP) (March 2008), *Legislative Newsletter* 30: 5.

18. See Constitution of Afghanistan, Articles 61 and 83. Article 83, in particular, stipulates that each new National Assembly's mandate "ends on the 1st of Saratan (June–July) of the fifth year after the elections and the new Assembly starts its work." While the wording is ambiguous, it is implied that elections for the new parliament should have taken place well in advance of this time, in order that results can be processed and the new parliament be ready to commence activities. Accordingly, parliamentary elections should be held around May, a month in which there is generally snow in the highlands, prohibiting movement.

Similarly, the constitution stipulates that the presidential term ends on 1 Jawza, and that elections for the presidency should take place thirty to sixty days beforehand (Article 61). This again would mean elections would take place in the winter months during which many regions would normally be inaccessible.

19. Cited in Noah Coburn and Anna Larson (2011), "Undermining Representative Governance: Afghanistan's 2010 Election and Its Alienating Impact," 8.

20. Many Pashtuns, however, claim to have a majority in the province.

21. Martine Van Bijlert (2011a), "Untangling Afghanistan's 2010 Vote: Analysing the Electoral Data," 6.

22. What was also particularly interesting was that this was not the first time that Hazaras had been elected to national public office in Ghazni without immediate Pashtun counterparts. In 1969, in Ghazni Center, a Hazara candidate was elected in what was widely known to be a Ghilzai-Pashtun area. Dupree (1971:9).

23. Government of Afghanistan (2005), "Rules of Procedure of the Wolesi Jirga," Rule 32.

24. Mujib Mashal (June 24, 2011), "Unseated Afghan MPs Threaten Protests," *Al Jazeera*.

25. For further analysis of the list of those included and excluded, see Thomas Ruttig (June 26, 2011), "Special Court Suggests to Change 62 MPs: The Outgoing and the Outcome (amended)."

26. Mashal (June 24, 2011).

27. *TOLO News* (July 26, 2011), "Karzai to Resolve Tensions Between Parliament, Special Tribunal."

28. For further analysis, see Martine Van Bijlert (2011b), "How to Read the Presidential Ruling."

29. Interview, Afghan political analyst.

9. INTERNATIONAL INTERVENTION AND ASPIRATIONS OF REPRESENTATIVE GOVERNANCE

1. For a similar argument, see Timor Sharan (November 17, 2012), "The Political Economy of Networked Politics: Three Decades of Elite Contestation, Cooperation and Control in Afghanistan." Paper presented at the 2012 American Anthropological Association Annual Meeting, San Francisco.

2. Barfield (2010).

3. G. Whitney Azoy, personal communication.

4. See, for example, Chesterman (2004), Paris (2004), Collier (2009), and Mac Ginty (2011).

5. This practice can be compared to early processes of state formation, in which, as James Scott argues, the allocation of recognizable fixed surnames to the populace was a critical means of states gaining control of the population through the means to identify individuals. Scott (1999), *Seeing Like a State: How Certain Schemes to Improve the Human Condition Have Failed*, 63–71. For further analysis of this point in relation to the Afghan context, see Sultan Barakat and Anna Larson (2013), "Fragile States: A Donor-serving Concept? Issues with Interpretations of Fragile Statehood in Afghanistan," *Journal of Intervention and Statebuilding* 8.1.

REFERENCES

Afghanistan Parliamentary Assistance Project (APAP). March 2008. *Legislative Newsletter* 30.

Alexander, Chris. 2011. *The Long Way Back: Afghanistan's Quest for Peace.* New York: HarperCollins.

Almond, Gabriel A. 1956. "Comparative Political Systems." *Journal of Politics* 18.3: 391–409.

Andersen, Louise, Bjørn Møller, and Finn Stepputat, eds. 2007. *Fragile States and Insecure People? Violence, Security and Statehood in the Twenty-First Century.* New York: Palgrave Macmillan.

Arendt, Hannah. 1969. *On Violence.* New York: Harcourt, Brace & World.

Asian Network for Free Elections (ANFREL). 2005. "Afghanistan Presidential Election: Report of International Observation Mission." Bangkok: ANFREL.

The Asia Foundation (TAF). 2010. "Afghanistan in 2010: A Survey of the Afghan People." San Francisco and Kabul: The Asia Foundation.

Barakat, Sultan and Anna Larson. 2013. "Fragile States: A Donor-serving Concept? Issues with Interpretation of Fragile Statehood in Afghanistan." *Journal of Intervention and State-building* 8.1.

Barfield, Thomas. 1981. *The Central Asian Arabs of Afghanistan: Pastoral Nomadism in Transition.* Austin: University of Texas Press.

——. June 2003. "Afghan Customary Law and Its Relationship to Formal Judicial Institutions." Washington, DC: The United States Institute of Peace (USIP).

——. 2005. "An Islamic State Is a State Run by Good Muslims: Religion as a Way of Life and Not an Ideology in Afghanistan." In Robert Hefner, ed., *Remaking Muslim Politics: Pluralism, Contestation, Democratization.* Princeton, NJ: Princeton University Press.

——. 2010. *Afghanistan: A Cultural and Political History.* Princeton, NJ: Princeton University Press.

Barfield, Thomas, Nemat Nojumi, and J. Alex Thier. 2006. "The Clash of Two Goods: State and Non-State Dispute Resolution in Afghanistan." Washington, DC: USIP.

Bourdieu, Pierre. 1977. *Outline of a Theory of Practice.* Cambridge: Cambridge University Press.

———. 1990. *The Logic of Practice*. Palo Alto, CA: Stanford University Press.

Brown, Michael E., Sean M. Lynn Jones, and Steven E. Miller. 1996. *Debating the Democratic Peace*. Cambridge: MIT Press.

Budge, Ian. 1996. *The New Challenge of Direct Democracy*. Cambridge: Polity Press.

Carter, Stephen and Kate Clark. May 2010. "'Snakes and Scorpions': Justice and Stability in Afghanistan." Kabul: Report Prepared for the Office of the High Commissioner for Human Rights.

Chesterman. Simon. 2004. *You, the People: The United Nations, Transitional Administration and State-building*. Oxford: Oxford University Press.

Chesterman, Simon, Michael Ignatieff, and Ramesh Thakur, eds. 2004. *Making States Work: State Failure and the Crisis of Governance*. Tokyo: United Nations University Press.

Civil-Military Fusion Center (CFC). 2012. "Afghanistan Agreements: A Collection of Official Texts from 2001–2011." Washington, DC: CFC.

Coburn, Noah. 2009. "Losing Legitimacy? Some Afghan Views on the Government, the International Community and the 2009 Elections." Kabul: AREU.

———. 2011a. *Bazaar Politics: Power and Pottery in an Afghan Market Town*. Palo Alto, CA: Stanford University Press.

———. 2011b. "The International Community and the '*Shura* Strategy' in Afghanistan." In Peter Albrecht, Helene Maria Kyed, Deborah Isser, Erica Harper, eds., *Perspectives on Involving Non-State and Customary Actors in Justice and Security Reform*. Rome: International Development Law Organization.

———. 2011c. "The Politics of Informal Dispute Resolution and Continued Instability in Afghanistan." Washington, DC: USIP.

Coburn, Noah and Anna Larson. 2009. "Voting Together: Why Afghanistan's 2009 Elections Were (and Were Not) a Disaster." Kabul: AREU.

———. 2011. "Undermining Representative Governance: Afghanistan's 2010 Election and Its Alienating Impact." Kabul: AREU.

Coburn, Noah and Shahmahmood Miakhel. September 2010. "Many Shuras Do Not a Government Make: International Community Engagement with Local Councils in Afghanistan." Washington, DC: USIP.

Coles, Kimberley A. 2004. "Election Day: The Construction of Democracy Through Technique." *Cultural Anthropology* 19.4: 551–80.

Collier, David and Steven Levitsky. 1997. "Democracy with Adjectives: Conceptual Innovation in Comparative Research." *World Politics* 49.3: 430–51.

Collier, Paul. 2009. *Wars, Guns and Votes: Democracy in Dangerous Places*. London: The Bodley Head.

Cox, Marcus. 2003. "Building Democracy from the Outside: The Dayton Agreement in Bosnia and Herzegovina." In Sunil Bastian and Robert Luckham, eds., *Can Democracy be Designed? The Politics of Institutional Choice in Conflict-Torn Societies*. London: Zed Books.

Dahl, Robert A. 1971. *Polyarchy: Participation and Opposition*. New Haven, CT: Yale University Press.

———. 1998. *On Democracy*. New Haven and London: Yale University Press.

Dahlerup, Drude. 2002. "Increasing Women's Political Representation: New Trends in Gender Quotas." In *Women in Parliament: Beyond Numbers, A Revised Edition*. Stockholm: International IDEA.

Dahlerup, Drude and Anja Taarup Nordland. 2004. "Gender Quotas: A Key to Equality? A Case Study of Iraq and Afghanistan." *European Political Science* 3: 91–98.

Dalton, Russell J. 1985. "Political Parties and Political Representation: Party Supporters and Party Elites in Nine Nations." *Comparative Political Studies* 18.3: 276–99.

Department for International Development (DFID). 2005. "Why We Need to Work More Effectively in Fragile States." London: DFID.

De Weijer, Frauke. 2007. "Afghanistan's Kuchi Pastoralists: Change and Adaptation." *Nomadic Peoples* 1.1: 9–37.

Diamond, Larry. 1999. *Developing Democracy: Toward Consolidation*. Baltimore: Johns Hopkins University Press.

Dobbins, James, Seth G. Jones, Keith Crane, and Beth Cole DeGrasse. 2007. *The Beginner's Guide to Nation Building*. Santa Monica, CA: RAND Corporation.

Dryzek, John S. 1990. *Discursive Democracy: Politics, Policy and Political Science*. Cambridge: Cambridge University Press.

Dryzek, John S. and Patrick Dunleavy. 2009. *Theories of the Democratic State*. Basingstoke, UK: Palgrave Macmillan.

Dryzek, John S. and Leslie Holmes. 2002. *Post-Communist Democratization: Political Discourses Across Thirteen Countries*. Cambridge: Cambridge University Press.

Dupree, Louis. 1960. "A Note on Afghanistan." *American Universities Field Staff Reports* 4.8, South Asia Series.

——. 1963. "Afghanistan's Slow March to Democracy: Reflections on Kabul's Municipal Balloting." *American Universities Field Staff Reports* 7.1, South Asia Series.

——. 1971. "Afghanistan Continues Its Experiment in Democracy: The Thirteenth Parliament Is Elected." *American Universities Field Staff Reports* 15.3, South Asia Series.

——. 1978. "Toward Representative Government in Afghanistan, Part II: Steps Six Through Nine—And Beyond?" *American Universities Field Staff Reports* 22.14, South Asia Series.

——. 1980 [1973]. *Afghanistan*. Princeton, NJ: Princeton University Press.

Edwards, David B. 1996. *Heroes of the Age: Moral Fault Lines on the Afghan Frontier*. Berkeley: University of California Press.

——. 2002. *Before the Taliban: Genealogies of the Afghan Jihad*. Berkeley: University of California Press.

Eide, Kai. 2012. *Power Struggle Over Afghanistan: An Inside Look at What Went Wrong—And What We Can Do to Repair the Damage*. New York: Skyhorse.

Electoral Complaints Commission (ECC). April 2010. "Final Report: 2009 Presidential and Provincial Council Elections." Kabul: ECC.

European Union Election Observation Mission. 2009. "Islamic Republic of Afghanistan, Presidential and Provincial Council Elections 2009: Preliminary Statement." Kabul: EU.

Evans-Pritchard, E. E. 1969 [1940]. *The Nuer: A Description of the Modes of Livelihood and Political Institutions of a Nilotic People*. Oxford: Oxford University Press.

Ferguson, James. 1994. *The Anti-Politics Machine: Development, Depoliticization, and Bureaucratic Power in Lesotho*. Minneapolis: University of Minnesota Press.

Foucault, Michel. 1991. "Governmentality." In G. Burchell, C. Gordon, and P. Miller, eds., *The Foucault Effect: Studies in Governmentality*. Chicago: University of Chicago Press.

——. 1995. *Discipline and Punishment: The Birth of the Prison*. New York: Vintage.

Franceschet, Susan, Mona Lena Krook, and Jennifer M. Piscopo, eds. 2012. *The Impact of Gender Quotas*. Oxford: Oxford University Press.

Free and Fair Election Foundation of Afghanistan (FEFA). 2009a. "FEFA's Brief Report on the First Phase of Voter Registration Process." Kabul: FEFA.

——. 2009b. "Observation Report from the Fourth Phase of the Voter Registration (VR) Process." Kabul: FEFA.

——. 2010. "Monitoring Campaign Finance in the 2010 Wolesi Jirga Elections." Kabul: FEFA.

——. 2011. "Afghanistan Parliamentary Observation Mission 2010: Final Report." Kabul: FEFA.

Freedom House. 2010. "Checklist Questions and Guidelines: Political Rights Checklist." Washington, DC: Freedom House.

Fukuyama, Francis. January/February 2004. "Nation-Building 101." *The Atlantic*.

Geertz, Clifford. 1973. *The Interpretation of Cultures*. New York: Basic Books.

Ghani, Ashraf and Clare Lockhart. 2008. *Fixing Failed States: A Framework for Rebuilding a Fractured World*. Oxford and New York: Oxford University Press.

Giustozzi, Antonio. 2007. *Koran, Kalashnikov, and Laptop: The Neo-Taliban Insurgency in Afghanistan, 2002–2007*. London: Hurst.

——. 2009. *Empires of Mud: Wars and Warlords in Afghanistan*. New York: Columbia University Press.

Giustozzi, Antonio, ed. 2012. *Decoding the New Taliban: Insights from the Afghan Field*. New York: Columbia University Press.

Giustozzi, Antonio and Simonetta Rossi. June 2006. "Disarmament, Demobilization, and Reintegration of Ex-combatants (DDR) in Afghanistan: Constraints and Limited Capabilities," Working Paper 2.2. London: Crisis States Research Centre.

Goodhand, Jonathan. 2004. "Afghanistan in Central Asia." In M. Pugh, N. Cooper, and J. Goodhand, eds., *War Economies in a Regional Context: Challenges for Transformation*. Boulder, CO: Lynne Rienner.

——. April 2005. "Frontiers and Wars: The Opium Economy in Afghanistan." *Journal of Agrarian Change* 5.2.

Goodhand, Jonathan, Christian Dennys, and David Mansfield. 2011. "A Dangerous Peace? Drugs, Post-conflict Statebuilding and Horizontal Inequalities in Afghanistan." In Arnim Langer, Frances Stewart and Rajesh Venugopal, eds., *Post-Conflict Reconstruction and Horizontal Inequalities*. London: Palgrave MacMillan.

Government of Afghanistan. 2003. "Political Parties Law." Kabul: n.p. [no publisher].

——. 2004. "Electoral Law." Kabul: n.p.

——. 2005. "Rules of Procedure of the Wolesi Jirga." Kabul: n.p.

——. 2009. "National Reconciliation, General Amnesty and National Stability Law." Kabul: n.p.

——. 2010. "Electoral Law," revised. Kabul: n.p.

Hansen, Thomas Blom and Finn Stepputat. 2005. "Introduction." In Hansen and Stepputat, eds., *Sovereign Bodies: Citizens, Migrants, and States in the Postcolonial World*. Princeton, NJ: Princeton University Press.

Herzfeld, Michael. 1992. *The Social Production of Indifference: Exploring the Symbolic Roots of Western Bureaucracy*. Chicago: University of Chicago Press.

Huber, Evelyne, Dietrich Rueschemeyer, and John D. Stephens. 1997. "The Paradoxes of Contemporary Democracy: Formal, Participatory, and Social Dimensions." *Comparative Politics* 29.3: 323–42.

Human Rights Watch. August 18, 2009. "Afghanistan: Human Rights Concerns in Run-Up to Elections."

Humayoon, Haseeb. 2010. "The Re-election of Hamid Karzai". Washington, DC: Institute for the Study of War.

International Crisis Group (ICG). 2002. "The Loya Jirga: One Small Step Forward?" *Asia Report* 17. Brussels: ICG.

——. 2003. "Afghanistan: The Constitutional Loya Jirga." *Afghanistan Briefing*. Brussels: ICG.

——. 2004. "Afghanistan: From Presidential to Parliamentary Elections." *Asia Report* 88. Brussels: ICG.

——. 2005. "Political Parties in Afghanistan." *Asia Report* 39. Brussels: ICG.

——. 2006. "Afghanistan's New Legislature: Making Democracy Work." *Asia Report* 116. Brussels: ICG.

International Institute for Democracy and Electoral Assistance (IDEA). 2011. "Voter Turnout Data for Afghanistan." Stockholm: IDEA.

International Republican Institute (IRI). 2005. "CEPPS/IRI Afghanistan Quarterly Report April–June 2005." Washington, DC: IRI.

Islamic Republic of Afghanistan Central Statistics Organization (CSO). 2010. "Estimated Population of Afghanistan 2010/2011." Kabul: CSO.

Jackson, Robert H. 1996. *Quasi States: Sovereignty, International Relations and the Third World*. Cambridge: Cambridge University Press.

Johnson, Chris and Jolyon Leslie. 2004. *Afghanistan: The Mirage of Peace*. London: Zed Books.

Kandiyoti, Deniz. 1998. "Gender, Power and Contestation: Rethinking Bargaining with Patriarchy." In C. Jackson and R. Pearson, eds., *Feminist Visions of Development*. New York: Routledge.

——. 2005. "The Politics of Gender and Reconstruction in Afghanistan." Geneva: UNRISD.

——. 2007. "Political Fiction Meets Gender Myth: Postconflict Reconstruction, 'Democratization' and Women's Rights." In Elizabeth Harrison, Andrea Cornwall, and Ann Whitehead, eds., *Feminisms in Development: Contradictions, Contestations and Challenges*. London and New York: Zed Books.

Kaplan, Seth D. 2008. *Fixing Fragile States: A New Paradigm for Development*. Westport, CT: Praeger Security International.

Karl, Terry Lynn. 1990. "Dilemmas of Democratization in Latin America." *Comparative Politics* 23.1.

Katzman, Kenneth. September 20, 2012. "Afghanistan: Politics, Elections and Government Performance." Washington, DC: Congressional Research Service.

Keane, John. 1996. *Reflections on Violence*. London: Verso.

——. 2009. *The Life and Death of Democracy*. New York: Norton.

Kertzer, David. 1989. *Ritual, Politics, and Power*. New Haven, CT: Yale University Press.

Kilcullen, David J. 2010. *Counterinsurgency*. Oxford: Oxford University Press.

Kippen, Grant. 2008. "Elections in 2009 and 2010: Technical and Contextual Challenges to Building Democracy in Afghanistan." Kabul: AREU.

Kitschelt, Herbert. 2000. "Linkages between Citizens and Politicians in Democratic Politics." *Comparative Political Studies* 33.6–7: 845–79.

Kouvo, Sari. February 22, 2010. "After 2 Years in Legal Limbo: A First Glance at the Approved 'Amnesty Law.'" Kabul: Afghan Analysts Network (AAN).

Krasner, Stephen D. 2009. *Power, the State, and Sovereignty: Essays on International Relations*. Abingdon (UK) and New York: Routledge.

Laakso, Markku and Rein Taagepera. 1979. "Effective Number of Parties: A Measure with Application to West Europe." *Comparative Political Studies* 12.1: 2–27.

Ladbury, Sarah. 2010. "Helmand Justice Mapping Study." Final Report for the Department of International Development. London: Coffey International Development.

Larson, Anna. 2009. "Toward an Afghan Democracy? Exploring Perceptions of Democratisation in Afghanistan." Kabul: AREU.

——. 2010. "The *Wolesi Jirga* in Flux: Elections and Instability 1." Kabul: AREU.

——. 2011a. "Assessing Democracy Assistance: Afghanistan." Madrid: FRIDE.

——. 2011b. "Deconstructing 'Democracy' in Afghanistan." Kabul: AREU.

——. 2012. "Collective Identities, Institutions, Security and State-Building in Afghanistan." In Franceschet, Krook, and Piscopo, eds., *The Impact of Gender Quotas*.

Lijphart, Abend. 1968. "Typologies of Democratic Systems." *Comparative Political Studies* 1.1: 3–44.

Lindberg, Staffan I., ed. 2009. *Democratization by Elections: A New Mode of Transition*. Baltimore: Johns Hopkins University Press.

Lindholm, Charles. 1982. *Generosity and Jealousy: The Swat Pukhtun of Northern Pakistan*. New York: Columbia University Press.

——. 1988. "Kinship Structure and Political Authority: The Middle East and Central Asia." *Journal of Comparative History and Society* 28: 334–55.

——. 2002. *The Islamic Middle East: Tradition and Change*. Rev. ed. Malden, MA: Blackwell.

Linz, Juan. 1990. "The Perils of Presidentialism." *Journal of Democracy* 1.1: 51–69.

Lipset, Martin Seymour. 2000. "The Indispensability of Political Parties." *Journal of Democracy* 11.1: 48–55.

Livingston, Ian S., Heather L. Messera, and Michael O'Hanlon. 2010. "Afghanistan Index: Tracking Variables of Reconstruction and Security in post 9/11 Afghanistan." Washington, DC: Brookings Institution.

Mac Ginty, Roger. 2011. *International Peacebuilding and Local Resistance: Hybrid Forms of Peace*. Basingstoke, UK: Palgrave Macmillan.

Mainwaring, Scott and Mariano Torcal. 2005. "Party System Institutionalization and Party System Theory: After the Third Wave of Democratization." Paper presented at the 2005 Annual Meeting of the American Political Science Association, Washington, DC.

Manin, Bernard. 1997. *The Principles of Representative Government*. Cambridge: Cambridge University Press.

Mansfield, Edward D. and Jack Snyder. 1995. "Democratization and the Danger of War." *International Security* 20.1: 5–38.

McCool, Carolyn. 2004. "The Role of Constitution-Building Processes in Democratization. Case Study: Afghanistan." Stockholm: International IDEA.

McGarry, John and Brendan O'Leary. Spring 2006. "Consociational Theory, Northern Ireland's Conflict, and Its Agreement 2: What Critics of Consociation Can Learn from Northern Ireland." *Government and Opposition* 4.2: 249–77.

Monsutti, Alessandro. 2005. *War and Migration: Social Networks and Economic Strategies of the Hazaras of Afghanistan*. New York: Routledge.

National Assembly of Afghanistan. 2006. "Rules of Procedures of the Wolesi Jirga." Accessed at www.sunyaf.org.

National Democratic Institute (NDI). 2006. "The September 2005 Parliamentary and Provincial Council Elections in Afghanistan." Kabul and Washington, DC: NDI.

Neumann, Ronald. 2009. *The Other War: Winning and Losing in Afghanistan*. Washington, DC: Potomac Books.

Oates, Lauren. 2009. "A Closer Look: The Policy and Lawmaking Process behind the Shiite Personal Status Law." Kabul: AREU.

Organization for Security and Co-operation in Europe (OSCE). 2004. "Election Support Team to Afghanistan: Recommendations, October 18 2004." Warsaw: OSCE.

Paley, Julia. 2002. "Towards an Anthropology of Democracy." *Annual Review of Anthropology* 31: 469–96.

Paris, Roland. 2004. *At War's End: Building Peace After Civil Conflict*. New York: Cambridge University Press.

Parkinson, John. 2006. *Deliberating in the Real World: Problems of Legitimacy in Deliberative Democracy*. Oxford: Oxford University Press.

Pedersen, Gorm. 1994. *Nomads in Transition: A Century of Change Among the Zala Khan Khel*. London: Thames and Hudson.

Phillips, Anne. 1995. *The Politics of Presence: The Political Representation of Gender, Ethnicity and Race*. Oxford: Clarendon Press.

Poole, Lydia. 2011. "Afghanistan: Tracking Major Resource Flows, 2002–2010." Somerset, UK: Development Initiatives, Global Humanitarian Assistance.

Przeworski, Adam. 1988. "Democracy as a Contingent Outcome of Conflicts." In J. Elster and R. Slagstad, eds., *Constitutionalism and Democracy*. Cambridge: Cambridge University Press.

——. 1999. "Minimalist Conception of Democracy: A Defense." In Shapiro and Hacker-Cordón, eds., *Democracy's Value*, 23–55.

Przeworski, Adam, Michael E. Alvarez, Jose Antonio Cheibub, and Fernando Limongi. 1996. "What Makes Democracies Endure?" *Journal of Democracy* 7.1.

Rashid, Ahmed. 2008. *Descent into Chaos: Pakistan, Afghanistan and the Threat to Global Security.* London and New York: Penguin Books.

———. 2012. *Pakistan on the Brink: The Future of America, Pakistan, and Afghanistan.* New York: Viking.

Reno, William. 1995. *Corruption and State Politics in Sierra Leone.* Cambridge: Cambridge University Press.

Reynolds, Andrew, Lucy Jones, and Andrew Wilder. 2005. "A Guide to Parliamentary Elections in Afghanistan." Kabul: AREU.

Reynolds, Andrew and Andrew Wilder. 2005. "Free, Fair or Flawed: Challenges for Legitimate Elections in Afghanistan." Kabul: AREU.

Roy, Olivier. 1994. *The Failure of Political Islam.* New York: Tauris.

———. 2003. "Afghanistan: Internal Politics and Socio-Economic Dynamics and Groupings." Geneva: UNHCR.

Rubin, Barnett R. 2002. *The Fragmentation of Afghanistan: State Formation and Collapse in the International System.* 2d ed. New Haven and London: Yale University Press.

———. 2004. "Constructing a Constitution for Afghanistan." *Journal of Democracy* 15.3: 5–19.

———. 2007. "Peace Building and State-Building in Afghanistan: Constructing Sovereignty for Whose Security?" In Mark T. Berger, ed., *From Nation-Building to State-Building.* New York: Routledge.

Rumsfeld, Donald. February 14, 2003. "Beyond Nation Building." 11th Annual Salute to Freedom, Intrepid Sea-Air-Space Museum. New York City: Department of Defense.

Ruttig, Thomas. 2006. "Islamists, Leftists and a Void in the Center: Afghanistan's Political Parties and Where They Come From, 1902–2006." Kabul: Konrad Adenauer Stiftung.

———. June 26, 2011. "Special Court Suggests to Change 62 MPs: The Outgoing and the Outcome (amended)." Kabul: AAN.

Saikal, Amin. 2004. *Modern Afghanistan: A History of Struggle and Survival.* New York: Tauris.

Sartori, Giovanni. 1968. "Representational Systems." In *The International Encyclopedia of the Social Sciences* 13: 470–75. New York: Macmillan.

———. 1976. *Parties and Party Systems: A Framework for Analysis.* Cambridge: Cambridge University Press.

Scott, James C. 1987. *Weapons of the Weak: Everyday Forms of Peasant Resistance.* New Haven, CT: Yale University Press.

———. 1999. *Seeing Like a State: How Certain Schemes to Improve the Human Condition Have Failed.* New Haven, CT: Yale University Press.

Schumpeter, Joseph A. 1942. *Capitalism, Socialism, and Democracy.* New York: Harper.

Semple, Michael. 2011. "The Taliban Movement and Prospects for Reconciliation in Afghanistan." Working Paper. Cambridge: Harvard Kennedy School.

Shapiro, Ian and Casiano Hacker-Cordón, eds., 1999. *Democracy's Value.* Cambridge: Cambridge University Press.

Sharan, Timor. November 17, 2012. "The Political Economy of Networked Politics: Three Decades of Elite Contestation, Cooperation and Control in Afghanistan." Paper presented at the 2012 American Anthropological Association Annual Meeting, San Francisco.

Stewart, Frances and Graham Brown. 2009. "Fragile States." CRISE Working Paper No. 51. Oxford: Centre for Research on Inequality, Human Security and Ethnicity (CRISE).

Suhrke, Astri. 2011. *When More Is Less: The International Project in Afghanistan.* New York: Columbia University Press.

Tilly, Charles. 1985. "War Making and State Making as Organised Crime." In Peter B. Evans, Dietrich Rueschemeyer, and Theda Skocpol, eds., *Bringing the State Back In.* Cambridge: Cambridge University Press.

———. 2007. *Democracy.* Cambridge and New York: Cambridge University Press.

Tinker, Irene. 2004. "Quotas for Women in Elected Legislatures: Do They Really Empower Women?" *Women's Studies International Forum* 27: 531–46.

United Nations. 1995. "Beijing Declaration and Platform for Action: Fourth World Conference on Women." New York: United Nations.

United Nations Development Program (UNDP). 2011. "Afghanistan Annual Report 2010." Kabul: United Nations.

United States Agency for International Development (USAID). 2005. "Fragile States Strategy." Washington, DC: USAID.

Van Bijlert, Martine. August 2009. "How to Win an Afghan Election." Kabul: AAN.

———. September 20, 2010. "Afghanistan's Elections: Let's Talk Turnout." *Foreign Policy.*

———. 2011a. "Untangling Afghanistan's 2010 Vote: Analysing the Electoral Data." Kabul: AAN.

———. 2011b. "How to Read the Presidential Ruling." Kabul: AAN.

Vanhanen, Tatu. 1984. *The Emergence of Democracy: A Comparative Study of 119 States, 1850–1979.* Helsinki: The Finnish Society of Sciences and Letters.

———. 1990. *The Process of Democratization: A Comparative Study of 147 States, 1980–1988.* New York: Crane Russak.

———. 2000. "A New Dataset for Measuring Democracy: 1810–1998." *Journal of Peace Studies* 37.2: 251–65.

Wafaey, M. Hassan with Anna Larson. 2010. "The *Wolesi Jirga* in 2010: Pre-election Politics and the Appearance of Opposition." Kabul: AREU.

Wardak, Ali. 2002. "*Jirga*: Power and Traditional Conflict Resolution in Afghanistan." In John Strawson, ed., *Law After Ground Zero.* New York: Routledge-Cavendish.

Weber, Max. 1919. "Politics as a Vocation." Lecture to the Free Students' Union, Munich University.

Weinbaum, M. G. 1972. "Afghanistan: Nonparty Parliamentary Democracy." *Journal of Developing Areas* 7.1: 57–74.

Wordsworth, Anna. 2007. "A Matter of Interests: Gender and the Politics of Presence in Afghanistan's Wolesi Jirga." Kabul: AREU.

World Bank. 2011. "Transition in Afghanistan: Looking Beyond 2014. Executive Summary." Washington, DC: World Bank.

Wilder, Andrew. 2005. "A House Divided? Analysing the 2005 Afghan Elections." Kabul: AREU.

Zakaria, Fareed. November–December 1997. "The Rise of Illiberal Democracy." *Foreign Affairs* 76.6: 22–43.

NEWS ARTICLES

American Free Press (AFP). March 19, 2009. "Bomb Kills Anti-Taliban Afghan MP."

Berak, Barry. April 29, 2002. "A Nation Challenged: A Warlord Takes His Revenge on a City, Launching an Attack That Kills 25." *New York Times.*

Boone, Jon. February 22, 2010. "Hamid Karzai Takes Control of Afghanistan Electoral Watchdog." *The Guardian* (London).

——. September 23, 2010. "Afghan Elections 'More Violent' Than Last Year's Presidential Poll." *The Guardian* (London).

British Broadcasting Company (BBC). December 27, 2007. "Diplomats Expelled by Afghanistan."

——. November 1, 2009. "Abdullah Pulls Out of Afghan Vote."

Burns, Robert. August 21, 2009. "Obama Lauds Afghan Vote, Warns of More Violence." Associated Press.

The Economist. June 10, 2010. "Reconciliation in Afghanistan: Outside the Tent."

Faiez, Rahim and Jason Straziuso. June 13, 2009. "Afghan Ballots to have 41 Candidates for President." Associated Press.

Farmer, Ben. September 17, 2010. "Afghans Face a Blizzard of Threats Ahead of Saturday's Parliamentary Elections." *The (London) Telegraph.*

Fisher, Ian. August 6, 2002. "Warlord Pushes for Control of a Corner of Afghanistan." *New York Times.*

——. March 24, 2003. "U.S. Returns 18 Guantanamo Detainees to Afghanistan." *New York Times.*

Gall, Carlotta. June 26, 2002. "Afghan Women in Political Spotlight." *New York Times.*

——. January 19, 2003. "Threats and Responses: Afghanistan; Warlord Is Said to Be Ready to End Standoff with Kabul." *New York Times.*

Gall, Carlotta and Jeff Zeleny. November 1, 2009. "Out of Race, Karzai Rival Is Harsh Critic of Election." *New York Times.*

Mashal, Mujib. June 24, 2011. "Unseated Afghan MPs Threaten Protests." *Al Jazeera.*

Rubin, Elizabeth. August 4, 2009. "Karzai in His Labyrinth." *New York Times.*

TOLO News. July 26, 2011. "Karzai to Resolve Tensions Between Parliament, Special Tribunal."

Tse, Archie. October 20, 2009. "Audit Finds Almost a Quarter of Afghan Vote Fraudulent." *New York Times.*

Wafa, Abdul Waheed. December 23, 2006. "Afghan Legislator Escapes Suicide Bombing." *New York Times.*

INDEX

Abdali Pashtuns. *See* Durrani Pashtuns

Abdullah, Abdullah: 2009 campaign/
election, 96, 105, 107, 119, 156, 157,
175, 247*n*19; appeal to international
community, 191–92; decision to forego
runoff, 104, 108, 192

Abdurrahman (king of Afghanistan), 70

absolute sovereignty, 17. *See also* sovereignty

accountability: decline of in Afghanistan,
189–90; historical modes of securing, 117;
in Loya Jirga, 240*n*18. *See also* checks and
balances

Administrative Board of Wolesi Jirga, 81–82

Afghan, Gul, 102–103

Afghan Star, 11, 237*n*15

Afghanistan: civil war, 22, 37, 39, 60, 63,
164, 221; coup (1973), 34; cultural norms
affecting election participation, 15;
debate over sovereignty, 18–23 (*see also*
sovereignty); democratization in, 16,
231; dependence on foreign aid, 68, 71,
241*n*7, 244*n*8; destabilization of, xiv–xv,
26, 27, 28, 40, 165–66, 170, 175; as "fragile
state," 236*n*9; future of, 219–23; GDP,
248*n*13; history of elections in, 10–11; jihad
period, 40; progress of intervention in,

xiii; recognition by League of Nations,
71; state-building projects, xiii–xiv,
44–48, 140–41, 228, 252*n*5 (*see also* Bonn
process). *See also* Afghans; election of
2004; election of 2005; election of 2009;
election of 2010; elections; international
intervention; Karzai, Hamid; parliament;
presidential system; senate; sovereignty;
Wolesi Jirga

Afghanistan Compact, 140

Afghanistan Research and Evaluation Unit
(AREU), xvii, 24, 91

Afghans: attitudes toward international
intervention, 142–44, 192; confidence in
national government, 47–48; confusion
over role of international community,
225–26; discontent with representatives'
performance, 130–31, 223; expectations of
state/representatives, 115–18; inability to
predict election outcomes, 185; insurgent
attacks on, 140; international actors' view
of, 150, 161; manipulation of elections
(*see* manipulation of elections); number
seeking asylum, 248*n*5; perceived distance
between state and, xv, 62, 99, 130, 185,
201, 223, 247*n*23; view of election fraud,

registration, 53–54, 109–110, 139, 145, 146, 156, 195, 229, 242n22. *See also* polling stations
technocratic figures, 181
territory, 22
terrorism, 45, 46, 241n1
terrorist groups, 239n47
Third Line group, 85, 87–88
traditional leadership, 115–18
transitional authority, 48
transitional governments, 16
transparency of elections, 23, 155, 168, 173, 224
tribal councils, 38, 39–40, 41
tribal elders, 7, 21, 127
tribal politics, 103
tribal ties: conflict within, 37; domination of communities, 121; effect on voting patterns, 8, 107; as source of political capital, 21, 76, 78, 178; sources of political capital, 23; symbols in campaign posters/ speeches referring to, 11; tension between state and, 18. *See also* kinship; lineages
troops. *See* international forces
Turkmen: bloc voting, 124; effect of position of on local politics, 26; expectations of representatives, 116; language barriers to trade, 2; opportunities to establish political connections, 113; political representation of, 3; settlements of, 1

United Kingdom, 141, 152
United Nations (UN): Afghans' view of role in elections, 187; financing of/interference in elections, 226–27; negotiations with Karzai over election law, 198; refusal to use electronic registration system, 53; training of parliamentarians, 206
United Nations Assistance Mission to Afghanistan (UNAMA), 52, 57, 76, 157–58, 225
United Nations Conference on Women, 61–62
United Nations Development Fund for Women (UNIFEM), 45
United Nations Development Program (UNDP), 99–100, 152–53, 154–55, 249n18

United Nations Office for Project Services (UNOPS), 144–45
United States: Afghanistan as component of foreign policy, 71; Afghanistan's dependence on aid from, 71, 80, 241n7, 244n8; Afghans' view of, 132; choice of institutional framework for Afghanistan, 67; debate over role in Afghanistan, 226; demands in post–Cold War world, 227; funding of stabilization programs in Afghanistan, 140; invasion of Afghanistan, 39, 99, 112, 217; lack of support of UNAMA, 225; position on nation-building in Afghanistan, 46; preparation for elections in Afghanistan, 152; rejection of constitutional monarchy in Afghanistan, 50; shift in focus to Iraq, xiii, 51, 160; support from Northern Alliance, 235n2; support of Ghani for president, 246n3; support of Hizb-Islami militant group, 239n47; unwillingness to remove warlords from leadership, 241n6; view of democracy in Afghanistan, 225–26
United States Agency for International Development (USAID), 19, 140–41, 148–49, 226, 246n1
urban areas, 189, 239n50, 250n24
Uzbeks, 196, 209–210

Vanhanen, Tatu, 243–44n4
village council elections, 247n14
village councils, 8
violence: in 2004 election, 168; in 2005 election, 80, 168; in 2009 election, 171, 228; in 2010 election, 161, 166–69, 189, 228; associated with Zadran, 162, 165, 167; disruptive impact of, 168–75; elections contributing to, 27, 165–66, 170, 171–72, 228; faith in elections undermined by, 173–75; within families, 43; function of in Afghanistan, 250n10; legitimate/ illegitimate, 167; manipulation of elections through, 168; as means of demonstrating political capital, 166, 168; as means of reshaping political systems, 7; as means of undermining government, 171;